INTIMATE MOBILITIES

Worlds in Motion

Edited by Noel B. Salazar, University of Leuven, in collaboration with ANTHROMOB, the EASA Anthropology and Mobility Network.

This transdisciplinary book series features empirically grounded studies from around the world that disentangle how people, objects and ideas move across the planet. With a special focus on advancing theory as well as methodology, the series considers movement as both an object and a method of study.

Volume 1
KEYWORDS OF MOBILITY
Critical Engagements
Edited by Noel B. Salazar and Kiran Jayaram

Volume 2
METHODOLOGIES OF MOBILITY
Ethnography and Experiment
Edited by Alice Elliot, Roger Norum and Noel B. Salazar

Volume 3
INTIMATE MOBILITIES
Sexual Economies, Marriage and Migration in a Disparate World
Edited by Christian Groes and Nadine T. Fernandez

Intimate Mobilities
Sexual Economies, Marriage and Migration in a Disparate World

Edited by

Christian Groes and Nadine T. Fernandez

First published in 2018 by
Berghahn Books
www.berghahnbooks.com

© 2018, 2020 Christian Groes and Nadine T. Fernandez
First paperback edition published in 2020

All rights reserved. Except for the quotation of short passages for the purposes of criticism and review, no part of this book may be reproduced in any form or by any means, electronic or mechanical, including photocopying, recording, or any information storage and retrieval system now known or to be invented, without written permission of the publisher.

Library of Congress Cataloging-in-Publication Data
Names: Groes, Christian, editor. | Fernandez, Nadine T., editor.
Title: Intimate mobilities : sexual economies, marriage and migration in a disparate world / edited by Christian Groes and Nadine T. Fernandez.
Description: New York : Berghahn Books, 2018. | Includes bibliographical references and index.
Identifiers: LCCN 2017053738 (print) | LCCN 2018015930 (ebook) | ISBN 9781785338618 (ebook) | ISBN 9781785338601 (hardback : alk. paper)
Subjects: LCSH: Intermarriage. | Sex. | Human behavior. | Emigration and immigration. | Intercultural communication.
Classification: LCC HQ1031 (ebook) | LCC HQ1031 .I885 2018 (print) | DDC 306.84--dc23
LC record available at https://lccn.loc.gov/2017053738

British Library Cataloguing in Publication Data
A catalogue record for this book is available from the British Library

ISBN 978-1-78533-860-1 hardback
ISBN 978-1-78920-825-2 paperback
ISBN 978-1-78533-861-8 ebook

Contents

Foreword — vii
Katharine Charsley

Introduction Intimate Mobilities and Mobile Intimacies — 1
Christian Groes and Nadine T. Fernandez

Part I. Migration Regimes and their Intimate Discontents

Chapter 1 Transnational Matchmaking: Marriage Practices of Chinese Migrants from Qingtian Living in Europe — 31
Martina Bofulin

Chapter 2 Temporary Intimacies, Incipient Transnationalism and Failed Cross-Border Marriages — 52
Nicole Constable

Chapter 3 Screening for Romance and Compatibility in the Brussels Civil Registrar Office: Practical Norms of Bureaucratic Feminism — 74
Maïté Maskens

Part II. Circuits of Sex, Race and Gendered Bodies

Chapter 4 Survival within a Multi-circuited Maze: Latin American Sex Workers in Spain — 101
Laura Oso

Chapter 5 Mobility through the Sexual Economy: Exchanging Sexual Capital for Respectability in Mozambican Women's Marriage Migration to Europe — 122
Christian Groes

Chapter 6 Fluid Sexualities beyond Sex Work and Marriage: Thai Migrants' Racialized Gender Performance in Copenhagen — 143
Marlene Spanger

Part III. Moralities of Money, Mobility and Intimacy

    Chapter 7 From *Programas* to Help and Marriage: Transnational Sexual, Economic and Affective Exchanges among Brazilian Women   167
Adriana Piscitelli

    Chapter 8 True Love and Cunning Love: Negotiating Intimacy, Deception and Belonging in Touristic Cuba   189
Valerio Simoni

    Chapter 9 The Masculine and Moral Self: Migration Narratives of Cuban Husbands in Scandinavia   213
Nadine T. Fernandez

Index   231

Foreword

Katharine Charsley

In many ways, this book represents the maturation of a field of study. The latter decades of the twentieth century saw researchers attempting to establish gender as a central issue in migration research, an effort that then facilitated the development of research interest in transnational families and family migration. Those previously dismissed as 'dependents' of (economic) migrants were recognized as themselves being legitimate subjects of academic interest, whilst there was also increasing recognition of the importance of gendered and familial dynamics in understanding migration more generally. In the context of tightening immigration regulations in Europe and demographic changes in East Asia, and with continuing interest in inter- vs. intra-ethnic marriage from an integration/assimilation perspective, cross-border marriage in particular emerged as one key focus of this new field.

In challenging the reductionism of previous economistic approaches to migration, however, there has been a danger of reifying new categories. In this volume, the focus broadens again to take in themes of intimacy, sexuality and emotion, which enables the contributors to continue the ongoing task of interrogating the categories (and their oft-implied binaries) that pepper policy, popular and academic discourses in this area. Should women migrating as wives or sex workers be considered as commodified or agentic? Should such women be seen as wives or workers? Is marriage-related migration best viewed through a lens of intimacy and relationships, or immigration tactics? This volume builds on and deepens such critiques, exploring the blurring of emotion and strategy, and of the boundaries of the category of marriage. It highlights areas that fall between the cracks of research reproducing immigration categories, such as relationships that do not lead to marriage, migration or long-term settlement, but that are nevertheless meaningful both for participants, and for researchers attempting to understand the dynamics of migration, gender and power. The book also draws valuable connections between fields not always brought into dialogue, such as those on sex work and marriage-related migration.

By approaching these topics anew, from differing perspectives and in varied empirical contexts, this collection provides a rich sense of the importance of issues of intimacy in migration. These defy relegation to a personal or domestic sphere. Instead we see emotional relationships and aspirations intimately entwined with livelihoods, mobilities and imaginaries – and not just for those for whom a relationship with someone from a different locality may offer imagined or actual material, emotional or sexual benefits. Emotion, it is apparent, may even be found in the workings of state controls over immigration and relationships between citizen and non-citizen, such that Belgian registrars are depicted as working with their feelings about couples in judgements over the genuineness or otherwise of marriages involving migrants.

All this plays out on terrain characterized by inequalities of resources and access to mobility. Sexuality may itself be seen as a resource with the potential to enable international mobility, but there are also more complex forms of playing with, and thinking with, emotions evident in these pages. Love has, unsurprisingly, been a key theme in the literature on cross-border relationships. Normative understandings of 'real' love often serve as a key technology in both the evaluation and display of such relationships to potentially critical others, including immigration officials and social networks, not to mention researchers. Emotional bonds between family members (other than intimate partners) also play a substantial role both in migration decisions and the enormous global remittance economy. But the chapters in this volume make plain that love is by no means the only emotion that needs to be taken into consideration – from the disgust at apparently mismatched transnational couples (the 'paunchy' older man with the younger bride) to the potential disapproval of relationships with foreigners by relatives on either side, less positive emotions may also come into play. Crucially, the rich material on diverse empirical contexts in this collection shows the importance of basing such understandings on an appreciation of the historical, socio-economic and cultural contexts in which relationships, emotions and aspirations are rooted. Diversity is also in evidence in gendered terms: much work in this field to date has been done on (and by) women; but in this volume we also hear from men – as prospective or actual migrants, as husbands or boyfriends, and as gendered selves negotiating the complex terrain of globalized relationships and imaginaries.

Migration as a topic may be approached from many angles, but what if all migration research was infused with an awareness of the centrality of relationships and emotions for understanding motivations, moralities and experiences of mobility and migration regimes? Researchers and activists have long attempted to inject such matters into depersonalized policy discourses around managing migration (for example, in the 'Love Letters to the Home Office' campaign to highlight the couples and families divided by British immigration requirements); but perhaps the time is ripe for scholars in this field to increase our efforts in engaging with those in migration studies more broadly. Recent years have seen a proliferation of workshops and conferences on migration and family, marriage, divorce, sexuality and intimacy, such as the one from which this volume has emerged. These events, at least in my experience, are not only immensely interesting and collegial, but highly productive, reflecting and generating a dynamic and growing research community brimming with activity and ideas. *Intimate Mobilities* presents the cutting edge of this dialogue, and should be a key resource for those already interested in these topics. But it is also an opportunity to introduce new audiences to the potential of an intimate perspective on migration in generating new insights and illuminating previously unexamined aspects of cross-border mobility and its regulation.

Katharine Charsley is Reader in Sociology at the School of Sociology, Politics and International Studies at the University of Bristol, UK. She is the author of *Transnational Pakistani Connections: Marrying 'Back Home'*, editor of *Transnational Marriage: New Perspectives from Europe and Beyond*, and has published widely on the topic of marriage-related migration.

INTRODUCTION

Intimate Mobilities and Mobile Intimacies

Christian Groes and Nadine T. Fernandez

In this age of globalization and transnational encounters, people's mobility often intersects with intimate issues such as love and sex, reproduction and obligation, and family and conjugal matters. Such intimate issues shape mobility across and between countries, and at the same time, transnational spaces and movements also shape people's intimate choices. Much migration research remains desexualized and overlooks emotional and intimate relationships. This book explores the entanglement of mobility and intimacy in various configurations, at various levels, and in diverse geographic locations. The purpose of the book is to cut across a disparate literature that treats various types of mobility and migration as distinct and unrelated phenomena rather than as variations of cross-border mobilities facilitated by and deeply entwined with issues of gender, power, kinship and sexuality that constitute the field and potential of intimacy in a disparate world.

For us, 'intimate mobilities' involve all forms of mobility shaped, implied or facilitated by bodily, sexual, affective or reproductive intimacy, spanning what has been coined as marriage migration, family migration, sexual migration, romance travel, erotic adventure, sex work migration and sex tourism, as well as any kind of mobility motivated by emotions, desires or pleasures, or conditioned by kinship, family ties or reproductive ambitions.

Until recently, different disciplinary interests and theoretical approaches have separated these fields of study and types of mobility. By contrast, the current volume highlights the cultural, social and political practices, structures and interests that bind these forms of mobility together by engaging the complex and yet powerful ways in which intimacy and mobility are entangled. Poor people migrating from the less affluent regions in the world to wealthier regions often share common challenges such as strict migration laws, social marginalization, racism and risks of deportation. Yet, such mobility also gives them a way of improving their living standards, pursuing personal dreams, finding new partners and lovers, living with loved ones or having the ability to support children, spouses or extended kin networks back home. At the same time, people from wealthier regions often move to places where their currencies are stronger and convert their privilege into adventures, love affairs and erotic encounters. The intimate encounters that ensue between rich and poor, women and men, black and white, old and young, as a consequence of new forms of mobility and immobility, give rise to all sorts of mixed relationships in which desire, lust, power, hope, romance, anxiety and the uncanny tend to blend and transform each other. Thus, this publication attempts to traverse fields of study that have hitherto been seen as separate by illustrating how transnational mobilities are often related to intimacy, and how intimacy enables people's movement.

Shifting governments of the Global North, especially in Europe, have inadvertently fostered different migration routes, which are all linked to intimacy. At a time when immigration policies, and control of labour migration in particular, have been tightened, the only loopholes left that will allow migrants legal access to European countries often entail some sort of intimacy. As scholars have argued, these can be seen as policies of exception, based on new forms of humanitarianism and biopolitics (Ticktin 2011; Fassin 2011; De Genova 2013; Loftsdóttir and Jensen 2016). Outside of family relations, only a few migrants are welcome due to extraordinary circumstances. Although high-skilled workers are often able to obtain temporary residence permits, unskilled or low-skilled persons generally cannot enter these countries legally, unless they perform highly unregulated work characteristic of the care sector, or can prove an intimate connection to citizens of the nation.

Au pairs and adoptees, for example, are desired migrants, and many nation states tolerate the immigration of family members and spouses of national citizens. The adoptee migrant is desired because of his or her perceived permanent attachment to the nation of her adoptive family, and the au pair migrant is desired precisely because of her more temporary attachment to the nation and the valuable care work she provides to the host family (Myong and Trige Andersen 2015). Marriage migrants and family migrants comprise an even more significant group that has become part of this process and these politics of exception. The family or spouse with citizenship in Europe or the United States, for example, in a sense becomes the nation's extended arm, as caretaker, protector and sponsor of the migrant-spouse or migrant-kin. Together these forms of alternative or exceptional attachments to the receiving nation point to an 'intimitization' of mobility, sometimes linked to national attachment of spouses and kin, encompassing particular notions of race, culture and gender (Groes 2016), and sometimes related to affective needs in, for example, European and American middle-class households (see also Ehrenreich and Hochchild 2004; Myong and Trige Andersen 2015).

Although most chapters address mobility and dreams of relocation from one place to another, the movement of the groups represented in this volume is certainly not unidirectional. Whether hoping to move out of Cuba through intimate liaisons, settling in the Spanish sex industry or being assisted by kin and family on the journey, people's movement is open-ended, and the conditions of mobility, physical or social, are constantly reshaped by social networks and political and economic changes, both locally and on the global stage. Ultimately, some migrants may return to their home countries to buy houses or set up family businesses with money saved from working abroad (Carling and Erdal 2014; Baldassar and Merla 2014).

At a time when a high number of refugees and migrants from the Middle East and North Africa are heading towards Europe to avoid conflict and war, some governments and populations are becoming evermore inclined to close the borders, thereby limiting the mobility of large groups of people (*Huffington Post* 2015; *The Guardian* 2016). The so-called 'refugee crisis' in 2015 highlighted the political challenges around immigration in the EU, and affected the ability of people to move between countries. The 'Brexit' vote in the UK in 2016 marked a new direction in Europe, where nationalist tendencies have put pressure on the political class to halt humanitarian policies and keep refugees and migrants from entering the EU. This sceptical attitude towards refugees and migrants is increasingly dominant, and yet, it is sometimes suspended allowing for intimacy-based migrations mentioned above. One reason for this is perhaps that citizens across Europe actively seek spouses from other parts of the world, and this affective need to marry non-Europeans and settle with them in a European country is taken into consideration when politicians form new and more strict immigration policies.

Besides entering and settling in the Global North through marriage, irregular migrants only receive attention and assistance in such rich countries when perceived as exceptional victims in the eyes of the public. The female subject of human trafficking or so-called sex trafficking is a case in point, precisely because she epitomizes the pure victim that the nation must protect to fulfil its image as an agent of justice, and ideas of humanitarian nationhood (Ticktin 2011). Notably, the majority of non-coerced sex workers who embark on the journey from Africa, Asia or Latin America to the Global North do not receive the same degree of attention or protection from the state (Agustin 2007). As some chapters in this volume point out, sexworker migrants have a hard time navigating the sex industry and finding ways to enter and remain in Europe by legal and legitimate means. The sexworker migrant going to Europe from Africa or Latin America responds at a structural level to an affective and sexual demand among a particular group of mostly male sex purchasers in the Global North. Yet, what the public often seem to ignore is that sex worker migrants also respond to an affective demand among poor families back home who benefit from a daughter selling sex on the streets of Europe in order to ensure the social reproduction of households (Casas 2010; Parreñas 2011; Peano 2013; Plambech 2014).

Conceptual Groundings and New Directions: (Im)mobilities and Intimacy

Conceptually, mobility and migration have very different genealogies and discourses attached to them. While migration has mainly referred to the actual physical, spatial and geographical movement of people, due to poverty, search for labour or seeking new lives in more affluent countries, regions or cities, the concept of mobility not only deals with people's movement but also the connected flux of materialities, money, ideas, images, knowledge and technologies, and the way such diverse mobilities are restricted, facilitated or understood.

Migration studies were initially marked by economic analysis of so-called push-and-pull factors, sometimes understood as part of a world system of rich centres and poorer peripheries. Lewis (1954) introduced the dual-economy models in the 1950 and 1960s, in which migration occurs as a result of differences in the supply and demand of labour between the rural and urban sectors. The Harris–Todaro models of the 1970 and 1980s augment these models to account for specific migration patterns. Other macro-theories included the world systems theory and dual labour market theory (Piore 1979), which explains migration as the result of a temporary pull factor, namely strong structural labour demand in developed countries. The world systems theory (Wallerstein 1974), which takes a historical structural approach, stresses the role of disruptions and dislocations in peripheral parts of the world – a result of colonialism and the capitalist expansion of neoclassical governments and multinationals. Only later, more intimate questions of family and gender were introduced. As Morokvasic (1984) pointed out, women migrate not only because of economic motives, but also to get married, due to social constraints, inadequate rights and lack of protection against domestic violence. Sandell (1977) and Mincer (1978) saw migration as a family decision, where the total income of the family and its ability to sustain the household was of central significance. Later scholars like Massey (1990) argued that the factors that influence migration to begin with could be very different from the conditions that make migration continue, or perpetuate. After an initial phase of pioneer migration, migration becomes more common in a community, with more and more people imitating earlier migrants and developing migrant communities. In another vein of literature, often with a more postcolonial or postmodern approach, migrant communities, identities, networks and politics were addressed as what has been referred to as diasporas (Hall 1990; Safran 1991; Clifford 1997; Van der Veer 1995). Overall, from various disciplinary perspectives and levels of analysis, (micro and macro) migration theory has largely taken a rationalist approach to understanding movement (Brettell and Hollifield 2014).

The concept of mobility is of more recent origin. It emphasizes the fluid nature of movement and offers a framework for understanding the relationships between movers and non-movers, and the irregular movement of not only people, but also goods, ideas, services and images (Hannam, Scheller and Urry 2006; Salazar 2010; Cohen and Sirkeci 2011). Rather than viewing people's cross-border movement as being a result of rational choice, pure necessity or merely an individual or collective strategy, mobility could encompass all sorts of journeys, including those sparked by hopes, obligations, nostalgia, desire, images, symbols, and cultural practice, or enabled by changing technologies, or triggered by broader unforeseeable life trajectories (Constable 2003; Olwig 2007; Vigh 2009; Piot 2010; Salazar 2010; Cohen and Sirkeci 2011). Mobility studies began in the 1990s when scholars began announcing the 'mobility turn' in the social sciences. Historian James Clifford (1997) advocated for a shift from cultural and social analysis of particular places to the routes connecting them, and anthropologist Marc Augé (1995) discussed the analytical potential of an anthropology of 'non-places' like airports and motorways that are characterized by constant transition and temporality. Mobilities emerged as a critique of contradictory orientations towards what was called 'sedentarism' on the one hand and 'deterritorialization' on the other. People had often been seen as static individuals tied to specific places, or by contrast as nomadic and placeless in an elusive and globalized existence (Hannam, Scheller and Urry 2006). Mobility studies criticized the focus on spatial mobility in migration studies because it tends to focus on movement in space-time rather than on the interaction between actors, structures and context. Thus, transitions and reconfigurations related to, for example, class, race and gender may become obscured. In order to address more clearly the close tie between spatial mobility and movement and social mobility, some scholars began to discuss the concept of 'motility', which they understood as the way entities such as goods, information and people become mobile in social and geographic space, or the way these entities apply the capacity for socio-spatial mobility according to circumstances (Kaufmann, Bergman and Joye 2004).

Empirical investigations of motility were supposed to focus fundamentally on the temporal changes that are sometimes overshadowed by addressing spatial changes and mobilities. In the same vein, several of the contributors to this volume make use of concepts such as circuits, trajectories and life narratives, which point equally to spatial and social mobility and the concrete experience and reconfigurations that take place in the intimate encounters and conflicts they address.

The link between mobility (or motility) and intimacy has only recently been explicitly addressed by scholars (González-López 2005; Mai and King 2009; Beck-Gernsheim 2011; Boehm 2012; Fernandez 2013; Cole and Groes 2016). In particular, scholars have unravelled the connection between social mobility, territorial movement and the intimacies that facilitate these or that these enable through transnational and binational mixed marriages, sex tourism, and the sex industry (Cole 2004; Brennan 2004, Piscitelli 2007) sometimes conditioned by 'alternative global circuits' (Sassen 2003) and highlighting the recurring feminization of mobility and immobility (Ehrenreich and Hochschild 2004; Gündüz 2013).

Overall, we hold, as do Hannem, Scheller and Urry, that 'the concept of mobilities encompasses both the large-scale movements of people, objects, capital and information across the world, as well as the more local processes of daily transportation, movement through public space and the travel of material things within everyday' (Hannam, Scheller and Urry 2006: 1). Even though this volume is mostly concerned with the movement and non-movement of people in and across specific national and transnational contexts, we also acknowledge the importance of the flow of money, images, knowledge and various cultural and social practices that move alongside people or independently of them (see Appadurai 1997). The 'mobility turn' has transformed the social sciences, in the sense that is cuts across disciplinary boundaries and questions the 'territorial' precepts and methodological nationalism of earlier approaches in social science (Wimmer and Glick Schiller 2002; Hannam, Scheller and Urry 2006; Beck and Beck-Gernsheim 2009; Glick Schiller 2013). Yet, mobilities cannot be understood without attention to the spatial and institutional moorings that configure, enable or constrain mobilities, since different hierarchies of power and questions of race, gender, age and class are ever present, and the ability and rights to travel, for example, are highly skewed (Hannam, Scheller and Urry 2006;

Glick Schiller and Salazar 2013). Clearly, and this is part of what we want to show, physical, spatial and geographical movement is closely related to upward or downward social mobility, to access to jobs and opportunities, and to personal senses of fulfilment and success, or isolation and failure. Such processes are closely linked to changing notions of gender and flexible performances, and pursuits of idealized masculinities and femininities. Moving to another place or country can be a source of status and power, and of new gendered expressions for business travellers and tourists, as well as for migrants seeking a better life for themselves and their families. Addressing mobility and immobility also requires that attention be given to the governance of mobility, in particular by nation states and supranational entities such as the UN and EU. At a time when the EU attempts to close off more and more borders through institutions like FRONTEX, in charge of surveillance and the control of entry points for member countries, the question now is how mobility is being affected and whether new journeys are made impossible.

This book extends these debates by challenging what Salazar and Smart (2011) have noted as some commonly held assumptions that mobility is implying an 'ease' of movement and that it leads to improvement or progress for migrants and their kin. The chapters in this volume engage in a range of new approaches, in which mobility is anything but 'self-evident', and the correlation between geographic movement and gains in financial or social status is not always straightforward. The empirical work here addresses how global power relations, policies, and economic flows intersect with gender, sexuality, kinship, race and class across national boundaries. The book does not argue that such divergent forms of mobility are necessarily part of the same global tendency to move across national boundaries. Instead it does point to certain ways in which we might talk about mobility being increasingly linked to intimacy, perhaps developing a set of ideals and norms that privilege some bodies and desires over others, and at the same time open for opportunities among hitherto immobilized people, whose mobility is conditioned by the mobility of others, such as tourists, expatriates men looking for future wives, and women looking for erotic adventure. The relation between intimacy and mobility is open-ended, just as the connection between social mobility and spatial or geographical mobility. Moving to another country can be seen as a step up the social ladder, but it may result in personal isolation and dependence, and can also lead to ruined relationships while benefiting one's family, all at the same time.

Several chapters tackle the thorny issue of interest and affect, questioning the line often drawn between sexual, emotional and monetary exchanges (e.g. chapters by Piscitelli and Simoni) and engaging with the grey zones of sex work and the multiple strategies of gender, race and kinship that women employ to migrate (e.g. chapters by Oso, Groes and Spanger). The latter are also grounded in research demonstrating the fundamentally gendered nature of transnational mobility (Mahler and Pessar 2006). Studies of the 'feminization of migration' have emphasized how an increasing number of women travel from developing countries to the Western world to earn incomes as maids, nannies, au pairs and sex workers (Ehrenreich and Hochschild 2004). The book extends this research by examining not only physical labour, but also how emotional/affective labour can be integral in the migration process for both female and male migrants. If some patterns of mobility can be seen as feminized, they can certainly also be addressed as part of a general movement conditioned by a variety of gender identities and sexualities. Thus, the attention to queer migration, and attempts to counter the heterosexual bias in migration studies (Gorman-Murray 2007; Luibhéid 2008), has been extremely important in order to understand how mobility can be tied to a pursuit of greater chance of personal fulfilment among gays, lesbians, bisexuals and transgender people, for example, or how mobility is sometimes motivated by harassment and persecution of homosexuality or what is seen as morally unacceptable behaviour in one's country of origin (Lewis 2014; Brown and Browne 2016). Although the chapters in this volume do not explicitly address these questions, we urge readers to keep such matters in mind when reflecting about the conundrums of intimate mobilities.

All the chapters are empirically grounded, drawing on original research and ethnographic studies by scholars across several continents (Asia, Europe, Africa, North and South America). The diverse disciplines and geographical perspectives represented in the book capture the flexibility, irregularity and messiness of intimate mobilities and migratory trajectories. The breadth of the research shows how such intimate mobilities are patterned by particular institutional and cultural contexts the migrants encounter at both ends of their trajectory.

Entangled Fields of Intimate Mobility: A Continuum with a Fractal Dimension

One can argue that with the increased possibility and necessity of mobility, social relations have become geographically dispersed, impersonal, and often mediated by broader political-economic or capitalist processes, and that intimate and personal relations have, at the same time, become more commodified, as shown, for example, in the case of so-called mail-order brides (Constable 2003; Plambech 2010), a booming sex industry, and the sex tourism sector (Brennan 2004; Cabezas 2009). In some places this commodification is seen as problematic and dangerous, while in others it is perceived as giving new hopes for social mobility since it provides new jobs and incomes (Constable 2009). In intimate encounters between a person from a part of the world where commodification is fought and seen as the root of evil and corruption, and a partner who holds other beliefs and exchange logics, conflicting views may cause severe challenges. Western values and principles of not mixing money and love, or sex and gifts, are questioned in intimate encounters with people from other social, cultural and ideological backgrounds, and as a result transnational couples may attempt to find a middle ground where these differences can be negotiated (see chapters by Simoni and Piscitelli in this volume; also Zelizer 2007; Cole 2014; Groes 2016).

A strong global reconfiguration of gender roles and division of labour is an equally urgent challenge to current mobilities research. Sassen (2003) discussed new processes of mobility and immobility as counter-geographies of globalization and the feminization of survival, which develop as unemployment in the South rises and opportunities shrink for formal male employment. Others have pointed to the disappearance of traditional sources of income and profit, with structural adjustment programmes leading to privatization and undermining national companies and formal labour markets (Ferguson 2006). In this situation households and communities are increasingly reliant on women for their survival and prosperity, and so allow or encourage them to embark on journeys to greener pastures for the benefit of those left at home (Ehrenreich and Hochschild 2004; Yeates 2012). By moving northwards, women from the Global South become providers instead of local men, and hope that their relocation to a wealthier setting can eventually bring with it some sort of social mobility and hope for themselves and their kin. In relations with Western men, as their husbands, sex customers, employers or patrons, power and gender inequality become tangible in everyday life. But such questions of power also apply to men and transgender people from the Global South when entering into intimate relationships with women from the Global North as a consequence of sex tourism, romance travel, marriage or sex work. Although power is often exercised by the stronger party in a strict sociological sense, in terms of financial power, gender privilege, race or nationality, it can sometimes, albeit often temporarily, be challenged or suspended by emotional, sexual or bodily performances, resources and 'love games'.

In attempting to shed light on and grasp the complexity of these issues, this volume addresses three highly entangled and interchangeable fields of intimacy and mobility, and these provide the headings for its three parts: (I) Migration Regimes and their Intimate Discontents; (II) Circuits of Sex, Race and Gendered Bodies; and (III) Moralities of Money, Mobility and Intimacy. We might see these three fields as part of a continuum with a fractal dimension. At one end of the continuum we have the field of marriage mobilities, with a focus on marriage practices within transnational movements, localized and place-bound or in liminal international (legal or illegal) spaces. At the other end of the continuum is the field of sex work mobilities, addressing the selling of sex in more or less formal settings, and exploring how this opens for or motivates journeys to others parts of the world and leaves sex workers in a very particular situation as foreigners or nationals, as exotic, stigmatized or socially situated. In between these two fields, associated with very different gender roles, sexualities, responsibilities, vulnerabilities and agency, we find what we call 'sexscape mobilities', characterized by a range of intimacies that cannot easily be reduced to either sex work or marriage/ love couples – that is, transactional sex and informal bodily and material exchanges in romance travel, erotic adventures, sex tourism, and transnational expat settings, for example. Yet, being engaged in one of these fields does not exclude being part of or active in the other, and the same person may in some cases be involved in all of them, and/or move between these fields over time, as shown by several authors in this book (see chapters by Spanger, Piscitelli, Oso, Groes and Simoni). Hence, intimate mobilities not only relate to spatial and social mobility, but are also enmeshed with mobility between different forms of intimacy. Traversing all these three fields are powerful actors that govern, facilitate or have an impact on mobilities and immobilities. These actors include states and supranational entities and their laws and policies of inclusion and exclusion when it comes to migration and intimacy; commercial institutions enacting certain labour demands and excluding others; and kin and family networks having a say in the extent to which intimacy and mobility is motivated or restricted, and creating senses of obligation or belonging. In most chapters in this book these actors figure centrally.

Migration Regimes and their Intimate Discontents

Policies increasingly restrict labour migration to richer parts of the world, such as Europe and North America, thereby limiting the immigration of people from poorer regions. In many cases legal entrance and permanent residence in these national spaces is only possible through marriage or other intimate arrangements and successful family reunification applications. These restrictions make intimate connections with, for example, an EU or US citizen one of the only gateways to enter these rich and privileged parts of the world (Fernandez 2013; Cole and Groes 2016). State regulations determine which binational couples can maintain their relationships and which ones will never be able to gain legal status. This can result in failed transnationalism where migrants are forced to creatively circumvent existing laws and regulations (e.g. chapter by Constable, this volume), or situations where state officials decide the legitimacy of intimate relations, and in so doing shape transnational family-formation strategies (e.g. chapters by Bofulin and Maskens, this volume). Global processes of migration regimes, economic redistribution and geopolitics exert influence on people's everyday intimate lives and decisions, but these decisions, actions and practices in turn sustain or transform the global flows. As Martina Bofulin shows in her chapter, the well-established migration flows and the networks that span the globe have been enabling young people to access foreign lands in various ways. One of the preferred options for decades, especially for Chinese women, was migration through marriage, often initiated through the practice of matchmaking, in which kin play a central role. Maïté Maskens, in her chapter, makes the case that the Belgium state, via its agents the civil registrars, applies new normative expectations of egalitarianism and romantic love when evaluating the 'veracity' of binational marriages between a Belgian citizen and a non-EU migrant. Marriages between people of different races, ages and nationalities in certain configurations become highly suspect. These new screening measures, Maskens argues, are evidence of European countries' attempts to limit the legal ways for migrants to enter so-called 'fortress Europe'. In this context, marriage is the 'last loophole' remaining in policies designed to restrict migration. These encounters between the state and binational couples make evident that the state is not an abstract entity, but is personified in the daily work of its agents, whose administrative perception of intimacy relies on an implicit idea of an 'acceptable romantic' relationship (see also Maskens 2013; Neveu Kringelbach 2013; Lavanchy 2014). This implicit idea becomes a practical norm in evaluating binational couples; it goes beyond the required legal framework, and illustrates the space between the official goal (to prevent marriage fraud as a means to enter Europe) and the biopolitical and civilizing project at work.

People moving to another part of the world in order to fulfil the dream of marriage and social mobility, or marrying in order to be able to remain in the country of one's loved ones, to help relatives back home, or kin arranging for their sons and daughters to get married abroad, are all commonplace in today's transnational space of opportunities (Palriwala and Uberoi 2008; Faier 2009; Beck and Beck-Gernsheim 2010; Charsley 2012; Constable 2005). As Bofulin's chapter illustrates, Chinese families encourage migrant kin living in Europe to visit their home region in order to marry a Chinese partner. In the regions heavily influenced by out-migration, families arrange for male migrants to come home and meet potential female partners at 'matchmaking ceremonies' (*xiangqin*). Chinese media expose the worrisome attitude – the 'problem' – that some facets of Chinese society have with young adults, particularly women, who fail to fulfil society's expectations to marry by their mid-twenties. The derogatory term 'leftovers' is common, and the imagined solution to this widespread gender conundrum is to have male migrants marry these women left at home, and take them with them to Europe. As Bofulin argues, such transitional transnational marriage practices become an innovative way of integrating marriage in a global arena into the social fabric of Chinese migrants' place of origin, including the role of parents, kin and friends, as well as a way of sustaining or negotiating transnational (and mostly male) migration. However, today, young people have much more to say in the matter of marriage than in the past, and their changing hierarchies of (desired) locations as well as desired lifestyles make marriage to a migrant a less attractive affair today than it was a decade ago. Still, for many young Qingtianese, a marriage to a migrant abroad remains the 'passage to hope' – a life overseas with freedom of movement and financial stability, if not affluence and social status. For others, though, marriage may rather represent the vision that this 'passage to hope' cannot be achieved in China.

Although not legally recognized, intimate arrangements by couples called 'marriages' or 'like-marriages' also take place within migratory spaces, and Nicole Constable (in Part I of this volume) turns our attention to this previously neglected topic. At best, she argues, these relationships are side issues in migration studies in general, and in studies of labour and marriage migration in particular. Focusing on women and men engaged in such relationships in Hong Kong, she contends that there is a lot to learn by putting these couples centre stage. They illustrate how migration experiences challenge normative expectations about marriage, intimate lives and social relationships. The marriage-like relationships Constable investigates provide insights into intimate lives that mobile people struggle to create within marginal migratory social spaces. Laws that prohibit temporary migrants or asylum seekers from becoming residents, and polices that allow migrant workers only one day off per week, in addition to employer-imposed curfews and rules against pregnancy, deter migrant women workers from having private lives, sex and children, and yet some manage to do so anyway. The intimate relationships of migrant workers and asylum seekers, and the experiences of those who migrate and later marry, show how conceptualizations of 'labour migrants' or 'marriage migrants' as two distinct categories are analytically too narrow and confining. As Constable argues, such divisions between categories of migrants obscure the connections between work and marriage migration. Often it also subordinates love to instrumental or material motives by assuming that women migrate either to gain material benefits through work or to gain them through marriage.

Each of the three chapters in Part I push beyond what Groes (2016) calls 'methodological conjugalism', which is a logical extension of methodological nationalism. While Wimmer and Glick Schiller criticized methodological nationalism as a perspective taking as a point of departure nation states, their policies and ideologies as an analytical framework when analysing cross-border migration (Wimmer and Glick Schiller 2002), Groes questions methodological conjugalism as a tendency to see marriage as the norm, the ideal, and the natural end of a migratory path of women from the Global South migrating with Europeans and settling in Europe. This perspective is powerfully reflected in European nation states' ideologies and policies where family reunification laws make immigration dependent on marriage, a perspective that scholars inadvertently risk reproducing if marriage is seen as the normative outcome of or means for mobility. By contrast, he argues, looking at migrants' exchanges with family and partners within the same framework allows for moving beyond an isolated focus on the migration of couples or individuals, and revealing a broader moral economy shaping women's choices. Thus, methodological conjugalism, with its tendency to focalize on marriage, couples and dyads within the framework of the nation state, should be replaced by addressing affective exchange triads and transnational ties in their multiplicity and potentiality. Moving beyond methodological conjugalism also means avoiding a view of migration as necessarily linear, planned, and agreed upon by two compatible partners, instead being attentive to unpredictable journeys sustained by ties to shifting partners and to kin or others to whom migrants are affectively related (Groes-Green 2014, Groes 2016).

Beck and Beck-Gernsheim point to another questionable tendency to focus on intimate migrations as either based on love or on interest – the former being the ideal, the latter being suspicious and instrumental. The former tends to be stuck in a Western conception in which marriage is the ideal form of relationship and love is the true foundation and condition of marriage (Beck and Beck-Gernsheim 2010). This line of thought upholds the Western nation state's privileging of egalitarian love-based marriage over and in opposition to partnerships defined by kin, rank and social inequality, or asymmetrical gendered exchanges between men and women (Fernandez 2013). As Fernandez argues in her study of Cuban–Danish marriages, 'these ideals of a love-based companionate marriage rooted in autonomy and individualism are evident in Danish family reunification policy and political discourses against forced migration and marriage of convenience', and unions not solely based on romance 'are seen as immoral and threatening to the state' (ibid.: 274). Thus, by approaching marriage migration as ideally love-based we risk reproducing the core principles of methodological nationalism by which states define, control and idealize some forms of migration over others. Consequently, we must be attentive to mechanisms in European state regulations through which methodological conjugalism and methodological nationalism simultaneously reinforce each other.

As demonstrated by a number of scholarly studies, sex work migration has been increasing between various regions of the world, in particular from Latin America, Asia and Africa to Europe (Spanger in this volume; Agustin 2007; Oso Casas 2010; Plambech 2014), but also increasing interregional movements to sex industries in larger cities around the globe (Fouquet 2007; Kempadoo et al. 2012). In general terms, however, much mobility and migration research has ignored the labour aspect of sex work migration in favour of an intense concentration on trafficking and the coercive aspects of sexual migration. As Agustin (2007) has argued, women have not been seen as voluntary migrants to the same extent as men, especially when it comes to working in intimacy or sex-related businesses. Some have addressed sex work mobility as part of global care chains, connecting emotional and sexual work in Western countries with the need for incomes to care for impoverished families in the Global South (Ehrenreich and Hochschild 2004; Yeates 2012). When it comes to sex work as part of care chains, scholars mention certain determining pull factors such as the demand for sex, particularly with exotic women, among men in these more affluent countries, and the demand for lower prices for sexual services. Push factors mentioned are poverty among women, lack of opportunities, male disengagement in household economies and childcare, often due to massive male unemployment (Sassen 2003; Ehrenreich and Hochschild 2004). Although such attempts at broader global analysis of sex work mobility have been of great significance, especially as a path towards labour- and rights-oriented understandings of prostitution and the transnational sex industry, the approach of this book is more directed at the highly complex interpersonal and translocal entanglements. In between or besides these often-cited push and pull mechanisms, which are sometimes perhaps too mechanic to reflect the reality of what conditions mobility according to recent ethnographic studies, there are sex work mobilities and migratory trajectories that are far from being unilineal, foreseeable or understandable from a macroeconomic labour perspective. As some chapters illustrate, personal incidents like breakdowns in love relationships, violent marriages at home, love for one's family, kin and friends, or images of wealth in foreign a country are sometimes cited by sex workers as decisive when they move abroad and sell sex at their (at least temporary) destination (Oso Casas 2010; Groes-Green 2014; Plambech 2014).

Women's migration for sex work has commonly been addressed in relation to trafficking (Kempadoo 2012; Carling 2006). Studies investigating sex trafficking from the perspective of migration often challenge the assumed correlation between sex trafficking and organized crime. These studies have also shown that such an understanding of trafficking fails to address the convergence between anti-trafficking and anti-immigration policies. Moreover, the international instruments set in place to counter trafficking (such as the Palermo protocol) have been criticized for actually facilitating the cooperation between states to prevent irregular migration, rather than protecting or giving restitution to the victims of crime or migrants in situations of labour exploitation (Agustin 2007). Building on this critique of immigration control and its challenge to the category of the 'victim', scholars have developed a more nuanced reading of the anti-immigration/sex-trafficking nexus in order to broaden the understanding of anti-trafficking policies beyond merely being tools for the straightforward exclusion of migrants, or for their inclusion under the respective headings of 'agents' or 'victims' (Andrijasevic 2010; Spanger 2013; Plambech 2014).

Circuits of Sex, Race and Gendered Bodies

Masculinities, as well as femininities, are affected in gendered ways by recent changes in global economies and globalized forms of intimacy, sometimes inverting gender stereotypes of the male breadwinner and the domestic woman. The focus on men highlights alternative forms of manhood and the specificities of the male migration experience in different settings (Donaldson et al. 2009). For both men and women, some migrations to other parts of the world emerge from sexual desires and orientations, curiosity and adventure, or are conditioned by sexual or gendered discrimination in the sending country. Some people go far away in order to escape the moral constraints or financial demands of communities and kin, or to seek cosmopolitan lifestyles as an alternative to patriarchal and oppressive heterosexual matrices at home (Mai 2013). In all of these cases, gender figures centrally. As migration and mobility research has for a long time mostly been attentive to female migration as survival strategy, or focused almost exclusively on the less skilled women (Kofman 2004), new approaches and frameworks are needed to understand inversions of gender roles and new gendered configurations (Hondagneu-Sotelo 1994). Race is equally central to understanding the inequalities and attractions that pave the way for social and geographical mobility and immobility. Being with a white woman or man may be seen as prosperous and a corporeal testimony of a person's success in the sexual economy or in life in places where whiteness is appraised and idealized due to specific colonial histories and postcolonial developments.

In Part II of this volume, Christian Groes shows how Mozambican women's use of sexual capital opens a path for mobility out of the country and towards Europe with white expatriates. What *curtidoras* strive for, whether in Mozambique or Europe, is a middle-class position where they feel 'respected'. In Mozambique this is within reach due to a combination of having easy access to rich expatriate men willing to support them, having the ability to move up in society, being respected as middle-class people with fashionable clothes, cars and conspicuous consumption, having a maid and benefiting from sustained kin support vis-à-vis their partners. However, by going to Europe they risk having their privileges reduced or reconfigured, which is why more and more migrants realize that unless certain criteria are met, it might be preferable to stay in Maputo with a husband. Studies of sex tourism, romance travel and transactional sex explore the intimate transnational encounters that occur in spaces such as tourist resorts and cosmopolitan cities. These encounters are not locally understood as or practised as prostitution or sex work, nor can they be seen as marriage-like or fulfilling ordinary notions of a romance-based egalitarian couple (Kempadoo 1999; Brennan 2004; Sanchez-Taylor 2006; Venables 2008; Cabezas 2009; de Sousa e Santos 2009; Bergan 2011; Frohlick 2013; Hoefinger 2013; Farrer and Field 2015; Hunter 2015; Meiu 2015).

The sharp distinction between sex work and other kinds of intimate labour or activity blurs the manifold and interchangeable identities and interests involved. Marriage, if seen as emotional labour, and wifehood as an occupation, as de Beauvoir ([1953] 2011) would have it, then the question is how this kind of labour is related to gendered bodies working with sexual services. Although performances of 'the housewife' and 'the prostitute' seen as work or gender roles are certainly distinct in many ways, the ways in which they are performed by the same person has largely been neglected. As Marlene Spanger notes in Part II of this volume, exchanges between female and transgender Thai migrants and Danish men take place in a space between sex work and marriage. Thus, the relationships existing between the Danish men and the Thai migrant sex workers are somewhat fluid, since sex work, friendship, marriage, love and patronage are not rigidly compartmentalized. For instance, the brothels and the bars do not just function as workplaces for the women, but also as a space of leisure; a place where they hang out and meet potential boyfriends and husbands. Sex work and prostitution must be seen as part of broader sexual economies or 'nightscapes', as she calls it, citing Farrer and Field (2015), pointing to a range of exchanges in married relationships and broader sexual networks, and relating to obligations towards children and kin at home. Another way in which this volume redirects the attention towards 'in-between' practices within an intimate and moral grey zone, and points to new gender, sexual and marriage configurations, is illustrated by Spanger's argument that Thai women and transgender people who have moved to Denmark and married Danish men identify as wives, workers and mothers all at once. They are, in a sense, both marriage migrants and sex worker migrants, and in another sense, they are neither. Although married to Danish men, they engage in selling sex services, more or less formally, at bars and nightclubs. Spanger shows how marriage is often juxtaposed to prostitution in Western and other contexts, and vice versa, but that female Thai migrants who are married to Danish men find ways to sell sex and strike a balance between the two by performing various roles in the nightscape of Copenhagen. By redirecting the attention away from ideas that marriage is necessarily equal to heterosexual Western notions of monogamous conjugal relationships, we also open up for a critique of some methodological challenges and biases in migration and mobility studies.

As recent studies show, people travelling to other countries to engage in sex work often share the same ideas, dreams and ambitions as other kinds of migrants. In her chapter, Laura Oso describes women, mainly from Colombia and Brazil, who as a strategy for economic or social mobility decide to travel to Spain, aware that they will be working as prostitutes, regardless of their means of entry, autonomously or by small-trade debt. She argues that the migratory projects are very similar to those of women who migrate in order to work in other sectors, such as domestic service. In both cases the driving force behind migration is typically the need to support a family or a desire for upward social mobility. Nevertheless, migrant women who decide to work in the sex industry and whose migration strategy is to pursue social mobility are no less exempt from abuse and exploitation by third parties. A trafficking discourse that points exclusively to pimps, prostitution rings and mafias as the 'baddies' overlooks the responsibilities of other social actors such as governments, politicians, business people, police, lawyers, clients and other parties governing intimate mobilities, especially with regard to the exploitation and poor working and living conditions of sex workers. The inclination to see all ties between mobility and sex work as instances of coercion and human trafficking has been criticized and nuanced by a number of studies, in particular by anthropologists and sociologists investigating the sex industry and following migrants from their home countries to their destinations, or through various countries and cities (Andrijasevic 2010; Jacobsen and Skilbrei 2010; Mai 2013; Plambech 2014). Along with these critical academic voices, Oso points to the inability of grand narratives about forced female victims to comprehend the complex reality and role of women who search for a better life for themselves and their families. The main objective of her chapter is to highlight that Latin American women in Spain, as the main providers for families in their homeland and in transnational households, can opt for sex work as a social mobility strategy; however, this decision leaves them to deal with a multi-circuited maze that perpetuates social and gender inequalities in the framework of global capitalism. The 'labyrinth' here is a complicated system of paths or passages that people try to navigate. This concept demonstrates the intersection between agency and barriers. Instead of being mere victims or becoming trapped by these circuits, the women opt for action strategies in order to try to find their way through. If stuck in one passage, they will seek other routes to move forward. Occasionally, navigating such mazes or circuits entails trajectories where women attempt to leave sex work through building more emotionally intimate ties to sex customers, who may eventually become their boyfriends or husbands.

Moralities of Money, Mobility and Intimacy

Another less investigated form of mobility is that involving so-called 'expats' or mobile professionals (Fechter and Walsh 2012). These people migrate to another country and settle there for a longer period in order to advance their career and/or experience the culture and conditions of another country. They are often middle class, have higher education and a cosmopolitan lifestyle or orientation (ibid.). Understanding intimate mobility, the encounters that occur between mobile professionals and locals must be attended to in a way that gives insight into the conditions for social mobility, and the status, fulfilment and despair experienced in these spaces. The term 'sexpatriates' has been applied to point to 'a strong vein of imperialism' in those relationships in which Western men find that their status as white men gives them the racialized privilege to pick and choose local women in order to fulfil erotic and exotic desires (Seabrook 1996: 33; O'Connell Davidson 2001). Yet, local men and women may be very aware of using exotic images in order to attract and seduce white expatriates and travellers (Meiu 2009; Groes-Green 2013) – images that are actively drawing on globalized tourist fantasies of the 'other' (Salazar 2010). Furthermore, mobile professionals and tourists do not only have sexual liaisons with locals or necessarily always reproduce colonial structures and stereotypes – they also often marry them and decide to stay in a place for longer than anticipated due to strong emotional attachments. Sometimes they bring back them to their home country to begin a new life together (Brennan 2004; Cole 2010; Groes-Green 2014).

Groes-Green (2014) has shown how rich white expatriate men in Maputo, Mozambique sometimes end up in a vulnerable and unstable situation when they fall in love with and are 'put in the bottle' by younger Mozambican lovers, who are better prepared to avoid the trap of emotional attachment to these men, supported by female kin and local healers. In such situations, using their erotic power and kin support allows them to extract money from the men and gain a degree of control in love affairs. This puts the younger women in a position where they can at least momentarily feel a sense of power that stands in contrast to the enormous structural inequalities between them and their partners. Mobility can be a privilege and an opportunity, but it can also be a curse – as can one's bodily and emotional resources that are applied in the process.

In his contribution to Part III of this volume, Valerio Simoni illustrates what is at stake in these 'sexscapes', where tourists going to Cuba and the locals with whom they engage need to figure out the trustworthiness and potential of lover relationships to avoid deception and falling in love with the wrong person. One of his informants, a Norwegian man called Jan who was dating younger women in Cuba, was tormented by negative experiences with Cuban girlfriends, one of whom was now carrying his child. According to Jan, local women he met were often deceptive and merely seeking material gain. His relationships with them had led him to confront the challenges and complications of 'falling in love', as a foreigner, with a Cuban. These 'failed relationships' had brought Jan 'back to earth', and made him realize the predominance of *jineterismo*, the local word for tourist hustling, which is why he had to seek proof of love and reliability among the women he encountered. Yet, Simoni also came across relationships that seemed to live up to – at least for a while – notions of 'true love'. The relationship between the Italian man Gianluca and Cuban Yara lasted for a longer time not only because he was assisting her financially while he was in Cuba but also through supporting her while he was away in Italy. Via mobile phone communication and monthly allowances, he was able to assure her of his dedication and help her with the money she required to satisfy her everyday needs, so that she would not have to continue hustling in Havana to get by. Gianluca treasured his feelings for Yara, and felt that such feelings were reciprocated, and they strove to build a path that could help them reach beyond the scenarios of a cunning and deceptive love. Simoni also shows how Cuban men struggle to find a balance between strategic seduction of white female tourists and intense emotional involvement. One of his male Cuban informants, Carlos, describes how falling in love with a female Swiss tourist made him lose control of the situation and forget his objective, which, the reasoning implied, was to get married and join his female lover in Switzerland. 'The error of the spy', as this excessive emotional involvement was called, made him lose track of his ultimately instrumental goal. The logic of the love game is that such relationships ought to be informed by cunningness, by skilful and detached playing with emotions and love, and not end up affecting the player to an extent where he might end up nowhere, in the sense of becoming too emotionally dependent on one woman or man and therefore losing control. In spite of his decade-old experience in dealing with tourists, Simoni shows, Carlos had obviously failed to maintain such detachment. However, Carlos was also torn between his attempt to build intimate relationships with tourists and making friends benefit from being in such relationships, by using the money from such affairs to party with other Cuban men. Because of the desire for 'pride' (*orgullo*), which can only be gained from other men by showing off girlfriends from abroad while taking advantage of them economically, he also forgot to play the love game properly – and so he lost his girlfriend.

In her chapter, Nadine Fernandez heads away from instrumentality and towards an emotional turn in migration studies. Cuban men's narratives of marriage migration reveal a moral discourse tied to self-making, which emerges in these heterosexual, and mostly interracial, unions. Using the concept of 'dialogic morality' she shows how the transformation of the post-Soviet Cuba has resulted not in a moral decline, but rather a dialogic reworking of ideas about people's obligations as they respond to changing economic conditions, social structures and social mores. Thus, she contributes to the growing literature on moralities of migration in which gender figures centrally (Åkesson, Carling and Drotbohm 2012 Gallo 2013; Groes 2014). In the Cuban men's narratives, we see a moral discourse of their migration experiences that shows an unfolding and interconnecting of self and different aspects of masculinity, such as the manly lover, the autonomous modern subject, and the family breadwinner. Shifting the gendered focus from mobile brides from the Global South, to mobile grooms from the Global South, she explores how the Cuban men themselves understand these relationships in terms of morality and masculinity. Adriana Piscitelli's chapter of this book provides another example of how certain ideals and notions of love, marriage and transactional sex are reconfigured. The trajectories of her informants suggest that with the transnationalization of sex markets, the modalities of sexual and economic exchanges are altered in diverse ways. And the shifting styles of affection are related to these changes. Some women move from informal sex work (*programas*), conducted on a cottage scale in Brazil, to sexual and economic exchanges in a European sex industry that require more intensive work, but which offer much higher incomes. In the tourist circuits of Fortaleza, sometimes the lines between prostitution and other sexual and economic exchanges are blurred. Some women shift from sexual and economic exchanges aimed at survival and consumption with local partners to relationships based on the logic of 'help' offered by foreign visitors that enlarge the possibilities to improve life in Brazil and could also pave the road to become part of the sexual economy in Southern Europe. The imbrications between material benefits and feelings present in the economic, sexual and affective exchanges analysed in her chapter point to multiple possibilities. The acknowledgement of inequalities connected to nationality, class, race and gender combined with the desire to 'improve one's life' are central elements of the relationships established in transnational spaces.

In summary, this book contributes to recent trends rethinking the fields of intimacy and transnational mobility, conceptually and methodologically. It adds to studies of intimate economies of mobility and migration that challenge widespread dichotomies and assumptions that separate money and sex, intimacy and power, love and labour, bodies and material resources (e.g. see Cabezas 2009; Piscitelli 2007; Mai and King 2009; Casas 2010). Furthermore, all the chapters explore how the 'intimitization' of migration has a radical impact on meanings of kinship, race and gender, which unsettle notions of family, equality and belonging.

Christian Groes, an anthropologist, is associate professor and head of studies at Cultural Encounters, Roskilde University, Denmark. He has co-edited two books: *Affective Circuits: African Migration to Europe and the Pursuit of Social Regeneration* (University of Chicago Press 2016) with Professor Jennifer Cole; and *Studying Intimate Matters: Engaging Methodological Challenges in Studies on Gender, Sexuality and Reproductive Health in Sub-Saharan Africa* with Barbara Ann Barrett (Fountain Publishers, Kampala 2011). He has published articles in *American Ethnologist, Journal of the Royal Anthropological Institute, Anthropological Theory, Men and Masculinities*, and several book chapters. In 2008 he was a PhD research fellow at Columbia University, and in 2012 he received the Young Elite Researcher Prize from the Danish Council for Independent Research.

Nadine T. Fernandez, a cultural anthropologist, is an associate professor and chair of the Social Science Department at the State University of New York/Empire State College. Her publications include *Revolutionizing Romance: Interracial Couples in Contemporary Cuba* (Rutgers University Press 2010), and several book chapters. Her articles appear in the *Journal of Ethnic and Migration Studies, Identities, Latin American Perspectives*, and *Temas*. She was a guest researcher at the Copenhagen University Anthropology Institute (2010), and the Danish National Centre for Social Research (2011). In 2015, she received the SUNY Chancellor's Award for Excellence in Scholarship and Creative Activities.

REFERENCES

Agustin, L.M. 2007. *Sex at the Margins: Migration, Labour Markets and the Rescue Industry*. London: Zed Books.

Åkesson, L., J. Carling and H. Drotbohm. 2012. 'Mobility, Moralities and Motherhood: Navigating the Contingencies of Cape Verdean Lives', *Journal of Ethnic and Migration Studies* 38(2): 237-60.

Andrijasevic, R. 2010. *Migration, Agency and Citizenship in Sex Trafficking*. New York: Palgrave Macmillan.

Appadurai, A. 1996. *Modernity at Large: Cultural Dimensions of Globalization*. Minneapolis, MN: University of Minnesota Press.

Augé, M. 1995. *Non-places*. London: Verso.

Baldassar, L., and L. Merla (eds). 2014. *Transnational Families, Migration and the Circulation of Care: Understanding Mobility and Absence in Family Life*. London: Routledge.

Beauvoir, S. de. (1953) 2011. *The Second Sex*. New York: Vintage.

Beck, U., and E. Beck-Gernsheim. 2009. 'Global Generations and the Trap of Methodological Nationalism for a Cosmopolitan Turn in the Sociology of Youth and Generation', *European Sociological Review* 25(1): 25-36.

———. 2010. 'Passage to Hope: Marriage, Migration, and the Need for a Cosmopolitan Turn in Family Research', *Journal of Family Theory & Review* 2: 401-14.

Beck-Gernsheim, E. 2011. 'The Marriage Route to Migration: Border Artistes, Transnational Matchmaking and Imported Spouses', *Nordic Journal of Migration Research* 1(2): 60-68.

Bergan, M.E. 2011. 'There Is No Love Here: Beach Boys in Malindi, Kenya'. PhD dissertation. Bergen: Department of Social Anthropology, University of Bergen.

Bloch, A. 2011. 'Intimate Circuits: Modernity, Migration and Marriage among Post-Soviet Women in Turkey', *Global Networks* 11(4): 502-21.

Boehm, D.A. 2012. *Intimate Migrations: Gender, Family, and Illegality among Transnational Mexicans*. New York: New York University Press.

Brennan, D. 2004. *What's Love Got to Do with It? Transnational Desires and Sex Tourism in the Dominican Republic*. Durham, NC: Duke University Press.

Brettell, C.B., and J.F. Hollifield (eds). 2014. *Migration Theory: Talking across Disciplines*. New York: Routledge.

Brown, G., and K. Browne. 2016. *The Routledge Research Companion to Geographies of Sex and Sexualities*. London: Routledge.

Cabezas, A.L. 2009. *Economies of Desire: Sex and Tourism in Cuba and the Dominican Republic*. Philadelphia, PA: Temple University Press.

Carling, J. 2006. *Migration, Human Smuggling and Trafficking from Nigeria to Europe*. Geneva: International Organization for Migration.

Carling, J., and M.B. Erdal. 2014. 'Return Migration and Transnationalism: How Are the Two Connected?', *International Migration* 52(6): 2-12.

Charsley, K. (ed.). 2012. *Transnational Marriage: New Perspectives from Europe and Beyond*. London: Routledge.

Clifford, J. 1997. *Routes: Travel and Translation in the Late Twentieth Century*. Cambridge, MA: Harvard University Press.

Cohen, J.H., and I. Sirkeci. 2011. *Cultures of Migration: The Global Nature of Contemporary Mobility*. Austin, TX: University of Texas Press.

Cole, J. 2004. 'Fresh Contact in Tamatave, Madagascar: Sex, Money, and Intergenerational Transformation', *American Ethnologist* 31(4): 573–88.

———. 2010. *Sex and Salvation: Imagining the Future in Madagascar*. Chicago, IL: University of Chicago Press.

Cole, J. 2014. 'Working Mis/Understandings: The Tangled Relationship between Kinship, Franco-Malagasy Binational Marriages, and the French State', *Cultural Anthropology* 29, no. 3 (2014): 527–551.

Cole, J., and C. Groes (eds). 2016. *Affective Circuits: African Migrations to Europe and the Pursuit of Social Regeneration*. Chicago, IL: University of Chicago Press.

Constable, N. 2003. *Romance on a Global Stage*. Berkeley, CA: University of California Press.

——— (ed.). 2005. *Cross-Border Marriages: Gender and Mobility in Transnational Asia*. Philadelphia, PA: University of Pennsylvania Press.

———. 2009. 'The Commodification of Intimacy: Marriage, Sex, and Reproductive Labour', *Annual Review of Anthropology* 38: 49–64.

De Genova, N. 2013. 'Spectacles of Migrant "Illegality": The Scene of Exclusion, the Obscene of Inclusion', *Ethnic and Racial Studies* 36(7): 1180–98.

Donaldson, M., et al. (eds). 2009. *Migrant Men: Critical Studies of Masculinities and the Migration Experience*. New York: Routledge.

Ehrenreich, B., and A. Hochschild (eds). 2004. *Global Women: Nannies, Maids and Sex Workers in the New Economy*. New York: Henry Holt.

Faier, L. 2009. *Intimate Encounters: Filipina Migrants and the Remaking of Rural Japan*. Berkeley, CA: University of California Press.

Farrer, J., and A.D. Field. 2015. *Shanghai Nightscapes: A Nocturnal Biography of a Global City*. Chicago, IL: University of Chicago Press.

Fassin, D. 2011. *Humanitarian Reason: A Moral History of the Present*. Berkeley, CA: University of California Press.

Fechter, A.-M., and K. Walsh (eds). 2012. *The New Expatriates: Postcolonial Approaches to Mobile Professionals*. New York: Routledge.

Ferguson, J. 2006. *Global Shadows: Africa in the Neoliberal World Order*. Durham, NC: Duke University Press.

Fernandez, N. 2013. 'Moral Boundaries and National Borders: Cuban Marriage Migration to Denmark', *Identities* 20(3): 270–87.

Fouquet, T. 2007. 'De la prostitution clandestine aux désirs de l'ailleurs: une "ethnographie de l'extraversion" à Dakar', *Politique Africaine* 3(107): 102–23.

Frohlick, S. 2013. 'Intimate Tourism Markets: Money, Gender, and the Complexity of Erotic Exchange in a Costa Rican Caribbean Town', *Anthropological Quarterly* 86(1): 133–62.

Gallo, E. 2013. 'Migrants and their Money are Not All the Same: Migration, Remittances and Family Morality in Rural South India', *Migration Letters* 10(1): 33–46.

Glick Schiller, N. 2013. 'The Transnational Migration Paradigm: Global Perspectives on Migration Research', in D. Halm and Z. Sezgi (eds), *Migration and Organized Civil Society: Rethinking National Policy*. London: Routledge, pp. 25–43.

Glick Schiller, N., and N.B. Salazar. 2013. 'Regimes of Mobility across the Globe', *Journal of Ethnic and Migration Studies* 39(2): 183–200.

González-López, G. 2005. *Erotic Journeys: Mexican Immigrants and their Sex Lives*. Berkeley, CA: University of California Press.

Gorman-Murray, A. 2007. 'Rethinking Queer Migration through the Body', *Social and Cultural Geography* 8(1): 105–21.

Groes, C. 2016. 'Men Come and Go, Mothers Stay: Personhood and Resisting Marriage among Mozambican Women Migrating to Europe', in J. Cole and C. Groes (eds), *Affective Circuits: African Migrations to Europe and the Pursuit of Social Regeneration*. Chicago, IL: University of Chicago Press, pp. 169–197.

Groes-Green, C. 2013. '"To Put Men in a Bottle": Eroticism, Kinship, Female Power, and Transactional Sex in Maputo, Mozambique', *American Ethnologist* 40(1): 102–17.

———. 2014. 'Journeys of Patronage: Moral Economies of Transactional Sex, Kinship, and Female Migration from Mozambique to Europe', *Journal of the Royal Anthropological Institute* 20(2): 237–55.

Guardian. 2016. 'Germany "won't change policy" after gains for anti-refugee AfD party'. http://www.theguardian.com/world/2016/mar/14/german-election-results-polarised-voters-choose-pro-refugee-stance.

Gündüz, Z.Y. 2013. 'The Feminization of Migration: Care and the New Emotional Imperialism', *Monthly Review* 65(7): 32–43.

Hall, S. 1990. 'Cultural Identity and Diaspora', in J. Rutherford (ed.), *Identity: Community, Culture, Difference*. London: Lawrence and Wishart, pp. 222–237.

Hannam, K., M. Scheller and J. Urry. 2006. 'Mobilities, Immobilities and Moorings', *Mobilities* 1(1): 1–22.

Hoefinger, H. 2013. 'Transnational Intimacies: Examples from Cambodia', in T. Sanger and Y. Taylor (eds), *Mapping Intimacies*. London: Palgrave MacMillan, pp. 15–26.

Hondagneu-Sotelo, P. 1994. *Gendered Transitions: Mexican Experiences of Immigration*. Berkeley, CA: University of California Press.

Huffington Post. 2015. 'How the Refugee Crisis Is Fuelling the Rise of Europe's Right'. http://www.huffingtonpost.com/entry/europe-right-wing-refugees_us_562e9e64e4b06317990f1922.

Hunter, M. 2015. 'The Political Economy of Concurrent Partners: Towards a History of Sex-Love-Gift Connections in the Time of AIDS', *Review of African Political Economy* 42(145): 362–75.

Jacobsen, C.M., and M.-L. Skilbrei. 2010. 'Reproachable Victims? Representations and Self-Representations of Russian Women Involved in Transnational Prostitution', *Ethnos* 75(2): 190–212.

Kaufmann, M., M. Bergman and D. Joye. 2004. 'Motility: Mobility as Capital', *International Journal of Urban and Regional Research* 28(4): 745–56.

Kempadoo, K. (ed.). 2012. *Trafficking and Prostitution Reconsidered: New Perspectives on Migration, Sex Work, and Human Rights*. London: Routledge.

Kempadoo, K. (ed.). 1999. *Sun, Sex, and Gold: Tourism and Sex Work in the Caribbean*. Lanham, MD: Rowman & Littlefield.

Kofman, E. 2004. 'Gendered Global Migrations', *International Feminist Journal of Politics* 6(4): 643–65.

Lavanchy, A. 2014. 'Regulating the Nation in Registry Offices: Love, Marriage and Racialization in Switzerland'. Presented at 'Of Love and Family, States and Borders: Comparative Perspectives on Afro-European Couples and Families' workshop, 13 December 2014. Paris, France.

Lewis, N.M. 2014. 'Moving "Out", Moving On: Gay Men's Migrations through the Life Course', *Annals of the Association of American Geographers* 104(2): 225–33.

Lewis, W.A. 1954. 'Economic Development with Unlimited Supply of Labour', *The Manchester School* 22(2): 139–91.

Loftsdóttir, K., and L. Jensen. 2016. *Whiteness and Postcolonialism in the Nordic Region: Exceptionalism, Migrant Others and National Identities*. London: Routledge.

Luibhéid, E. 2008. 'Queer/Migration: An Unruly Body of Scholarship', *GLQ: A Journal of Lesbian and Gay Studies* 14(2–3): 169–90.

Mahler, S.J., and P.R. Pessar. 2006. 'Gender Matters: Ethnographers Bring Gender from the Periphery toward the Core of Migration Studies', *International Migration Review* 40(1): 27–63.

Mai, N. 2012. 'The Fractal Queerness of Non-heteronormative Migrants Working in the UK Sex Industry', *Sexualities* 15(5–6): 570–85.

_____. 2013. 'Embodied Cosmopolitanisms: The Subjective Mobility of Migrants Working in the Global Sex Industry', *Gender, Place & Culture: A Journal of Feminist Geography* 20(1): 107–24.

Mai, N., and R. King. 2009. 'Love, Sexuality and Migration: Mapping the Issue(s)', *Mobilities* 4(3): 295–307.

Maskens, M. 2013. 'L'amour et ses Frontières: Régulations Étatique et Migrations de Mariage (Belgique, France, Suisse et Italie)', *Migrations Société* 25(150): 43–60.

Massey, D.S. 1990. 'Social Structure, Household Strategies, and the Cumulative Causation of Migration', *Population Index* 56(1): 3–26.

Meiu, George P. 2009. '"Mombasa Morans": Embodiment, Sexual Morality, and Samburu Men in Kenya', *Canadian Journal of African Studies* 43(1): 105–21.

_____. 2015. '"Beach-Boy Elders" and "Young Big-Men": Subverting the Temporalities of Ageing in Kenya's Ethno-Erotic Economies', *Ethnos* 80(4): 472–96.

Mincer, J. 1978. 'Family Migration Decisions', *Journal of Political Economy* 86(5): 749–73.

Morokvasic, M. 1984. 'Birds of Passage are also Women', *International Migration Review* 18(4): 886–907.

Myong, L., and N. Trige Andersen. 2015. 'From Immigration Stop to Intimizations of Migration: Cross-Reading the Histories of Domestic(ated) Labor Migration and Trans-national Adoption in Denmark, 1973–2015', *Retfærd* 38(3): 62–79.

Neveu Kringelbach, Hélène. 2013. 'Mixed Marriage, Citizenship, and the Policing of Intimacy in Contemporary France'. Working Paper 77, International Migration Institute, University of Oxford. http://www.imi.ox.ac.uk/publications/working-papers/wp-77-2013.

O'Connell Davidson, J. 2001. 'The Sex Tourist, The Expatriate, His Ex-Wife and Her 'Other': The Politics of Loss, Difference and Desire', *Sexualities* 4(1): 5–24.

Olwig, K.F. 2007. *Caribbean Journeys: An Ethnography of Migration and Home in Three Family Networks*. Durham, NC: Duke University Press.

Oso Casas, L. 2010. 'Money, Sex, Love and the Family: Economic and Affective Strategies of Latin American Sex Workers in Spain', *Journal of Ethnic and Migration Studies* 36(1): 47–65.

Palriwala, R., and P. Uberoi (eds). 2008. *Marriage, Migration and Gender*. New Delhi: Sage.

Parreñas, Rhacel. 2011. *Illicit Flirtations: Labor, Migration and Sex Trafficking in Tokyo*. Palo Alto, CA: Stanford University Press.

Peano, I. 2013. 'Opaque Loves: Governance and Escape in the Intimate Sphere of Nigerian Sex Workers', *Etnografia e Ricerca Qualitativa* 3: 359–84.

Piore, M.J. 1979. *Birds of Passage: Migrant Labor and Industrial Societies*. Cambridge: Cambridge University Press.

Piot, C. 2010. *Nostalgia for the Future: West Africa after the Cold War*. Chicago, IL: University of Chicago Press.

Piscitelli, A. 2007. 'Shifting Boundaries: Sex and Money in the North-East of Brazil', *Sexualities* 10(4): 489–500.

Plambech, S. 2010. 'From Thailand with Love: Transnational Marriage Migration in the Global Care Economy', in T. Zheng (ed.), *Sex Trafficking, Human Rights, and Social Justice*. New York: Routledge, pp. 47–61.

_____. 2014. 'Points of Departure: Migration Control and Anti-trafficking in the Lives of Nigerian Sex Worker Migrants after Deportation from Europe'. PhD thesis. Copenhagen: Department of Anthropology, University of Copenhagen.

Rytter, M. 2013. *Family Upheaval: Generation, Mobility and Relatedness among Pakistani Migrants in Denmark*. New York: Berghahn Books.

Safran, W. 1991. 'Diasporas in Modern Societies: Myths of Homeland and Return', *Diaspora: A Journal of Transnational Studies* 1(1): 83–99.

Salazar, N. B. 2010. 'Towards an Anthropology of Cultural Mobilities', *Crossings: Journal of Migration & Culture* 1(1): 53–68.

Salazar, N.B., and A. Smart. 2011. 'Anthropological Takes on (Im)mobility', *Identities* 18(6): 1–9.

Sanchez-Taylor, J. 2006. 'Female Sex Tourism: A Contradiction in Terms?', *Feminist Review* 83: 42–59.

Sandell, S.H. 1977. 'Women and the Economics of Family Migration', *The Review of Economics and Statistics* 59(4): 406–14.

Sassen, S. 2004. 'Global Cities and Survival Circuits', in B. Ehrenreich and A. Hochschild (eds), *Global Women: Nannies, Maids and Sex Workers in the New Economy*. New York: Henry Holt, pp. 254–274.

Seabrook, J. 1996. *Travels in the Skin Trade: Tourism and the Sex Industry*. London: Pluto Press.Sousa e Santos, D. de. 2009. 'Reading beyond the Love Lines: Examining Cuban Jineteras' Discourses of Love for Europeans', *Mobilities* 4(3): 407–26.

Spanger, M. 2013. 'Doing Love in the Borderland of Transnational Sex Work: Female Thai Migrants in Denmark', *NORA* 21(2): 92–107.

Ticktin, M. 2011. *Casualties of Care: Immigration and the Politics of Humanitarianism in France*. Berkeley, CA: University of California Press.

Van der Veer, P. (ed.). 1995. *Nation and Migration: The Politics of Space in the South Asian Diaspora*. Philadelphia, PA: University of Pennsylvania Press.

Venables, E. 2008. 'Senegalese Women and the Cyber Café: Online Dating and Aspirations of Transnational Migration in Ziguinchor', *African and Asian Studies* 7: 471–90.

Vigh, H.E. 2009. 'Wayward Migration: On Imagined Futures and Technological Voids', *Ethnos* 74(1): 91–109.

Wallerstein, I. 1974. *The Modern World-System: Capitalist Agriculture and the Origins of the European World Economy in the Sixteenth Century*. New York: Academic Press.

Wimmer, A., and N. Glick Schiller. 2002. 'Methodological Nationalism and Beyond: Nation-State Building, Migration and the Social Sciences', *Global Networks* 2(4): 301–34.

Yeates, N. 2012. 'Global Care Chains: A State-of-the-Art Review and Future Directions in Care Transnationalization Research', *Global Networks* 12(2): 135–54.

Zelizer, V. 2007. *The Purchase of Intimacy*. Princeton, NJ: Princeton University Press.

PART I

Migration Regimes and their Intimate Discontents

CHAPTER

1

Transnational Matchmaking
Marriage Practices of Chinese Migrants from Qingtian Living in Europe

Martina Bofulin

During the 2013 Chinese Spring Festival period, the Oushinet.com (*Ouzhou Shibaowang*) Internet portal for Chinese migrants living in Europe published an article by a Hangzhou-based journalist with a somewhat curious title: 'The "Leftovers" Spring Festival: a 36-year-old emigrant businessman from Italy returns to Qingtian to meet eighteen potential spousal candidates' (Oushinet.com 2013). The article goes on to introduce several cases of 'leftover' men and women (*shengnan* or *shengnü*) who are over the age of twenty-seven and (still) unmarried. The case of Wang Zheli, which features in the title of the article, is particularly telling. A native of Qingtian, a district in the south-eastern province of Zhejiang, and owner of a small Chinese restaurant enterprise in Italy, returned to his hometown during the Spring Festival festivities not only to vacation and reunite with his family members, but also to find a wife through *xiangqin*, a practice that could be dubbed as 'matchmaking'. Following his relatives, Wang left China at the age of twenty-six to work as a waiter in a Chinese restaurant in Vicenza in northern Italy, and gradually established his own restaurant business. Although he experienced success in his professional life, he was not as lucky when it came to matters of the heart. The article said: 'His "personal problem" became the target of family and friends' criticism'. While he was in Italy his parents would call him and talk exclusively about who was getting married, who had given birth and who would be getting grandchildren. His parents believed that it would be best for him to marry a girl from home, and knowing he would be returning for Spring Festival they immediately started the search for a suitable marriage candidate. Wang's one-month holiday thus became a series of eighteen consecutive meetings with potential brides, among them nurses, teachers, clerks and private entrepreneurs. Most of these meetings were unsuccessful, which drove his family members to despair. However, among all the candidates, there was one girl he really liked. But when asked if it might lead somewhere, he responded: 'I still have a few days and quite a few girls to meet. I have to be sure that there will be no problems in the future'. 'After all,' he said, 'these things cannot be hurried. Meeting potential spouses is not like going to the market to buy food. After successful negotiations you cannot simply exchange money for the goods' (Oushinet. com 2013).

This vignette is illustrative of the interplay of various elements that concern contemporary marriage patterns in China, particularly in the regions heavily influenced by out-migration. Recently, media across the globe exposed the worrisome attitude that different facets of Chinese society hold towards young adults, particularly women, who fail to fulfil society's expectations to marry in their mid-twenties. The derogatory term 'leftovers' has been coined for these men and women, and is frequently used not only in public and media discourses but also in official parlance (Fincher 2012). In general, in the last decades of rapid social and economic transformation, finding a good marriage partner has become increasingly important since marriages are seen as a vehicle for social mobility (Fan and Li 2002). In the small rural district of Qingtian, where roughly half of the inhabitants have left to work in Europe, Japan, USA and lately Africa and South America, these national trends are given an additional spin. Here marriage can also be a way for young people to migrate legally to different parts of the world, as well as a possibility to lead an economically more prosperous and independent life. In other cases, however, these marriages, once actively sought after, are no longer the preferred option.

Addressing how young people, native to Qingtian, look for and make decisions about their future spouses, this chapter will illustrate how marriage practices are integrated into the social fabric of Chinese migrants' place of origin, including the role of parents and kin, as well as how these different actors sustain or negotiate transnational migration. In particular, it looks at spousal choice, which is often mediated by kin and friends. This type of marriage selection has been widely problematized in the countries of settlement as supporting segregation and patriarchal structures, as well as serving as a legal but not necessarily legitimate means of immigration

(Strasser 2014). Here the matchmaking activities and the resulting conjugal unions are not exposed with the aim of 'exaggerating cultural difference' (Khandelwal 2009) or to contrast these practices with purportedly more Western 'love marriages', but rather to unveil the intimate economies of Qingtian's young people, which are shaped by local, national and transnational socio-economic structures as well as their own imaginations and initiatives. Through close ethnographic account, I address the role of matchmaking in the process of out-migration from Qingtian, its changing meaning among the Qingtianese elders and youth, as well as how the complex intertwining of structure and subjectivity produces different responses from the actors to matchmaking activities and subsequent marriages. I have observed marriage practices across national borders – that is, in the place of origin, as well as in the multiple places of settlement. The data for this chapter were gathered as a part of my doctoral research on different aspects of migration between the People's Republic of China (PRC) and Slovenia, and my postdoctoral project on the entrepreneurial practices and family lives of Chinese migrants in Belgrade, Serbia. Multi-sited ethnographic fieldwork was applied in three sets of locations: in different localities in Slovenia and Serbia where migrants from Zhejiang live and work, and in their place of origin in Qingtian district in the south-eastern part of Zhejiang province, PRC.[1]

Marriage Practices in the Chinese Context

The transnational turn in social studies and migration studies has highlighted the presence of practices, institutions and modes of belonging across national borders and the creation of concomitant transnational social spaces (Basch, Glick Schiller and Szanton Blanc 1994; Faist 2000; Levitt 2001), while feminist perspectives not only revealed the gendered and racialized nature of migration but also challenged the prevailing view of migrants pursuing only economic gains (Kofman at al. 2000). Moreover, scholars from diverse disciplinary backgrounds provided foundational work for overcoming some of the binaries that seemed to hinder a deeper analysis of the human condition and social processes in migration research including: local/global (Massey 1994) mobility/immobility (Urry 2007), economic transactions/intimate relationships (Zelizer 2007), family (private)/work (public) (Hochschild 1997). All this is reflected in the recent proliferation of research on marriages and migration that, according to Charsley (2012), examines several distinct aspects of migration studies: transnationalism, gender and power (Ballard 1990; Piper and Roces 2003; Constable 2005), regulating marriage migration (Wray

2012) and marriage, migration and integration (Alba and Nee 2003; Khoo 2011).

In the context of China, the literature on the marriage migration nexus covers mostly two areas: rural to urban marriage migration within China (Min and Eades 1995; Gaetano and Jacka 2004; Davis 2007) and Chinese women's transnational marriages to husbands from economically prosperous countries, mostly Taiwan and Japan (Liu and Liu 2008; Friedman 2010; Lu 2012). Much less attention is paid to marriages between members of Chinese diasporas or migrant communities and between them and Chinese living in PRC, which can also be seen as a form of transnational marriage. Among notable exceptions are contributions by Oxfeld (2005) and Schein (2005), who focus on transnational marriage networks of the Hakka and Miao minority populations living in PRC and other countries of settlement, and by Bao (2005) looking at Chinese diaspora in Thailand.

In China, it was daughters who traditionally married 'out' and had to be integrated into the new family (Baker 1979). Also, Davin (2007) writes that marrying outside the village was the general rule in much of China, although different communities observed this rule with various degrees of strictness. Oxfeld (2005) has thus observed that marriage was always a form of migration in the Chinese context, at least for the women. For them, marriage was also the main route to socio-economic mobility, hence the economic conditions in the husband's village were seen as important, and spatial hypergamy (marrying someone in a more affluent area) was prevalent (Lavely 1991). Furthermore, Fan and Li (2002: 623) argued that the role of location as one of the attributes for consideration in the spouse selection process increased during the period of socialist transition, marked by increased household opportunities and risks as well as the widening gap between regions within China, making marriage choices more crucial than in the pre-reform era.

In the distant past, arranged marriages had been a dominant tradition in China, which applied equally across social classes. In most cases, parents were the exclusive marriage decision makers to the extent that the couple often met for the first time on the day of their wedding (Xu and King Whyte 1990). At the beginning of the twentieth century, however, the practice came under heavy criticism from revolutionaries and reformists alike. After the Communists took power in 1949, they started to propagate 'free love' (*ziyou lian'ai*) and partner selection that did not involve parents or other intermediaries. However, Xu and King Whyte's (1990: 716) study showed that although the role of the parents consequently declined, 30–50 per cent of younger female respondents never or rarely dated their future husbands (in the sense of meeting in a private setting), and even for those who did, the dates almost always came after the decision to marry had been made.

Hence, the role of 'introducers' (*jieshao ren*), if not professional matchmakers (*hongniang*), as go-betweens for the prospective partners, remained important. Together with relatives, they strived to find a good match by evaluating each candidate's personal attributes (*tiaojian*) including age, education, occupation, income, family background, physical characteristics (especially height for men and appearance for women), personality, health and resources (Fan 2000).

Chu and Yu's (2009) study showed that in contemporary China marriage patterns have changed considerably in the post-reform decades. Regarding the marriage decision-making process, they found a substantial decline in marriages arranged by relatives and parents (14.40 per cent of marriages before 1970, to 7.37 per cent after 1990), but only a slight increase in marriages where the spouses met on their own (14.55 per cent before 1970 to 21.82 per cent after 1990). The surprising aspect was that the percentage of marriages arranged by a matchmaker remained high (36.64 per cent before 1970 to 24.75 per cent after 1990), but when reviewed for geographical distribution, the number of marriages that were the result of spouses meeting on their own was considerably higher in urban areas than in rural areas. These data also confirm numerous media reports that matchmaking practices are still widespread in China. In the big cities, people attend large-scale matchmaking parties, which are often organized for the parents rather than the unmarried men and women. Parents come en masse to the parks and other venues with homemade posters detailing their child's age, occupation, education and other 'marketable' characteristics, hoping to find a suitable candidate for a blind date (Jiang 2007; Jing 2010). The other, somewhat more low-key version of matchmaking is *xiangqin*, a meeting of potential partners organized by parents or close family members and friends. In the past, *xiangqin* referred to the meeting of potential partners and heads of households (*jiazhang*) before the arranged marriage took place. Contemporary versions of this practice may range from non-binding suggestions of marital candidates by family members, to more forceful persuasions. Although parents' total control of their child's marital choice is increasingly rare, a study by Riley (1994) confirmed that parents remained involved in the decision-making process, especially in rural areas where young people are more segregated and there is less dating culture.

Local Matchmaking for Global Audiences: Qingtian County and its Transnational Community

The relatively private and family-oriented nature of *xiangqin* matchmaking seems to be very well suited for this small rural district in Zhejiang province, which has had strong out-migration for more than a century. Qingtian's mountainous location with deposits of semi-precious green steatite stone, and its proximity to the port of Wenzhou,[2] initiated at the turn of the twentieth century a chain migration process not only to various places within China, but especially to foreign countries, both far and near (Ye 1986; Thunø 1999). Through peddling stone carvings and other miscellaneous objects, the Qingtianese managed to form communities across Europe as early as 1910 (Ye 1986; Thunø 1999; Beltrán 2003). Large-scale emigration, though, began in the 1980s with China's opening-up reforms. Local sources estimate that out of the half a million inhabitants roughly 42 per cent emigrated – mostly to Europe, but also to the Americas, and to parts of Asia and Africa (Zhou 2006). Consequently, emigration became the prevalent economic activity and the migrants became the 'main production force' (*shengchan li*) in the district. Migrants from this part of Zhejiang province are not only the main driving force of development locally, but are also responsible for internationalizing the 'Wenzhou economic model' based on labour-intensive family firms with a strong emphasis on manufacturing export goods (Tomba 1999). In short, emigration and the subsequent return flow of people, objects, information and money has thoroughly transformed a once backward region, and has shaped local mentality such that migration is perceived as a prestigious career option; and, despite the recent economic development within China, for many it is still the *only* career option.

If marriages in wider Chinese society are a vehicle for social and geographic mobility (usually the woman's) as mentioned earlier, in Qingtian this phenomenon is only more accentuated. Marriages connected to out-migration are particularly sought after since they not only offer material security and remittances but also spatial mobility, which is seen in Qingtian as integral to social mobility, affluence and access to foreign travel. During my fieldwork in China and Europe, I met many couples who became married through *xiangqin*. While this was openly discussed in Qingtian, my interlocutors in Europe were at first more apprehensive to explain how they had met their spouse. If I discretely suggested that it might have been through *xiangqin*, they often wondered how I might have known about that, but then relaxed and told me more about it. A person can participate in a number of these meetings with various potential candidates, and depending on the circumstances, they will either meet alone at a public venue (restaurant or coffee bar) or, less often, in the presence of a friend or a younger relative. As I will show, communication technologies are becoming an increasingly important part of this practice. The following stories illustrate how *xiangqin* fits into the everyday practices of the Qingtianese, and what the connection is between this practice and migration. While both cases feature women, this is not the rule. Men also, albeit in smaller numbers, partake in *xiangqin* with migrant women, get married and then join them in the country of settlement. The first case shows the rather typical pattern of matchmaking performed by friends that results in marriage, and also reveals the strong and geographically dispersed social networks among the Qingtianese. The second case portrays an unsuccessful *xiangqin*, which is the result of the young woman's strong standpoint that goes against her parents' wishes. Both cases thus convey the wide range of responses among young people taking part in these matchmaking activities, as well as how these responses are conditioned by an individual's social location and the changing structures in the world around them.

The Case of Lan: From Worker to Boss through Marriage

I met twenty-eight-year-old Lan, a mother of two, during my fieldwork at the Chinese market in New Belgrade, Serbia. Two decades ago, the relatively high immigration levels of Chinese nationals resulted in the formation of a vast wholesale and retail market for inexpensive goods in the suburbs of Serbia's capital (Chang 2012). Lan was a native of Qingtian, which she left at the age of sixteen to find work (*da gong*) in Hangzhou, the capital of Zhejiang province. One of her acquaintances, a fellow townsman (*laoxiang ren*), secured her a job in a large department store in the northern province of Shandong. There she met Weiwei, also a native of Qingtian, and the two became good friends. After some time, Weiwei returned to her village of birth for a visit and met a young man who had just returned from Serbia to spend vacation time with his grandparents. They immediately 'liked each other', Weiwei said, and after a short courtship they got married and moved to a small town in northern Serbia where his parents owned a small store. The young couple would go regularly to New Belgrade to buy from wholesale merchants at the Chinese market. There they learned that one of their regular suppliers, a fifty-year-old female manager (*laobaniang*) was looking for a bride for her son, Chun. Weiwei immediately thought of Lan, whose last romantic relationship had gone sour. She persuaded the manager that hardworking and humble Lan would be a good choice for her son. After obtaining the mother's approval, Weiwei proceeded to introduce the potential partners through QQ, China's most widely used Internet instant messaging tool. Lan and Chun started to talk regularly online over webcam, and exchanged photos and music files. She, squeezed into a small cubicle in a large clothing store in Shandong, and he, from behind a desk in a cramped family shop in New Belgrade. They talked extensively about their lives away from home, interrupted only by the occasional customer. He often talked about the beauties of his native village in the mountains over Qingtian. While talking he would perform the *qigong* movements, which he believed would keep him in good shape until old age. She shared details about her harsh life with her paternal grandmother (who did not like her) and about the pain of losing her mother at a very early age. These online chats and meetings eventually led to a binding decision. In January of the following year, when the busiest business period in Serbia had subsided, Chun travelled to China where the two met for the first time 'in the flesh' in the romantic setting of Hangzhou's Western Lake. One month later the wedding took place. After a few weeks he left his new wife and returned to Serbia. Lan soon discovered that she was pregnant and seven months later she delivered her first son. When he had reached three months old, she also left China to join her husband in Serbia, while the infant stayed behind in the care of her husband's younger sister.

This detailed description of one particular pathway to marriage of two Qingtian natives reveals several elements that are crucial for understanding the intimate migrations of individuals as well as the workings of century-long migration traditions in areas characterized by strong out-migration flows in China. This out-migration has vastly expanded the local youth's horizons of desire, albeit in a particular way: to seek fortunes abroad rather than looking for opportunities in the economically bustling areas of Eastern China.

Lan's migration to Europe might not have happened if it had not been for her friend Weiwei's intervention. In matchmaking, the role of the intermediary is crucial; usually, she has to be a person trusted by both parties to know the backgrounds of potential partners. She then has to evaluate the potential partners' 'conditions' (*tiaojian*) in the light of both families' expectations, as well as in accordance with the more general norms. The role of the intermediary is also to convince both sides to participate in *xiangqin*, and this usually requires some tactical consideration as to how to present the candidates to the respective families. In the case of Chun, it was his mother who first needed to be convinced that Lan was hardworking and sincere, while Lan, due to the distant relationship with her only surviving parent, did not consult her father. This is similar to Fan and Li's (2002) studies of marriages within the Chinese context: for long-distance marriage migration, an intermediary is often involved who provides information on the prospective spouses *and* on the location of the couple's future residence. Often the result is 'snowballing' or chain migration that leads to focused migration streams, from specific places of origin to specific destinations (Han and Eades, in Fan and Li 2002).

This often also leads to the formation of communities where the practice of marriage between members of the same group is prevalent. Indeed, as Beck-Gernsheim (2007) observed, a large body of literature seems to indicate that this is a persistent trend across migrant groups and different countries of settlement. There are a number of reasons for this. Firstly, there are the structural conditions in the countries of settlement – mainly immigration policies. The regulations regarding entry into some countries of settlement can favour family reunification, so it can be easier to enter a country legally as the wife or the husband of an already established migrant (ibid.). Similarly, overly restrictive immigration regimes can close other avenues of immigration. According to Kibria (2012), increasingly stringent immigration laws in the UK actually raised the importance of intra-group marriages for community building in the case of the Bangladeshi Muslim diaspora in Britain.

Moreover, the migrant's family members often prefer a marriage partner from their own community. Sometimes the men and women 'back home' are seen as less affected by perceived bad influences of modernity – that is, they are less spoiled, less emancipated, more caring and more family-oriented. Strasser (2014) describes that in Austria, Turkish parents believe that men in Turkey are more caring, thoughtful and reliable and thus more appropriate for their daughters than local men. Also, migrant men and women are often at the bottom of social hierarchies in the countries of settlement, having been at the top in the countries of origin. In the case described by Thai (2005), a Vietnamese man in the United States turned to his home country to find a bride because there is a severe shortage of women in the Vietnamese diaspora in the United States, and he, a low-wage worker, was at the bottom of the marriage market there. In another case of British Pakistanis, Ballard (1990) describes the spousal choice from the home country as advantageous for family honour, the consolidation of assets and the continued immigration of kinsfolk. This community building can result in considerable status enhancement for families who are able to facilitate cross-border migration for other kinsfolk.

In Qingtian, this preference on a discursive level takes the form of interfamily intimacy only possible through usage of a common language. Parents thus insist that their prospective son/daughter-in-law speaks the local dialect, *Qingtian hua*, which is locally understood as synonymous with being a Qingtianese. There are at least three underlying reasons for this. Firstly, parents prefer somebody who has been socialized in the Qingtianese transnational social space (including Qingtian), and who will understand and accept migration as a necessary and indispensable part of his/her life. Therefore, he or she will be able to 'eat bitter' (*chi ku*) – that is, be able to endure hardships, while at the same time be prepared to share possible rewards with family and kin through remittances. Secondly, as described by Oxfeld (2005), in the case of Hakka Chinese migrating to India a century ago, some migrant husbands never returned home or did not remain in contact with family members in China. Parents can therefore insist on intra-group marriage, because they know it is easier to exert social control over somebody whose family still lives in Qingtian, and ensure continuous support from overseas in the form of regular contact and remittances. Thirdly, as already mentioned, it also ensures continuity in the migration process for the in-group members, especially kin. Chinese citizens' mobility to most countries, especially Western ones, is still heavily obstructed through restrictive immigration policies. Relatives and friends abroad are thus extremely valued since they provide access to a legal way of entering the countries of settlement. It is a widely shared belief in Qingtian that the 'kin brings kin, friends bring friends' (*qinqi dai qinqi, pengyou dai pengyou*) – or in other words, the in-group members have priority over others in sponsoring the immigration.

Another point is the technologies that mediate these relationships. Although new technologies (Internet calling and video services, instant messaging services, social media) are widely recognized as an important tool in sustaining transnational lives (Madianou and Miller 2012), it is also true that migrants in the past succeeded in keeping a lively exchange of information with their near and dear across borders (Morawska 2001). Nonetheless, as regards Qingtianese migrants, the spread of the Internet to rural China, with its instant messaging tools and multiple ways to exchange data, has made it possible for them to connect across large distances with not only kin and friends but also with other fellow townsmen, in China or beyond, whom they might not have met previously in the flesh. Moreover, Internet and mobile applications like Tencent QQ or Weixin are viewed as appropriate and convenient mediums for the equivalent of the 'first date'. Online meetings may be perceived as being much less stressful or embarrassing than 'live' meetings, and they are well suited for migrants' busy lives. Since matchmaking activities are embedded in migrants' everyday practices, virtual dating also saves time.

Often the relationship is well established online before the first actual meeting takes place. This might happen when the migrant returns home for a visit, as seen in the example above. If the visit falls over a festive period or on an auspicious day (e.g. Chinese New Year), this is an additional bonus. The local Qingtianese newspaper reported that the number of couples who registered their wedding day at the local government magistrate's office on Valentine's Day has been growing in recent years, and in 2012 it surpassed the 2011 record of eighty weddings on that day. According to the report, many of the couples had returned to China from abroad for this very occasion (Shao 2012).

Lastly, Lan's case also confirms the traditional pattern of women 'marrying up' in China. Lan married a financially better-off migrant entrepreneur living in Europe, and gained access to foreign travel. Once a wage-worker (*dagong ren*), she managed to become a 'young woman manager' (*xiao laobanniang*) through marriage – a status distinction crucial in mobility perceptions among the inhabitants of Qingtian and the wider Zhejiang region. Although she was performing much the same work as before as a sales clerk, she was no longer perceived as a worker but as part of the entrepreneurial family. But her moving from a 'worker' position in China to a 'boss' position abroad is not only a case of hypergamy, but also of 'spatial hypergamy' (Lavely 1991), where movement to a more prosperous area is one of the ways an individual can move up the social ladder.

Not all Qingtianese migrants marry through *xiangqin* or other matchmaking practices. Weiwei's marriage, for example, was a product of a chance encounter and subsequent 'free love' (*ziyou lian'ai*), as are the marriages of many, especially younger, Qingtianese migrants. Two of my interlocutors, both twenty-year-old male migrants in Belgrade, explained that 'free love' in the realm of the Chinese migrant community in Belgrade has much to do with appearance. They said if a girl is beautiful, she will be pursued by many suitors in this micro-marriage market and she will choose one quite early on, resulting in marriage at a fairly young age. According to them, everyone else needs to rely on 'introductions' (*jieshao*) by family and kin, especially since there are only limited numbers of young, unmarried and suitable candidates available locally. Their understanding of a 'suitable' candidate obviously does not include the local Serbian and other minority candidates, and it also expresses the gendered patterns of desire, where appearance is still a key attribute for a female candidate.

However, it is true that young Qingtianese have considerably more freedom to choose their spouse up until they reach the age that is perceived as critical in relation to marriage more or less across different social groups in China. The social pressure of being unmarriageable has always existed in China, and women over twenty-five were and still are considered 'old' for marriage (Gaetano 2009).[3] But in the last decade of turbulent and far-reaching socio-economic change, the public discourses on young men and women who have not married by the age of thirty and twenty-seven, respectively, became increasingly channelled in the form of moral panic about lost generations and population imbalance, culminating in defamatory portraits of unmarried people in their late twenties as 'leftover women' (*shengnü*) and, less commonly, 'leftover men' (*shengnan*) (Fincher 2012).

The Case of Jin: Does Marrying a Migrant Necessarily Mean Marrying Up?

The fear that their daughter might be turning into a *shengnü* drove the parents of twenty-five-year-old Qingtian native Jin to resort to matchmaking.

She was perceived as a beauty with an education well above the average, a promising job and a good family background. But these traits also worked against her since the pattern of women marrying up is still prevalent in China. Her degree from a good university, her talent and her good job, a combination often referred to as the 'three highs' (*san gao*) in China, created the expectation that she had to find a husband who would in some way surpass these. Her parents thus believed that a union with an heir of a well-off local overseas Chinese might be the best solution for Jin. She detested the idea at the beginning, but slowly agreed to matchmaking. Her aunts were soon calling on a regular basis to inform her parents of various available candidates. If her parents felt a candidate was suitable, they would slowly begin to persuade her to meet him online via QQ.

The first candidate was the son of Qingtianese restaurant owners from Austria, arranged by Jin's aunt in Austria. He was twenty-seven at that time, and held a high school diploma. She described their first conversation online as awkward, with long moments of silence when neither of them knew what to say. He complained that his life was dull (*wuliao*) and that he mostly spent it between the first and the second floor, meaning that his life consisted of working in his parents' restaurant on the first floor and living in his room on the second floor. Jin later commented on this statement saying: 'When I heard that... Just to imagine that this could become my life... I asked him if he had some other plans for the future, to do something different than restaurant business... He just said: "What kind of plans? Can you tell me what I could do?"'

Jin was less than impressed by what she saw as a lack of ambition, and felt that he was too immature. Her aunt pressed her for a decision, stressing that he was a good candidate whose family was interested in a quick wedding. His mother had already booked an air ticket for her son to return to China and so the wedding could happen within a month. In one of their QQ chats, the Austrian suitor suggested that they could go on a romantic trip to Hangzhou and get to know each other better. Jin declined the invitation to the provincial capital, and finally also his and his family's propositions. She said that she could not decide so quickly and that he should not come to China and spend money on something that may not come true. After this they exchanged a few more, short online talks, but it was clear that nothing substantial would come of it. Jin's parents were not very happy, but their pleas for Jin to reconsider her decision fell on deaf ears, with her mostly staying in her room and not talking to her parents. As Constable (2005) noted, Chinese women nowadays have much more say in choosing their own marriage partner than they had in the past, and they are able to decline a potential match. In Oxfeld's (2005) words: 'While elders could suggest, everyone has to agree'.

But Jin's parents did not give up. Within a week, her mother's older sister had found another candidate. He was a twenty-five-year-old Qingtianese living on an island off the African coast, where his parents had a large supermarket. His mother was in town and was meeting girls who might be suitable for her son. She invited Jin to tea where she explained that they live in a beautiful place where the sky touches the turquoise sea. 'The island is scarcely populated but all the people are rich', she said, and 'all the people there, including me and my son, hold French citizenship'. Jin left quite enthusiastic and agreed to meet her son online. They talked a few times but his mother turned out to be too demanding. She wanted Jin to visit her again so that she could have one more look at her and wanted to know her birth date to see if she was compatible with her son.[4] Jin felt that this was inappropriate, and her parents agreed. They declined the second invitation, saying that their daughter was too busy and the matter was closed. Jin remarked: 'I'm sure she is feverishly collecting, comparing and judging the girls right now. To me this seems as it was in America when they brought the slaves from Africa. They would compare them on the basis of their appearance and ability to work. Disgusting'.

Jin's education in an urban centre on the bustling east coast of China gave an alternative to her hometown's vision of success and modernity, which did not entail years of waiting tables, working fingers to the bone in a factory or peddling cheap merchandise in Europe or elsewhere. Rather than marrying and going abroad, as thousands from her hometown had done, she envisioned a future for herself where young college professionals find jobs that will allow them to develop their independent careers with modern urban lives. In her view, modern life did not mean being tucked away in a restaurant far away in a foreign place, nor did she think that a successful match could be based on the horoscope. This is not to say that her choices excluded any practical consideration about marriage. She still subscribed to the prevailing model of 'marrying up' – that is, marrying a better educated, financially secure male with abilities (*nengli*) – but her expectations went beyond 'conditions'; or, as Constable (2005) puts it, practical consideration (financial security) does not preclude feelings (love). In China today, Farrer (2004: 180) argues, women participate in the moral economy in which love and money are the two values that must be balanced against each other.

What stands out in Jin's story is her rather strong and vocal agency that rests on her, not her parents', vision of personal development. She told me that consenting to matchmaking was a way to negotiate with her parents as well as with her potential future partner in order to fulfil at least some of her wishes. Her greatest wish was to continue her studies, preferably abroad, or at least to start her independent life in one of the big cities of Eastern

China. At that time, she said: 'Basically, I now have two possibilities. I can find a stable job and a husband here, in Qingtian, or marry an overseas Chinese and go abroad. I used to joke with my mother that I would marry an overseas Chinese if she gives me two years of overseas studies'. Although presented as a joke, she was actually testing the ground for turning her wishes into reality. By subjugating herself to her parents' matchmaking she was inventively manipulating the practice in order to obtain some benefits for herself, while still keeping a good relationship with her kin. After all, she knew she could play this game of matchmaking for quite some time, since her parents would not give up easily. They will persist until a spouse is found, as illustrated by the insistence of the parents of the restaurant owner mentioned earlier.

At the heart of Jin's story is the conflict between her own ideas of what it means to 'marry up' and that of her parents' generation. Her parents believed she would secure her future and social status by marrying a wealthy overseas migrant – a pattern that has been common among local youth for the last thirty years. Because of her good looks, her education and her family's social status, she is able to choose from candidates who are largely inaccessible to the vast majority of Qingtian girls with a lower social status, although soon she might be considered too old. Jin, on the other hand, does not believe that marriage to a poorly educated, albeit wealthy, migrant equals marrying up. She still favours the 'marrying up' model, however, but one that is more in alignment with post-reform China's modern, urban and cosmopolitan notions of personal development. She wants 'independence', to 'develop herself' (*fazhan ziji*) and pursue her dreams – and, in her view, marriage should allow her to do that. It is undoubtedly this insistence on independence that made the parents of the Austrian candidate wonder if she was 'capable of bitter life' (*hui chi ku*), a personal characteristic of endurance and perseverance highly valued by Qingtianese migrants, often necessary for economic survival in labour-intensive Qingtianese businesses in Europe and elsewhere.

Entanglements of Spousal Choice in Post-reform China

The two stories illustrate some of the key issues in the research on intimacy and mobility with special regard to marriages and migration nexus: the changing nature of spousal selection, the contested meaning of a good match, and the intertwining of structure and subjectivity in the context of spousal choice. Matchmaking, in this chapter presented in the form of *xiangqin*, was in the past the core of an arranged marriage in China (Bao 2005). The main function of this practice was to connect two young individuals with matching familial backgrounds, as in the popular saying 'the doors match the doors, and the window matches the window' (*mendang hudui*). However, in post-reform China this practice has undergone considerable transformations in the sense that it has become more democratic as well as fraught with intergenerational conflict. As we have seen, today all parties have to agree on the selection, and this is backed by the legal framework as well as the greater autonomy of the youth. The result is that the practice has changed from being the parents' decision forced on the children to no more than the consultation of parents (and other relatives) in the pre-selection process. Even though the practice has changed, the goal has remained the same: to find the best possible spouse for one's child. But the key question, which echoes Constable's (2005) reflections on what constitutes upward mobility in the context of marriage, is not who might the best possible match be, but who determines what 'the best' is in this context. And the answer lies in the generational perspective of spousal selection.

Emily Chao (2005: 35), in the context of marriage strategies in a village populated by Naxi in south-western China, reports tensions arising from conflicting generational views of marriage and mobility informed by the experiences of two very different economic periods. Jin's story channels this insight. While her parents and other elders emphasized the importance of the family, financial security and even divine forces through horoscope speculations, Jin's college years in the urban and cosmopolitan East China infused her with ideas of independence and self-fulfilment as crucial elements of the modern marriage. For the inhabitants of Qingtian, the most desired path to social mobility in the last three decades was through physical mobility to Europe and other countries of settlement, but the development of a market economy provided the Qingtianese with alternative means of economic mobility. Educated Jin was among the young people who embraced these transformations wholeheartedly and felt in charge of her destiny. But Lan, an uneducated migrant worker in Shandong with a humble background, was in a more precarious position. Her response to matchmaking and the marriage promise with a relatively successful migrant was thus much more welcome. Following this, it could then be argued that within the younger generation of Chinese there are disparate groups that may have very different views on marriage, intimacy and desire, and hence also different responses to matchmaking and spousal selection by their elders. As argued elsewhere (Constable 2003), the agency of the potential bride is heavily dependent on her social location.

What is more, Chao (2005) argues, that from the point of view of parents, marriage fixes one's position in both the hierarchy of place and the economic hierarchy. Fixing one's child abroad has in the past been mostly a good thing in the case of the Qingtianese. The strong out-migration consequently transformed the place of origin, so that despite being quite rural, Qingtian was seen as a cosmopolitan place par excellence in the region, and a desired place to live for many of the inhabitants of the surrounding counties between about 1990 and 2005. But it seems that in these restless times locations are also moving, at least in the hierarchies of modern and cosmopolitan places. A small county cannot compete with a big metropolis in East China, and for the young Qingtianese the hometown's narratives of bitter-life yielding-wealth may no longer be enough to convince them to follow the beaten path of migration. Marriage to a migrant is therefore no longer the preferred choice of most locals, especially those who are relatively well-off, and this trend may grow with the current economic stagnation in many of the countries of settlement. This is likely to be true not only for Qingtian, but for numerous other 'hometowns of overseas Chinese' in Eastern China (see Oxfeld 2005).

Although the younger generations can now exert considerable agency with regards to the past, and may desire very different partners than their parents would choose for them, young people would still prefer to negotiate some form of common ground than revolt against their parents. Hansen and Pang (2005) explain that social transformation in China has brought about individualization that demonstrates itself in the remarkable sense of personal responsibility that young adults have. In practice, this means that when finding a marriage partner is not yet considered urgent, young people stress their own individual role and right to make demands regarding their intimate relationships. But as soon as they start to consider marriage and think about the criteria that a spouse ought to live up to, the opinions of their parents and siblings become more important. Jin, similar to many of my interlocutors, was first against partaking in *xiangqin*, but later changed her mind. While she saw the *xiangqin* as an opportunity to negotiate with her parents to get what she desired, other interlocutors often simply stated that their parents act in their best interests and consequently used the practice as a kind of 'family-mediated dating'.

This does not appear to be limited to the Chinese context only. Kibria (2012: 235) reports on a very similar phenomenon among Bangladeshi Muslims in the United States, and sees it as 'hybrid cultural forms that integrate tradition and modern impulse'. The modern impulse entails the emotions and romantic feelings that may occur during or after these arranged meetings. *Xiangqin* in Qingtian thus increasingly takes place in expensive, foreign-looking establishments that not only convey the financial standing of the male candidate, but also hints at some sort of cosmopolitan romance. In the cases of my interlocutors, *xiangqin* and subsequent marriage are not thought of as a practical arrangement devoid of emotion.

It is rather an arrangement that needs to be filled with romantic feelings, hence the frequent use of Hangzhou's Western Lake as the setting for the first meeting of potential spouses. Lan's photos from that time are just the same as the millions of photos of other happy young couples: laughing, posing and flirting. These photos point to the increasingly blurred lines between matchmaking and dating, as well as between arranged marriages and romantic relationships, and illustrate how immensely reductive these binary categories are (see Constable 2005; Fernandez and Jensen 2013).

Conclusion

Global processes of migration regimes, economic redistribution and geopolitics exert influence on people's everyday intimate lives and decisions, but these decisions, actions and practices in turn sustain or transform the global flows. In Qingtian, the well-established migration flows and the networks that span the globe have been enabling young people to access foreign lands in various ways. One of the preferred options for decades, especially for women, was migration through marriage, often initiated through the practice of matchmaking.

In this chapter, I have presented two detailed ethnographic cases of matchmaking between Qingtianese migrants and potential spouses from the place of origin. Each case was then situated into the particular complexity of the structural conditions and subjectivity to expose the main aspects of this practice and how they deepen our understanding of marriages and migrations, and the connection between them. While similar practices exist in many migration contexts (e.g. in the Turkish, Vietnamese, Pakistani and Bangladeshi communities abroad), the cases from Qingtian reveal different responses to matchmaking among the youth that are contingent on their social position. What is more, matchmaking has an increasingly generational perspective, where the elders' understanding of what constitutes a suitable candidate is very different to the younger generations' desires and expectations. Young people, however, have much more say in the matter than in the past, and their changing hierarchies of (desired) locations as well as desired lifestyles make marriage to a migrant a less attractive affair today than it was a decade ago. Still, for many young Qingtianese, a marriage to a migrant abroad remains the 'passage to hope' (Beck and Beck-Gernsheim 2010) – a life overseas with freedom of movement and financial stability, if not affluence and social status. For others, though, marriage may rather represent the hope that this passage can be achieved in China.

Martina Bofulin is a researcher at the Slovenian Migration Institute, Research Centre of Slovenian Academy of Sciences and Arts. Previously, she was a JSPS postdoctoral fellow at the University of Osaka in Japan, and a postdoctoral fellow at the University of Belgrade, Serbia, where she carried out extensive fieldwork among Chinese migrants. She is an author of the monograph *Home Away From Home: Migration from PR China to Slovenia* (in Slovene language).

NOTES

1. I applied the participant observation method, and took an active part in the lives of the Zhejiangese in Slovenia as a community interpreter and mediator. In Belgrade, while I also occasionally acted as community interpreter, I taught English to several families on a regular basis. Moreover, in their place of origin in China, semi-structured interviews and informal discussions were conducted with the relatives of Zhejiangese migrants in Slovenia as well as with representatives of migrant- and education-related local institutions. In addition, media reports and commentaries on the topic of emigration/immigration in China, Slovenia and Serbia were analysed.
2. Wenzhou is a large port city in the south-eastern part of Zhejiang province that has, similar to Qingtian, been an important source area for Chinese migrants to Europe.
3. After the establishment of the People's Republic of China, a legal age of marriage was set. At that time, men could get married at twenty years of age and women at eighteen. The law was later changed, and in the 1980 and 2000 versions, the legal age of marriage was raised to twenty-two for men and twenty for women. Raising the legal marriage age was seen as an important part of birth control policies.
4. Many people in China believe in auspicious days and harmonious unions, calculated on the basis of the Chinese Almanac Calendar (*huangli*). Often parents consult a taoist priest or fortune-teller to determine who would be a good match and when the most important ceremonies should take place (e.g. wedding) in order to ensure a stable marriage and a prosperous life.

REFERENCES

Alba, R., and V. Nee. 2003. *Remaking the American Mainstream*. Cambridge, MA: Harvard University Press.

Baker, H. 1979. *Chinese Family and Kinship*. New York: Columbia University Press.

Ballard, R. 1990. 'Migration and Kinship: The Differential Effect on Marriage Rules on the Processes of Punjabi Migration to Britain', in C. Clark, C. Peach and S. Vertovec (eds), *South Asians Overseas*. Cambridge: Cambridge University Press, pp. 219–49.

Bao, J. 2005. *Marital Acts: Gender, Sexuality and Identity among the Chinese Thai Diaspora*. Honolulu, HI: University of Hawaii Press.

Basch, L., N. Glick Schiller and C. Blanc Szanton. 1994. *Nations Unbound: Transnational Projects, Post-colonial Predicaments and Deterritorialized Nation-States*. Langhorne, PA: Gordon and Breach.

Beck, U., and E. Beck-Gernsheim. 2010. 'Passage to Hope: Marriage, Migration, and the Need for Cosmopolitan Turn in Family Research', *Journal of Family Theory and Review* 2: 401–14.

Beck-Gernsheim, E. 2007. 'Transnational Lives, Transnational Marriages', *Global Networks* 7(3): 271–88.

Beltrán, A.J. 2003. *Los Ocho Inmortales Cruzan el Mar: Chinos en Extremo Occidente*. Barcelona: Edicions Bellaterra.

Chang, F.B. 2012. 'Myth and Migration: Zhejiangese Merchants in Serbia', in F.B. Chang and S.T. Rucker-Chang (eds), *Chinese Migrants in Russia, Central Asia and Eastern Europe*. Abingdon, Oxon and New York: Routledge, pp. 137–53.

Chao, E. 2005. 'Cautionary Tales: Marriage Strategies, State Discourse, and Women's Agency in a Naxi Village in Southwestern China', in N. Constable (ed.), *Cross-Border Marriages: Gender and Mobility in Transnational Asia*. Philadelphia, PA: University of Pennsylvania Press, pp. 17–33.

Charsley, K. 2012. 'Transnational Marriage', in K. Charsley (ed.), *Transnational Marriage: New Perspectives from Europe and Beyond*. New York: Routledge, pp. 3–23.

Chu, C.C.Y., and R. Yu. 2009. *Understanding Chinese Families: A Comparative Study of Taiwan and Southeast China*. Oxford: Oxford University Press.

Constable, N. 2003. *Romance on a Global Stage: Pen Pals, Virtual Ethnography, and 'Mail Order' Marriages*. Berkeley, CA: University of California Press.

———. 2005. *Cross-Border Marriages: Gender and Mobility in Transnational Asia*. Philadelphia, PA: University of Pennsylvania Press.

Davin, D. 2007. 'Marriage Migration in China and East Asia', *Journal of Contemporary China* 16(50): 83–95.

Faist, T. 2000. 'Transnationalization in International Migration: Implications for the Study of Citizenship and Culture', *Ethnic and Racial Studies* 23(2): 189–222.

Fan, C.C. 2000. 'Migration and Gender in China', in C.M. Lau and J. Shen (eds), *China Review 2000*. Hong Kong: Chinese University Press, pp. 217–48.

Fan, C.C., and L. Li. 2002. 'Marriage and Migration in Transitional China: A Field Study of Gaozhou, Western Guandong', *Environment and Planning* 34: 619–38.

Farrer, J. 2004. 'The Changing Moral Economy of Chinese Sexuality: An Archeology of Ethical Discourse in Recent Chinese Popular Discourse', *Revista* Española del Pacifico 16: 169–90.

Fernandez, N.T., and T.G. Jensen. 2013. 'Intimate Contradictions: Comparing the Impact of Danish Family Unification Laws on Pakistani and Cuban Marriage Migrants', *Journal of Ethnic and Migration Studies* 40(7): 1136–53.

Fincher, L.H. 2012. 'China's Leftover Women', *New York Times*, 11 October. Retrieved 10 February 2013 from http://www.nytimes.com/2012/10/12/opinion/global/chinas-leftover-women.html?_r=0.

Friedman, S.L. 2010. 'Determining "Truth" at the Border: Immigration Interviews, Chinese Marital Migrants, and Taiwan's Sovereignty Dilemmas', *Citizenship Studies* 14(2): 167–83.

Gaetano, A.M. 2009. 'Single Women in Urban China and the "Unmarried Crisis": Gender Resilience and Gender Transformation', Working paper 31, Center for East and South-East Asian Studies. Retrieved 12 October 2013 from http://www.ace.lu.se/upload/Syd_och_sydostasienstudier/pdf/Gaetano.pdf.

Gaetano, A.M., and T. Jacka. 2004. *Women and Rural-to-Urban Migration in Contemporary China*. Columbia: Columbia University Press.

Hansen, Halskov M., and C. Pang. 2005. 'Me and My Family: Perceptions of Individual and Collective among Young Rural Chinese', *European Journal of East Asian Studies* 7(1): 75–99.

Hochschild, A.R. 1997. *The Time Bind: When Work Becomes Home and Home Becomes Work*. New York: Metropolitan Books.

Jiang, W. 2007. 'The New Model Matchmaking', *China Pictorial*, October. Retrieved 12 March 2012 from http://www.rmhb.com.cn/chpic/htdocs/english/200710/7-1.htm.

Jing, M. 2010. 'Matchmaking Flourishing in City Parks among Parents', *ChinaDaily.com*, 12 February. Retrieved 12 May 2012 from http://www.chinadaily.com.cn/cndy/201002/12/content_9466082.htm.

Khandelwal, M. 2009. 'Arranging Love: Interrogating the Vantage Point in Cross-Border Feminism', *Signs Journal of Women in Culture and Society* 34(31): 583–609.

Khoo, S. 2011. 'Intermarriage, Integration and Multiculturalism: A Demographic Perspective', in M. Clyne and J. Jupp (eds), *Multiculturalism and Integration: A Harmonious Relationship*. Sydney: ANU E Press, pp. 101–19.

Kibria, N. 2012. 'Transnational Marriage and the Bangladeshi Muslim Diaspora in Britain and the United States', *Religion and Culture* 13(2): 227–40.

Kofman, E., et al. 2000. *Gender and International Migration in Europe: Employment, Welfare, and Politics*. New York: Routledge.

Lavely, W. 1991. 'Marriage and Mobility under Rural Collectivization', *in* R.S. Watson and P.B. Ebrey (eds), *Marriage and Inequality in Chinese Society*. Berkeley, CA: University of California Press, pp. 286–312.

Levitt, P. 2001. *The Transnational Villagers*. Berkeley, CA and London: University of California Press.

Liu, L., and H. Liu. 2008. 'Boundary-Crossing through the Cyberspace: Chinese Women and Transnational Marriages since 1994', in K.E. Kuan-Pearce (ed.), *Chinese Women and Cyberspace*. Amsterdam: Amsterdam University Press, *pp.* 249–70.

Lu, M.C. 2012. 'Transnational Marriages as a Strategy of Care Exchange: Veteran Soldiers and their Mainland Chinese Spouses in Taiwan', *Global Networks* 12(2): 233–51.

Madianou, M., and D. Miller. 2012. *Migration and the New Media: Transnational Families and Polymedia*. London and New York: Routledge.

Massey, D. 1994. *Space, Place, and Gender*. Minneapolis: University of Minnesota Press.

Min, H., and J.S. Eades. 1995. 'Brides, Bachelors and Brokers: The Marriage Market in Rural Anhui in an Era of Economic Reform', *Modern Asian Studies* 29(4): 841–69.

Morawska, E. 2001. 'Immigrants, Transnationalism, and Ethnicization: A Comparison of This Great Wave and the Last', in G. Gerstle and J.H. Mollenkopf (eds), *E Pluribus Unum? Contemporary and Historical Perspectives on Immigrant Political Integration*. New York: Russell Sage, pp. 175–212.

Oushinet.com. 2013. 'The "Leftovers" Spring Festival: 36-year-old Emigrant from Italy Returns to Qingtian to Meet with 18 Potential Marriage Candidates'. Retrieved 12 March 2013 from http://www.oushinet.com/182-544-214243.aspx. Also available at http://qjwb.zjol.com.cn/html/2013-02/12/content_2003286.htm?div=-1 (last accessed 15 January 2018).

Oxfeld, E. 2005. 'Cross-Border Hypergamy? Marriage Exchanges in a Transnational Hakka Community', in N. Constable (ed.), *Cross-Border Marriages: Gender and Mobility in Transnational Asia*. Philadelphia, PA: University of Pennsylvania Press, pp. 17–33.

Piper, N., and M. Roces. 2003. *Wife or Worker? Asian Women and Migration*. Lanham, MD: Rowman & Littlefield.

Riley, N. 1994. 'Interwoven Lives: Parents, Marriage and Guanxi in China', *Journal of Marriage and Family* 56(4): 791–805.

Schein, L. 2005. 'Marrying out of Place: Hmong/Miao Women Across and Beyond China', in N. Constable (ed.), *Cross-Border Marriages: Gender and Mobility in Transnational Asia*. Philadelphia, PA: University of Pennsylvania Press, pp. 53–79.

Shao, Y. 2012. 'Zhejiang Qiaoxiang Qingtian: Qingrenjie Huan Jiehun Dengji Gaofeng', *ChinaNews.com*. Retrieved 12 October 2013 from http://www.chinanews.com/df/2012/02-13/3665551.shtml.

Strasser, S. 2014. 'Repressive Autonomy: Discourses on and Surveillance of Marriage Migration from Turkey to Austria', *Migration Letters* 11(3): 316–28.

Thunø, M. 1999. 'Moving Stones from China to Europe', in F. Pieke and H. Mallee (eds), *Internal and International Migration: Chinese Perspectives*. Richmond, UK: Curzon Press, pp. 159–79.

Thai, H.C. 2005. 'Globalization as a Gender Strategy: Respectability, Masculinity, and Convertibility across the Vietnamese Diaspora', in R.P. Appelbaum and W.I. Robinson (eds), *Critical Globalization Studies*. New York: Routledge, pp. 76–92.

Tomba, L. 1999. 'Exporting the "Wenzhou Model" to Beijing and Florence', in F.N. Pieke and H. Mallee (eds), *Internal and International Migration: Chinese Perspectives*. Richmond, UK: Curzon Press, pp. 280–94.

Urry, J. 2007. *Mobilities*. Cambridge: Cambridge University Press.

Wray, H. 2012. 'Any Time, Any Place, Anywhere: Entry Clearance, Marriage Migration and the Border', in K. Charsley (ed.), *Transnational Marriage: New Perspectives from Europe and Beyond*. New York: Routledge, pp. 41–59.

Xu, X., and M. King Whyte. 1990. 'Love Marriages and Arranged Marriages: A Chinese Replication', *Journal of Marriage and the Family* 52: 709–22.

Ye, Z.M. 1986. 'Qingtian Qiaoxiang Tuanyuan', *Qingtian Wenshi Ziliao* 2: 64–77.

Zelizer, V. 2007. *The Purchase of Intimacy*. Princeton, NJ: Princeton University Press.

Zhou, H.L. 2006. *Qiao Xing Tianxia*. Beijing: Dazhong wenyi chubanshe.

CHAPTER
2

Temporary Intimacies, Incipient Transnationalism and Failed Cross-Border Marriages

Nicole Constable

Introduction

Migration studies have been criticized for treating migrants as discrete categories (such as labour migrants *or* marriage migrants); for lack of attention to the importance of love, emotion and sexuality; and for privileging certain heteronormative perspectives (Piper and Roces 2003; Manalansan 2006; Ahmad 2009; Mai and King 2009; Constable 2014). This chapter explores an ethnographic and analytic gap at the intersection of migration, transnationalism and marriage. Relationships that are described by couples as 'marriages' or 'like marriages', but that are not legally recognized, and take place within migratory spaces between mobile people without legal rights to permanent residency, have been neglected. At best these relationships are minor side issues in migration studies. Taking my studies among women and men engaged in such relationships in Hong Kong as my point of departure, I contend that there is much to learn by putting such relationships centre stage. As I argue, they illustrate how migration experiences challenge normative expectations about intimate lives and social relationships.

They do not resist normative experiences of heterosexuality – indeed, many couples embrace heteronormative ideals – but they nonetheless challenge normative migratory expectations and categorizations that exist both within the academy and within sending and receiving societies.

Such marriages, or marriage-like relationships, provide insights about intimate lives that mobile people often struggle to create within marginal migratory social spaces. Laws that prohibit temporary migrants or asylum seekers from becoming residents, and polices that only allow migrant workers one day off a week, in addition to employer-imposed curfews and rules against pregnancy, deter migrant women workers from having private lives, sex and children, yet some manage to do so anyway (Constable 2015). The intimate relationships of migrant workers and asylum seekers, and the experiences of those who migrate and later marry, show how conceptualizations of 'labour migrants' or 'marriage migrants' as two distinct categories are analytically too narrow (see also Piper and Roces 2003). Such divisions between categories of migrants obscure the connections between work and marriage migration. Often it also subordinates love to instrumental or material motives by assuming that women migrate to gain material benefits, either through work or through marriage.

The men and women described below are not 'marriage migrants' per se. Unlike the subjects of most studies of marriage migration, neither partner travelled to Hong Kong for the purpose of marriage or as a result of marriage, and nor did they marry as part of a pre-existing transnational community. Yet, the transnational context, as discussed below, shapes and is shaped by their work opportunities and romantic encounters. The women in the study migrated to Hong Kong from Indonesia and the Philippines, and were among over 300,000 migrant workers in 2012 who do cooking, cleaning, or child and elderly care work, holding temporary 'foreign domestic helper' (FDH) visas. The men in the study are mostly among the thousands of men who migrated from South Asia and Africa for work; some entered the region surreptitiously, while others entered as visitors, overstayed, and worked 'illegally'. Others arrived as asylum seekers; some worked illegally while others did not work for fear of jeopardizing their chances of acquiring refugee status.[1]

It is widely recognized that both labour migrants and refugees can be motivated to go abroad out of love or commitment to family members or partners back home. Labour migrants often express familial obligations as the primary reason for migration. 'I am here to earn money for my family…' is something I often heard, especially in initial conversations with women. Although such economic and familial reasons are the expected and socially acceptable explanations, they are not the only ones (Constable 2007). These answers hide less easily expressed motivations that come out later:

'I came for the adventure'; 'I could not afford to go to school'; 'I came to escape my husband's abuse'; 'My parents were pressuring me to get married'; 'My heart was broken'; 'My fiancée got someone else pregnant'. Migratory categories such as 'labour migrant' and 'asylum seeker' obfuscate not only the fact that these two categories can and do overlap, but they also draw attention away from the existence of love, sex, desire and intimacy in migrants' lives, 'back home' and abroad.

Foreign domestic workers in Hong Kong, as in many parts of the world, are expected to be 'just workers' and to devote themselves solely to labour-related tasks and to their employer's families (Constable 2014). As a Hong Kong High Court judge wrote:

> a foreign domestic helper's stay in Hong Kong is for a very special, limited purpose from society's point of view – to meet society's acute demand for domestic helpers which cannot be satisfactorily met by the local labour market. Hence, their stays in Hong Kong are highly regulated so as to ensure that *they are here to fulfil the special, limited purpose for which they have been allowed to come here in the first place, and no more.* (Cheung 2012: 50, emphasis added)

As live-in domestic workers, they are meant to work, and are 'not allowed to love' (Moukarbel 2009). They are prohibited from bringing family members with them, and warned not to form intimate relationships with anyone, except perhaps their employer's children. Migration studies scholars have been criticized for rarely viewing migrants 'as complex social beings, willing and able to experience the full range of human emotions the rest of us take for granted' (Ahmad 2009: 310). Outside of the academy, similar assumptions of migrant asexuality prevail. From the point of view of the local Hong Kong community, especially employers, as well as from the perspective of many other migrant workers, foreign domestic workers should not feel love, other than for their charges or for their own family members back home, and they should not have sexual desires or local romantic experiences.[2]

The 'marriage' stories of migrant workers and asylum seekers, recounted below, illustrate how a categorical divide between the work lives and intimate/sexual lives of mobile people is often untenable. Their stories also show how these migrants' lives exceed the narrow and one-dimensional ideas common in both the sending and receiving states about what migrants' lives 'should' be. Contrary to what is expected, they often sacrifice their employment and legal status and resist the bounds of official, legal or conventional notions of marriage in Hong Kong, opting for love or intimacy instead. Furthermore, they challenge the notion that sex and family are the exclusive privilege of locals. To do so often requires living outside of the law, in unregulated spaces, with 'irregular', 'undocumented', or other marginal status.

This chapter is divided into three sections. The first lays out the ethnographic context and provides some key definitions, concepts, and theoretical issues relating to marriage, migration and transnationalism. The second provides ethnographic examples from Hong Kong, and depicts two Pakistani–Indonesian couples' relationships, exploring their shifting roles as intimate partners, parents and workers, their shifting migratory status, and the transnational and intimate space(s) they temporarily occupy. The third discusses how the concepts introduced in the first section relate to the ethnographic stories of the two couples in the second section, and reveal analytic gaps and theoretical questions for scholars of migration.

Context and Concepts

Between 2010 and 2013 I spent eighteen months conducting ethnographic fieldwork among Indonesian and Filipina migrant mothers in Hong Kong. I interviewed, talked and spent time with migrant women, men, asylum seekers and refugees, as well as staff members at non-governmental organizations and others associated with migrants (Constable 2014). I found that that intimate sexual relationships develop between South East Asian women (mainly Indonesians and Filipinas) who enter Hong Kong as migrant workers, and African or South Asian men who work, seek asylum, or overstay (or all three). Couples commonly meet in Hong Kong's many migratory spaces – outside mosques, in parks, at restaurants or pubs, at boarding houses, and other locations where non-locals socialize and do business among their co-ethnics. A Pakistani–Indonesian couple, for example, might introduce his or her friends to each other. Other couples might meet by chance on trains or buses, or during their daily routines.

Many such relationships are conceived of as temporary, ranging from hook-ups to boyfriend–girlfriend relationships that may last weeks or possibly years. Other relationships become more serious, and in some cases couples describe these relationships as 'marriages'. Several hundred children are born in Hong Kong from both short- and long-term liaisons each year (PathFinders 2012). Filipinas are said to mostly return home to deliver (Ullah 2010), whereas Indonesians are more likely to give birth in Hong Kong. Some domestic workers take maternity leave, to which they are legally entitled, and then return to work. However, most women I knew were dismissed or felt they had no choice but to resign once their pregnancies became apparent.

The line between 'marriage' and other sorts of intimate relationships was somewhat arbitrary. Those who proclaimed they were 'married' usually used the term to assert the heteronormative legitimacy and moral validity of their relationships. They emphasized their relatively long-term mutual commitment, having a child together, expectations of monogamy, cohabitation, shared subsistence, and often also 'love'. Some Muslim couples had a *nikah* (marriage blessing ceremony) to legitimize their union. Others, however, said the *nikah* was not a 'real marriage', but a way to render their sexual relationship, and any child that might result from it, *halal* (permissible) as opposed to *haram* (prohibited). *Nikah* blessings are not legally binding in Hong Kong. Legal marriages require proof of marriageability (single status) and other bureaucratic procedures that few migrant workers, overstayers or asylum seekers can afford. Moreover, without identification cards, or with expired cards, going to the marriage registry can be risky. At the time of my research, few couples considered official marriage registration in Hong Kong to be a necessary or feasible step, unless one of the partners was a Hong Kong resident, which then enabled the non-resident partner to apply for legal residency.

Such marriages are asserted by the couples, and sometimes accepted as such by acquaintances in similar situations, but they may not be sanctioned by family members in their home countries. Family members may be reluctant to recognize a marriage if one of them is already married, or because of the partner's religion, race or nationality. Anticipating familial disapproval, some migrants delay telling their families about their 'marriage' until they are about to leave Hong Kong.

As noted above, these relationships do not easily fit the categories of migrant workers, marriage migrants, or 'migrants' in general. Are they really 'married'? And if we accept that they are, then are they 'marriage migrants' – that is, migrants who have married, as opposed to those who migrated specifically for marriage? And if they are 'married', then do they count as 'cross-border marriages' or 'transnational marriages'? The women, at least, *were* labour migrants, but most no longer worked or did not do so 'legally', and some had become asylum seekers or torture claimants. Under those circumstances are they still 'migrants' or do they better fit some other category of mobility?

In *Transnational Marriages: New Perspectives from Europe and Beyond* (see Charsley 2012 and Williams 2012), Lucy Williams and Katharine Charsley distinguish between 'cross-border' and 'transnational' marriages. Williams considers cross-border marriages to be the larger category, of which transnational marriages are but one type. She proposes that cross-border marriages form a continuum between those that are firmly transnational and those that are not (Williams 2012: 23). She uses 'cross-border marriage' to refer to marriages in which one partner migrates and lacks citizenship in the marital country of residence (ibid.: 24). As Williams aptly explains, the partners' citizenship is of critical importance, creating a qualitative difference from couples who share local citizenship and belonging in their country of residence. She argues that 'marriages in which one or both partner lacks formal status or citizenship, that is when one or both partners are classified as 'migrant' by the state, should be viewed as cross-border marriages' (ibid.: 24).

'Transnational' marriages, according to Williams, are a narrower category of cross-border marriages. They are marriages that take place 'within established, transnational communities' (Williams 2012: 24). These communities are characterized by pre-existing kinship and community ties, and shared cultural, ethnic, national or religious belief systems that are linked to the process of establishing or arranging cross-border marriages. In other words, kinship ties and social networks between migratory communities and homeland communities are often integrated into marriage introductions. A pre-existing intra-ethnic community is what makes the marriage transnational, according to Williams (2012: 24–25). Charsley and Williams' prime example of transnational marriages (within an established, transnational community) is of Pakistanis in Britain who marry partners from other parts of the Pakistani diasporic community. Such migrations unambiguously produce and are produced by a transnational 'community'. They are intra-ethnic marriages that cross national borders and are linked to wider ethnic ties and processes.

Much of the literature on South Asian cross-border marriages, and marriage migration to Europe, emphasizes intra-ethnic connections and transnational chain migrations through marriage. These migrations are often linked to xenophobia, social anxieties about migration, and ever-more restrictive migration policies in host communities that fear a flood of migration of foreigners through marriage. Studies of inter-ethnic marriage migration in East Asia and from South East Asia also reflect anxieties about migration, as illustrated by Taiwan's policy restrictions on marriage migrants from particular regions, especially women from mainland China (Friedman 2015). But overall, scholars of East and South East Asia have paid more attention to inter-ethnic patterns that point to 'new' migratory flows and new technologies that facilitate such marriages (Constable 2003, 2005; Kim 2010; Yang and Lu 2010).

Among the examples of cross-border marriages that Williams considers less transnational, or only 'incipiently transnational', most are inter-ethnic and involve East and South East Asian men and women of different ethnic and national origins, who are not part of a pre-existing transnational community. Citing several contributors to *Cross-Border Marriages* (Constable 2005), Williams points to marriages between Filipinas and men from Korea, Japan and the United States as cross-border marriages. In these cases,

Filipinas migrate to marry and are (at least at first) non-citizens in their husband's country.[3] Such inter-ethnic marriages are either not transnational at all, by Williams' definition, and certainly not as transnational as those linked to a 'transnational community' such as the Pakistani diaspora, or they are 'incipiently transnational' in the sense that a transnational community can potentially develop from them later on, such as among US–Filipina couples who live in the Philippines. As Charsley notes, the contributors in her volume (including Williams) have been most influenced by Basch, Glick Schiller and Szanton Blanc's (1994: 7) conceptualization of migrant transnationalism as 'the processes by which immigrants forge and sustain multistranded social relations that link together their societies of origin and settlement' (Charsley 2012: 17).

The problems with this conceptualization, however, relate to the differences between transnational *communities* and transnational *spaces*, and with types and degrees of transnationalism. While 'community' focuses clearly on social relations or networks, the notion of a space, I would argue, allows for greater attention to the movement of ideas, goods, capital and people. This draws from Arjun Appadurai's conceptualization of transnationalism in terms of global ethnoscapes, technoscapes, financescapes (Appadurai 1991) and I what I call 'marriagescapes' (Constable 2005). While Basch, Glick Schiller and Szanton Blanc highlight migrants' political and economic ties between place of origin and place of settlement, which is critically important for understanding the ongoing ties of migrants to their home communities, it gives greatest emphasis to sociological, lasting, established and functional patterns of social relationships. This obscures the more subtle and creative yet often dysfunctional, non-functional, or short-lived aspects of global intimacies, which are also transnational. Indonesian or Filipina women and South Asian or African men who once had intimate relationships or marriages and maybe children in Hong Kong, for example, sometimes communicate through Facebook. Their online community is part of the global marriagescape. Even though they might not form day-to-day, face-to-face 'functioning' communities, they are nonetheless important transnational inter-ethnic spaces.

Shifting Migratory Categories and the Stories of Temporary Intimacy

The stories of Anti and Ali, and Lilik and Rashid provide a glimpse of their marriages in Hong Kong, and in the case of Anti and Ali the short-term aftermath of their relationship after Anti returned to Indonesia. Fundamentally, these sketches point to the intimate lives of Indonesian domestic workers and Pakistani asylum seekers in Hong Kong, which I claim cannot be fully understood with either a work- or a marriage-focused approach to migration. Most of the relationships I knew of that did not involve a Hong Kong resident lasted no more than a few years, like that of Anti and Ali. Those that lasted longer, like that of Lilik and Rashid, seemed rare. Most women I knew took their children home after the relationship ended, and within a few years many had returned abroad – perhaps to Singapore or to Taiwan – to work again. Some went home only when they had exhausted all channels to prolong their stay in Hong Kong. Migrant men who remained in Hong Kong, or who returned home after their partners and children had left, rarely provided material support or stayed in close touch with their partner. In most cases, relationships did not last beyond the time and space of Hong Kong. Are these 'cross-border' marriages, and if so, at what point do they cease to be? Are they 'transnational', and if so, when and how is it manifested? Even if one were to answer 'no' to both of these questions (which I am not inclined to do), I would nonetheless argue that such examples and experiences should be considered alongside the more normative examples of transnational marriages and migration.

Anti and Ali

Anti, a Muslim from rural Central Java, was sixteen when she completed her domestic worker training and left Indonesia to work as a maid in Singapore with a passport that made her seem three years older than her real age. At eighteen she then went to Hong Kong where she could earn more money. While there, she met Ali, a friendly young Pakistani man her age, who was doing mechanical repair work nearby, and they exchanged mobile phone numbers. Ali was an 'economic migrant' who had come to Hong Kong to earn money. After his visitor visa expired he filed an asylum claim and continued to work illegally for a Pakistani relative who was a Hong Kong resident. This provided him with a measure of protection from getting caught working 'illegally'.

Anti and Ali spent their weekly day off together for a year, and were married at a local mosque with a *nikah* ceremony after she became pregnant. Unaware that as a domestic worker she was entitled to maternity leave, Anti left her employer when her pregnancy began to show and went to live with Ali in a tiny flat. She overstayed her visa by two months, then, in anticipation of needing to give birth in a government hospital, she surrendered to Immigration and filed a 'torture claim', which (like an asylum claim) allowed her to remain in Hong Kong for the birth (at little or no cost), but did not permit her to work. Sadly, she delivered a stillborn baby.

Shortly afterwards, Anti went to work in a restaurant while her torture claim was being processed. As she explained, Ali was 'becoming more responsible and faithful' to her, their relationship 'grew stronger' and they decided to have another baby. Early in her second pregnancy she was arrested for working illegally and received a six-month prison sentence, which was reduced to four, then two when her pregnancy became evident. While she was in prison, Ali remained committed to her and their relationship deepened. After their daughter was born, as Anti explained, Ali would not let her work because it was 'too risky' and he 'did not trust anyone else' to care for their child. He took on a second job to support them, and continued to support his parents and siblings in Pakistan.

Meanwhile, Anti witnessed the rejection of many other Indonesian women's torture claims and their subsequent departures from Hong Kong. She knew she could not ultimately win her case. Her parents knew about their granddaughter and encouraged her to come home. Despite Ali's many tearful pleas that she remain in Hong Kong, or that she go with him to Pakistan (where he said he would likely have to marry a Pakistani woman as well to appease his parents), Anti chose to return to Central Java with nine-month-old Eni. When I asked her why she did not want to see her torture case through to the end and remain in Hong Kong as long as possible, she explained: 'My husband says he loves us very much and begged me to stay. But my parents are worried. It will be even harder to leave [Hong Kong] when Eni is older and will miss her father. The longer I wait the harder it will be for Eni'. Her husband promised to come to Indonesia when his claim had been finished, but Anti said she would only believe it if it happened. Ali's parents had opposed their relationship from the start, and had pressured him to forget Anti and go back to Pakistan to marry a Pakistani. Anti knew many Pakistani men who had found new girlfriends as soon as their Indonesian partners had left Hong Kong. 'Most men are like that', she sighed. Her return to Indonesia seemed inevitable, and it was better, she reasoned, to leave Hong Kong on her own terms than be deported.

When I visited her in Central Java, Indonesia, in 2012, seven months after she had left Hong Kong, her situation was worse than anticipated. She had known it would be hard to return home as a single mother, and she had expected criticism for the shame she brought to her family. But when she left Hong Kong she was unaware that she was pregnant again, and she gave birth to another girl just before my visit. Having another daughter did nothing to convince Ali's parents in Pakistan to accept their marriage (perhaps a boy would have made a difference). It also thwarted her longer-term plans to spend a year in Java, allowing Eni to get used to her relatives, and then return to work abroad again. At first, Ali occasionally sent money, but not enough to make a difference in Anti's situation. When Anti worked in Singapore and then later in Hong Kong, she had sent money home with which her family was expected to buy land. She had planned to farm it to support herself and her children, but instead her grandmother had appropriated the land and Anti was afraid to reclaim it without causing more conflict within the family.

Anti was frequently criticized or shunned for the shame she brought on her family – for being a single mother and a financial burden rather than an asset as intended when she went to work abroad. Anti's family's home was the poorest and shabbiest in the village; during fieldwork there I witnessed how their home was one of the few remaining ones with a dirt floor, thatch roof, and split bamboo and thin board walls where light and bugs easily passed through, as opposed to the mostly concrete homes with cement floors of her neighbours. She was watched by her elders, and not permitted to leave her home alone or after dark. Her depression was obvious. When I asked about other single mothers nearby, with whom she might find support, she said there were several women with babies from the Middle East, but they avoid each other, for fear that being seen with other 'bad women' would further tarnish their reputations. The situation for returned single mothers, though not unusual or unheard of, was worse than Anti had anticipated. In Hong Kong, she had said that her parents would welcome her back. This hope was echoed by many women whose parents 'forgave them' and eventually urged them to come home with their children, but who failed to appreciate just how difficult it would be for single mothers in Java to be seen as anything other than 'loose' or 'fun' women. They remained a shame and a failure unless they managed to find a way to go back to work abroad, remit money home, and (re)enter what I have called 'the migratory cycle of atonement' (Constable 2014).

In the face of the criticism that Anti faced from relatives, especially her grandmother and neighbours, she insisted that she was married; but the chorus of 'Where is this husband of yours?' and 'Why isn't he sending more money?' continued. Anti said, 'I told them that Ali has a job and it is too difficult to get a visa to come here'. But she held out little hope. She evoked her husband's arrival, she explained, just to keep the critics at bay and to protect Eni, but she no longer believed that he would visit or remain faithful to her. His phone calls and remittances were becoming few and far between.

At that time, Anti was still unaware that Ali had made plans to marry a Chinese Hong Kong resident. He told Anti's close friend, whom I knew well, 'Please don't tell Anti. I am doing it for her and our family and the future'. His imagined future – after the many years it would require for him to gain residency, divorce his Hong Kong wife, and establish the financial means to sponsor Anti and their daughters as his dependents – seemed highly unlikely. Indonesian women repeatedly told me that they had never heard of a Pakistani man moving to Indonesia, and only rarely of Indonesian women going to live with husbands in Pakistan. Pakistani men understood it was difficult enough for local men to make a living in Java; as foreigners they would be further disadvantaged. Women feared going to Pakistan because they heard stories of how difficult life is for women there (especially for daughters-in-law). As one woman said, 'there we would be just like maids, but unlike Hong Kong it would be hard to leave or go home when you want to'. Women also feared becoming a second wife in a foreign country, and the husband leaving them behind. Most Pakistani partners return home only for short visits, but hope to return to Hong Kong, or go to England, Canada or elsewhere to earn money.

Neither Anti nor Ali had been married before they went to Hong Kong, and both initially went there to work to help to support their families back home. Both were single, and neither had been actively seeking a romantic relationship – but like many others I spoke to, they said they fell in love, she got pregnant and they got married. Then they encountered many obstacles that prevented them from remaining as a family in Hong Kong or imagining how to be one elsewhere. Lilik and Rashid's story bears some resemblance, but it also differs in significant ways.

Lilik and Rashid

While working on this chapter in 2012, I received a text message from Lilik, an Indonesian woman in her mid-twenties living in Hong Kong. She wrote:

> So sad to say that I have already finished my torture claim interview and am just waiting for screening to see if Immigration accepts my claim or not... Last week they also call Rashid [her partner] to make an appointment for his interview... He got sad and he got sick because he is worried about us... he doesn't want to get far from Husain [their child]. But he promises to visit us in Indonesia and I believe him because he never lied to me before.

A year and a half later, Lilik and Rashid were still in Hong Kong. Her torture claim was rejected soon after she wrote to me, and she filed an appeal. That too was rejected, and she filed an asylum claim with the UNHCR. When her asylum claim was rejected, she contemplated a claim on the basis of cruel, inhuman, degrading treatment or punishment that had recently come to the attention of asylum seekers and torture claimants (Vision First 2013). Most Filipino, Indonesian and Pakistani applicants I knew had no illusions that they would win their asylum or torture cases. Only one torture claim has – as of writing – been approved in Hong Kong. Lilik and Rashid's claims did not fit the UN definition of torture.

Lilik had come to Hong Kong on a two-year FDH visa, against her parents' wishes, and in the wake of a failed marriage. She met Rashid, a Pakistani in his late twenties, on her Sunday off in a crowded fast food restaurant, where he asked to share her table. Both were lonely new arrivals and they began to meet regularly every Sunday. Rashid had travelled overland from Pakistan through China and then taken a boat from Guangdong province to enter Hong Kong surreptitiously. When they met, he worked in a small factory run by Hong Kong resident relatives. He told Lilik he had 'immigration papers', the unofficial name of recognizance papers given to asylum seekers and torture claimants while their cases are under review. At the time, Lilik did not know the difference between immigration papers and legal residency, and Rashid did not explain. Like many others, Rashid had little hope of winning his claim; the purpose of filing it was to remain in Hong Kong to work (illegally) for as long as he could. Only if he married a local resident, like Ali did, could he ever gain the right to eventually remain there, a process that took at least seven years.

After several months, and with the encouragement and support of one of Rashid's close relatives, they took part in a Muslim *nikah*. His relatives warned them that a sexual relationship between an unmarried couple is *haram* according to Muslim law. By then, Lilik knew Rashid was already married in Pakistan: 'He told me he was married, but only after it was too late and we were already in love. He said theirs [his first marriage] was an arranged marriage, not like ours which is a love marriage'. Lilik's parents in Indonesia very reluctantly gave their consent and Rashid's cousin, who resided in Hong Kong, gave his approval. By contrast, Rashid's parents and his first wife in Pakistan, as well as his wife's relatives in Hong Kong, knew nothing of their marriage, and Rashid and Lilik worked hard to keep it secret.

After they married, Lilik continued to live and work with her employer as required by law with her FDH visa, and she met Rashid on her day off. A year later, Lilik was pregnant. When Lilik's employer illegally terminated her contract because she was pregnant, she consulted an NGO and filed a claim against her employer. She was permitted to stay in Hong Kong on a series of short-term renewable visas (which she had to pay for, and that did not allow her to work) while she pursued her case of wrongful termination. By the time she won her claim, and was awarded a small sum of money as compensation, her pregnancy was advanced. She gave birth to Husain and then moved into a tiny two-bedroom, sixth-floor, walk-up apartment, which she and Rashid shared with another Pakistani–Indonesian couple and their child, in an ethnically mixed Kowloon neighbourhood. Lilik could not find a new employer within the allowed two-week period after her visa expired. Her difficulty stemmed partly from the fact that all foreign domestic workers (FDWs) in Hong Kong are required to 'live in' with their employers. The agencies and employers she contacted would not let her live out, and also did not like the idea of having a domestic worker with a child in Hong Kong. After her visa expired, Lilik overstayed for a few days and then surrendered to Immigration and filed a torture claim, as Rashid had done several months earlier. She received 'immigration papers' while her case was assessed. For those migrants who had applied in 2005 or 2006, the process often took several years, but by 2010 the process had accelerated and Lilik's case took less than a year to evaluate. Rashid's case was rejected a few months later, but his appeal has been delayed, and is still ongoing a few years later.

Lilik and Rashid were more successful at building a family in Hong Kong than many other couples I knew, but their story is not entirely unique. I met over a hundred Filipina and Indonesian domestic workers who had babies in Hong Kong, many with men from South Asia and West Africa. Some such couples had fleeting sexual relationships or very short-lived relationships, while others, like Lilik and Rashid, had *nikah* ceremonies and considered themselves 'husband and wife'. In some cases, the women were more committed to the relationship than the men. Petty jealousies between women, and betrayal by 'friends' who were blamed for seducing a husband or boyfriend, were common. In other cases, like that of Lilik and Rashid, the relationship endured at least while both partners remained in Hong Kong.

Rashid had told Lilik several months after they met that he had a cousin-wife in Pakistan and a child there as well. That marriage, he assured her, was an arranged one that he had been obligated to accept out of respect for his parents. His marriage in Pakistan, he insisted, was far different from his 'love marriage' to Lilik. This fits the pattern of 'dual marital aspirations' described by Charsley and Liversage of young Pakistani or Turkish men who want to have 'a "love match" of their own choosing, as well as to please their family and fulfil their filial duties by marrying the spouse selected for them' (Charsley and Liversage 2013: 67). When Rashid's Pakistani wife heard rumours about Lilik and Husain, she barraged him with angry, jealous phone calls and threatened to tell his parents. He told her it was all just idle gossip. According to Lilik, he did not mind his Pakistani friends and relatives in Hong Kong knowing he had a girlfriend, but he did not want them to know he had a 'wife and child' until he was ready to tell his parents and his wife himself. Rashid's close cousin, the one who had encouraged them to marry, knew of the marriage, but Rashid intentionally hid Lilik from another uncle who he feared would tell his wife or parents in Pakistan 'before he was ready'. Lilik was alternately angry and understanding of the situation: 'If his wife finds out, she will be angry and so will her family. Her relatives will have Rashid arrested for illegal work. Then we won't be together at all'. She also complained that he had not told her about his wife until after they were romantically involved. Once, Rashid's uncle paid a surprise visit. Lilik and the baby had to climb out a window onto the rooftop and wait for hours in the sweltering hot stairway of the adjoining building until he left.

Rashid assured Lilik that he would support her and Husain, and would visit when she returned to Indonesia, but few of the similar cases I knew or had heard about bore out the likelihood of such plans. I knew women like Anti who initially received a small remittance, but it was often less than the promised sum and insufficient to counteract the stigma of returning home as a single mother. When the husband left Hong Kong, the woman's chances of receiving support diminished further. Rashid speculated that when he has to leave Hong Kong he would return to Pakistan, then to go to work elsewhere, perhaps England. He could not settle in Indonesia because he could not earn enough there to support Lilik, Husain, and his family in Pakistan. Lilik believed he would visit because of their bond and his deep attachment to Husain, who Rashid referred to as his 'gift from God'.

In response to my question about whether such relationships can last, Hakim, another Pakistani man, expressed it better than anyone else: 'These are real marriages. They can last for as long as both are still in Hong Kong'. His Indonesian 'wife' (who he had not married in a religious ceremony) had eventually gone back home after he asked her to marry him. As he told me, 'She said she couldn't because there was no future for us. I did not want to go to Indonesia and she did not want to stay here [in Hong Kong]'. Like Rashid, Hakim had a wife and child in Pakistan when he came to Hong Kong, but he divorced his Pakistani wife, and like Ali he married a Chinese Hong Kong resident. Given his strong feelings for his Indonesian ex-partner, I asked if he loved his Chinese wife. He said, 'If you live with a dog for fifteen months you will learn to love a dog'. Yet his Hong Kong Chinese wife offered him the precious opportunity to eventually obtain residency, and to work in Hong Kong legally.

Discussion: Global Intimacies, Temporary Marriages, and Transnational Spaces

These stories, which speak to the wider arena of global intimacies, raise questions about the transnational aspects of temporary marriage relationships. If the prototype of transnationalism involves intra-ethnic diasporic communities, then we can see why inter-ethnic relationships (like those described above) are excluded or on the very periphery of two transnational communities. In the case of the Pakistani transnational community, Ali and Rashid's parents disapprove or do not know about their Indonesian wives and children. And while Lilik and Anti's families know about their partners, they are loath to accept them unless they are there in person or send significant sums of money, neither of which are likely. Yet rather than consider these as 'failed' transnational marriages (failed marriages *and* failed transnationalism) it is important to consider how they may be transnational in a temporal and spatially limited sense, at least within the migrant spaces of Hong Kong.

A conservative approach to transnationalism would consider Rashid and Ali's remittances as evidence of their participation in a Pakistani transnational space, and Anti and Lilik's in an Indonesian one. But transnationalism involves far more than political and economic connections. Fantasies of 'modern' romantic relationships with handsome men and attractive women who resemble Bollywood stars, and ideas about future migrations and reunions are produced within Hong Kong's inter-ethnic transnational spaces. Such ideas will not necessarily sustain long-lasting social ties or 'communities' after the women return to Indonesia with their children. But to conflate 'community' links with transnationalism ignores both the 'incipient communities' (Williams 2012) that may still form and be formed, and ideological and discursive aspects of transnationalism, such as direct or indirect communication with or about partners or former partners by phone or on Facebook.

A narrow view of transnationalism might lead us to dismiss the relationships described above. Instead we might ask whether, and in what ways, they are or might be or become more transnational. What new questions do inter-ethnic cross-border marriages raise about transnational flows of ideas, fantasies, desires, children, remittances, people, and family relations? How do the physical migratory spaces outside of the Kowloon Mosque and Kowloon Park serve as a transnational space? And how do virtual communicative spaces offer future possibilities of reconnecting with partners, or in the future, distant parents?

The heterosexual 'marriages' I describe above, moreover, do not simply reinforce heteronormativity. They also undermine more conventional localized forms of marriage, reshaping and challenging expected norms of Hong Kong and of home countries. Elsewhere I have written about the ways in which migration allows for temporary escape from heteronormative expectations, as migrant workers may become involved with same sex partners (Constable 2000, 2010). Here I suggest that seemingly heteronormative and conventional marriages may not be so conventional.

Anti was unmarried when she came to Hong Kong, and like many others, her parents were eager for her to return home within a few years to marry a partner of their choice. For many young women, going to Hong Kong is a way to escape their parents' watchful eyes and to delay or escape the transition from obedient daughter to obedient wife. Migration offers romantic and sexual opportunities and choices that are not available at home, including greater freedom to have sexual relationships outside of marriage, and same sex relationships.

Many women I knew in Hong Kong took part in *nikah* ceremonies so that their relationships and children would not be *haram* in the eyes of the local Muslim community. Others had sex and children, but never married, because one or both partners did not want to. The possibilities of sexual liberation in Hong Kong are far greater than in these migrants' home countries. However, Anti and Ali and Rashid and Lilik did not want their relationships to be *haram*, so they married. They nonetheless understood that their relationships were likely to be short-term, bounded by the time and space of Hong Kong. As temporary marriages, these relationships go against certain conventional expectations. Couples speak of their relationships as 'marriages', disrupting existing local and hegemonic notions of marriage as the official and exclusive privilege of locals and 'legals'. Against local Chinese perceptions of migrant workers and asylum seekers as asexual and alone, they struggle to love, have sex, marry, and form families. Such relationships are conventionally heteronormative and heterosexual, with their aspirations of modern romance and their legitimacy through marriage rituals, but they are also transgressive. The lives of Anti, Lilik, Rashid and Ali (let alone those of Hussain and Eni) cannot be fully understood through the rubrics of labour migrants or marriage migrants. Nor do they fit into narrow, one-dimensional local constructs of migrants who are solely workers. While many migrant workers devotedly labour, make and save money, and lead ascetic lives while they fulfil their employers' needs, others resist this narrow existence, have meaningful intimate relationships, and even – against the odds – marry and have families in Hong Kong. In so doing, they challenge migratory expectations, living outside of the normative and expected parameters of migratory life.

It is important to consider not only the transnational aspects of such relationships, but also the different gendered implications. Married women, with bad or failed marriages back home, can imagine more fulfilling and love-based modern relationships in Hong Kong. Many women know these relationships are temporary, whereas others, like Anti, at first 'refuse to think about it' until it becomes inevitable. While in Hong Kong it is possible for women to be 'single mothers', and despite criticism from peers and negative attitudes from some staff in government offices, they often express surprise that torture claimants and asylum seekers and their children are entitled to some social welfare support (including food, shelter and medical care). In Java, their reception is often quite different and they are stigmatized. Upon her return, Anti was secluded in her home and compound. Other single mothers reported being harassed by men who asked them to 'come out and have fun' (a euphemism for having sex) because they are assumed to be promiscuous. Assumptions about these women's promiscuity are associated with assumptions about the sexual freedom and decadence of Hong Kong.

For men like Ali and Rashid, by contrast, there is little danger of returning to Pakistan with a sense of shame. Both men faithfully provided their families with financial support, and as long as they continue to do so, kin were unlikely to criticize their sexual liaisons. Ali was expected to eventually marry in Pakistan. Rashid, who was already married in Pakistan, feared that if his in-laws knew about Lilik and Husain they might report him to immigration, resulting in his detention and deportation from Hong Kong. But ultimately, they cannot report him or they risk their own well-being as well, as if he is detained he can no longer send home remittances. Moreover, as the men explained (a view shared by their family members), it is expected for migrant men to have sex abroad. It is accepted and tolerated as long as those relationships do not threaten the well-being of families back home. The personal, social and economic costs for women who return home with children as 'single mothers' are much greater than for their male partners.

Conclusion

Patterns of global capitalism are linked to patterns of mobility, desire, and the wider movement of ideas, people, money, labour and goods across national borders. Increasingly these are not unidirectional or binary movements. New patterns of intimacy reflect both local idiosyncrasies and intersecting global histories. The meeting of Filipinas, Indonesians, Pakistanis, Nigerians, Somalis and many others, within what I have described as the transnational and migratory spaces of Hong Kong, grow out of colonial histories and postcolonial legacies that inform Hong Kong's migratory policies and shape its social spaces. These in turn shape and are shaped by new patterns of inter-ethnic intimacies. Such intimate relationships are often overlooked or ignored because they seem fleeting or inconsequential (to all but perhaps the individuals involved), but they have longer-term repercussions, especially when children are born. As concrete artefacts of desire or material embodiments of transnational relations, children like Eni and Husain – and the growing number of minority or 'mixed race' children in Hong Kong kindergartens – represent possible agents for the 'incipient' transnational communities Williams (2012) describes. Discourses that circulate among and about these children, and about their distant foreign fathers or mothers, will no doubt shape the transnational dimensions of the future, and the place of these children within an evermore globalizing world.

Building on the work of Piper and Roces (2003), Mai and King (2009), Charsley (2012) and Williams (2012), I have argued that it is important to consider all sorts of marriage migrations, including those that fall outside of the most common patterns and definitions, and that might be questioned as being 'marriage' at all. This includes migrations that result in marriage but are not motivated by a wish or a plan to marry in the destination country. It includes relationships that are not long lasting and that are unlikely to be or to become part of a transnational 'community' in the classic sense. If transnational marriages are defined primarily in relation to their existing or insipient connections to wider transnational communities or social fields, then we risk echoing earlier tendencies of placing our analytic emphasis on the enduring aspects of social structures. This risks missing the significance of temporary, fleeting or failed transnational connections that are better understood in relation to wider structures of globalization and ideology as well as individual subjectivities and experiences. How marriages are linked to wider transmigrant communities or social fields is important, often marking differences between patterns of particular geographic regions and different ethnic or national heritage or diasporic groups.

Drawing from my recent work on failed or temporary marriages between migrants and asylum seekers in Hong Kong, however, I caution against conceptualizations of transnational marriage that exclude relationships that appear at first glance to produce only seemingly temporary or failed transnational communities or networks. Marriages and intimate relationships that are neither supported by or serve to create long-term transnational communities of co-ethnics, nonetheless illustrate important transnational patterns of gendered intimacy. Such relationships might fall outside of the ideal-type categories of transnational marriages but they can still stretch our understandings of the multiple contemporary forms of global inequalities of race, class and gender that fuel real, imagined and aborted trajectories of migration and return.

I have also argued that, within a wider context, these marriages or marriage-like relationships between mobile people – labourers, asylum seekers, and overstayers – challenge conventional migratory scripts and categories. Contrary to local assumptions and academic approaches that treat migrants as one-dimensional people whose sole purpose is to work hard and earn money, and contrary to the norms and expectations in their home countries, some foreign domestic workers and their partners go to great lengths to marry and have families in Hong Kong. They do so despite the restrictions aimed at preventing them from having sexual lives and intimate relations. In many cases 'being married' requires breaking laws, overstaying visas, working 'illegally', or resorting to strategies that allow them to stay longer but offer little hope of remaining together permanently. In these cases, neither partner has the legal right to remain permanently in Hong Kong, neither partner provides the other with substantial material benefits, and neither one is very interested in settling in their partner's home country. It is thus difficult for this analysis to privilege instrumental or strategic factors over desire, love and sexuality.

In sum, much has been written about linear and planned patterns of marriage migration, and about inter- and intra-ethnic cross-border marriages in relation to transnationalism and transnational processes. These patterns of migration are often discussed and analysed as though they are separate from, or take place at some distance from, other forms of migration. More attention should be paid to less patterned, less planned and less institutionalized cross-border marriages that also take place within the context of globalization, but that intersect with or result from other forms of migration and mobility.

Little attention has been paid to intimate relationships and marriages that do not result from or contribute in obvious ways to existing transnational communities. Temporary marriages and intimate relationships that take place within migratory contexts are not institutionalized like other forms of 'marriage migration', which have received most of the scholarly attention; and to the extent that they are 'patterned', it is only on a very small, and usually local, scale. Yet, as we have seen in Hong Kong, these relationships develop out of other forms of mobility such as labour migration and asylum seeking. Marriage was not the motivation or the goal of migration; marriage and the birth of children are, in a sense, side effects of migration. They reflect non-normative intimate patterns in relation to home and host communities, and are a challenge to and a reshaping of migratory categories and expectations.

Acknowledgements

I gratefully acknowledge the assistance of many individuals in Hong Kong, the financial support from the Dietrich School of Arts and Sciences at the University of Pittsburgh, and the comments from Nadine Fernandez, Christian Groes, Joseph Alter and the anonymous reviewers.

Nicole Constable is professor of anthropology at the Dietrich School of Arts and Sciences and research professor at the University Center for

International Studies at the University of Pittsburgh, in Pennsylvania, USA. She is author of numerous articles and several books on gender, labour and marriage migration, including *Romance on a Global Stage: Pen Pals, Virtual Ethnography, and 'Mail Order' Marriages* (2003); *Maid to Order in Hong Kong: Stories of Migrant Workers* (2007); and, most recently, *Born Out of Place: Migrant Mothers and the Politics of International Labor* (2014).

NOTES

1. Hong Kong does not accept refugees for resettlement.
2. Sexuality, love and desire are discussed in studies of migrant entertainers, sex workers, sexual and romance tourism, and marriage migration, which often raises questions about how love and material desire are intertwined (Constable 2003; Brennan 2004; Padilla et al. 2007; Faier 2009; Freeman 2011; Cheng 2013).
3. Inter-ethnic cross-border marriages include relatively new patterns of South East Asian and East Asian marriages (e.g. Constable 2005; Faier 2009; Hsia 2009; Belanger 2010; Yang and Lu 2010; Ishii 2016).

REFERENCES

Ahmad, A.N. 2009. 'Bodies That (Don't) Matter: Desire, Eroticism and Melancholia in Pakistani Labour Migration'. *Mobilities* 4(3): 309–27.

Appadurai, A. 1991. 'Global Ethnoscapes: Notes and Queries for a Transnational Anthropology', in James Fox (ed.), *Recapturing Anthropology*. Santa Fe, NM: SAR Press, pp. 191–210.

Basch, L., N. Glick Schiller and C. Szanton Blanc. 1994. *Nations Unbound: Transnational Projects, Post-colonial Predicaments and Deterritorialized Nation-States*. New York: Routledge.

Belanger, D. 2010. 'Marriages with Foreign Women in East Asia: Bride Trafficking or Voluntary Migration?' *Population and Societies* 469 (July–August): 1–5.

Brennan D. 2004. *What's Love Got to Do with It? Transnational Desires and Sex Tourism in the Dominican Republic*. Durham, NC: Duke University Press.

Charsley, K. (ed.). 2012. 'Transnational Marriage', in *Transnational Marriage: New Perspectives from Europe and Beyond*. London: Routledge, pp. 5–22.

Charsley, K., and A. Liversage. 2013. 'Transforming Polygamy: Migration, Transnationalism and Multiple Marriages among Muslim Minorities'. *Global Networks* 13(1): 60–78.

Cheng, S. 2013. *On the Move for Love: Migrant Entertainers and the U.S. Military in South Korea*. Philadelphia, PA: University of Pennsylvania Press.

Cheung, C.J.H.C. 2012. CACV 204/2011 in the High Court of the Hong Kong Special Administrative Region Court of Appeal, Civil Appeal No. 204 of 2011.

Constable, N. 2000. 'Dolls, T-birds and Ideal Workers: The Negotiation of Filipino Identity in Hong Kong', in S. Dickey and Kathleen Adams (eds), *Home and Hegemony: Domestic Service and Identity Politics in South and Southeast Asia*. Ann Arbor, MI: University of Michigan Press, pp. 221–47.
_____. 2003. *Romance on a Global Stage: Pen Pals, Virtual Ethnography, and 'Mail Order Marriages'*. Berkeley, CA: University of California Press.
_____ (ed.). 2005. *Cross-Border Marriages: Gender and Mobility in Transnational Asia*. Philadelphia, PA: University of Pennsylvania Press.
_____. 2007. *Maid to Order in Hong Kong: Stories of Migrant Workers*. Ithaca, NY: Cornell University Press.
_____. 2010. 'Telling Tales of Migrant Workers in Hong Kong: Transformations of Faith, Life Scripts, and Activism'. *The Asia Pacific Journal of Anthropology* 11(3): 311–27.
_____. 2014. *Born Out of Place: Migrant Mothers and the Politics of International Labor*. Berkeley, CA: University of California Press.
_____. 2015. 'Temporary Shelter in the Shadows: Migrant Mothers and Torture Claims in Hong Kong', in Sara Friedman and Pardis Mahdavi (eds), *Encountering the State: Intimate Labor Migrations across Asia*. Philadelphia, PA: University of Pennsylvania Press, pp. 92–112.
Faier, L. 2009. *Intimate Encounters: Filipina Women and the Remaking of Rural Japan*. Berkeley, CA: University of California Press.
Freeman, C. 2011. *Making and Faking Kinship: Marriage and Labor Migration between China and South Korea*. Ithaca, NY: Cornell University Press.
Friedman, S. 2015. *Exceptional States: Chinese Immigrants and Taiwanese Sovereignty*. Berkeley, CA: University of California Press.
Hsia, H.C. 2009. 'Foreign Brides, Multiple Citizenship and Immigrant Movement in Taiwan'. *Asia and the Pacific Migration Journal* 18(1): 17–46.
Ishii, S.K. (ed.). 2016. *Marriage Migration in Asia: Emerging Minorities at the Frontiers of Nation-States*. Singapore: National University of Singapore Press / Kyoto, Japan: Kyoto University Press.
Kim, M. 2010. 'Gender and International Marriage Migration'. *Social Compass* 4(9): 718–31.
Mai, N., and R. King. 2009. 'Introduction. Love, Sexuality and Migration: Mapping the Issue(s)'. *Mobilities* 4(3): 295–307.
Manalansan IV, M.F. 2006. 'Queer Intersections: Sexuality and Gender in Migration Studies'. *International Migration Review* 40(1): 224–49.
Moukarbel, N. 2009. 'Not Allowed to Love? Sri Lankan Maids in Lebanon'. *Mobilities* 4(3): 329–47.
Padilla, M.B., J.S. Hirsch, M. Muñoz-Laboy, R.E. Sember, and R.G. Parker (eds.) 2007. *Love and Globalization: Transformations of Intimacy in the Contemporary World*. Nashville, TN: Vanderbilt University Press.
PathFinders. 2012. '2011 Annual Report'. Hong Kong.
Piper, N., and M. Roces. 2003. *Wife or Worker? Asian Women and Migration*. Lanham, MD: Rowman & Littlefield.

Ullah, A.K.M. 2010. 'Premarital Pregnancies among Migrant Workers: The Case of Domestic Helpers in Hong Kong'. *Asian Journal of Asian Studies* 16(1): 62–90.

Vision First. 2013. 'Immigration Department's Refusal to Entertain CIDTP Claims'. http://visionfirstnow.org/2013/06/10/immigration-departments-refusal-to-entertain-cidtp-claims/ (last accessed 5 November 2013).

Williams, L. 2012 'Transnational Marriage Migration and Marriage Migration: An Overview', in K. Charsley (ed.), *Transnationalism Marriage: New Perspectives from Europe and Beyond*. London: Routledge, pp. 23–35.

Yang, W., and M.C.W. Lu. 2010. *Asian Cross-Border Marriage Migration: Demographic Patterns and Social Issues*. Amsterdam: Amsterdam University Press.

CHAPTER
3

Screening for Romance and Compatibility in the Brussels Civil Registrar Office
Practical Norms of Bureaucratic Feminism

Maïté Maskens

This chapter explores the normative expectations of romantic love utilized by civil registrars in Brussels, Belgium when evaluating a binational marriage between a Belgian citizen and a non-EU migrant. During the last four decades, legal ways to migrate into so-called 'fortress Europe' have narrowed. From the perspective of most European states, marriage is perceived as the last remaining 'loophole' in policies designed to control migration (Wray 2006). In these encounters between the state and binational couples, the state is not seen as an abstract entity, but as an institution personified in the daily work of its agents (Fassin et al. 2013: 15). The state agents' administrative perception of intimacy relies on an implicit idea of an 'acceptable romantic' form of shared intimacy determined by two major criteria. First, each partner's recounting of their relationship must correspond exactly, and second, state agents rely on a 'practical norm' (Olivier de Sardan 2008: 13) to assess the veracity of the relationship. 'Practical norms' refer to invisible social regulations that are constituted in those specific state encounters by particular ideas of freedom, equality and choice that I call 'bureaucratic feminism'. The use of this practical norm, which goes beyond the required legal framework, illustrates the space between the official goal (to prevent cheaters who use marriage to cross European boundaries) and the civilizational project at work. This takes place, for example, when some binational couples seen as 'modern' are favoured, while those perceived as 'unmodern' are rejected.

This chapter also aims to explore three professional dimensions of administrative work: the *subjective and reflexive perspective* of state employees on the reliability of the method they use to distinguish real from sham marriages; the analysis of the *moral dilemmas* they experience daily in their role as gatekeepers; and the *material dimension* of their work illustrated by the transformation of tense interviews into official documents.

Beginning with an analysis of this unprecedented encounter between binational couples and state authorities, I will explore romantic love and the ideal of companionate marriage as dominant moral categories in Euro-American societies, and discuss how these moral categories are operationalized through the practical norm of *bureaucratic feminism* applied by state agents evaluating potential binational marriages. These agents are nation's cultural regulators whose decisions rest upon subjective feelings and the daily management of individual or collective moral dilemmas.

As Wray (2006: 10) has noted, to question these boundaries in the study of binational couples is equivalent to identifying, in various contexts, implicit hierarchies (unofficial and unarticulated) of acceptable marriages, highlighting a hidden politics of belonging and exclusion. In this implicit hierarchy encapsulated by the notion of bureaucratic feminism, what is at stake is not only different conceptions of migration, migrants and citizenship, but also love, marriage and romance, as well as the intersection of these realms. After describing the suspicion device defined below, and objectifing these implicit criteria, I also analyse what disappears between the original interview and the official document produced by state agents.

This chapter is based on fieldwork carried out between January 2012 and June 2013 in various civil registrar offices in Brussels. The main focus of the fieldwork was observing everyday administrative procedures, and fifteen in-depth interviews with binational couples.[1] Municipal authorities accepted my presence in their office under the condition that I was not to enter into contact with any of the couples. I thus only had access to the bureaucrats' definition and vision of the situation. Drawing on observations of couples' meetings with civil registrars and interviews with fifteen members of staff in these offices, I witnessed the practical application of what I call 'administrative suspicion'. I argue that the context of broader suspicion based on a perceived polarization between the wealthy North and the poor South affects the daily work of agents. The agents' work is also embedded in what Groes calls 'methodological conjugalism' (Groes 2016).² The invention of the term 'grey marriage' encapsulates this generalized suspicion because it implies the existence of a 'self-interested' southern migrant deluding a naive European citizen by simulating affection in order to gain legal status in Belgium. Hélène Neveu Kringelbach notes that it was in 2007 that the French integration minister, Eric Besson, coined the term 'grey marriage' to describe a union between a French partner marrying for love and a foreign partner marrying solely for 'migratory purposes' (Neveu Kringelbach 2013: 1). She adds that this 'term has since made its way into parliamentary debates, legal texts and bureaucratic practices, and the public debate around the notion has contributed to the emergence of a generalized climate of suspicion towards French–foreign couples'.

The use of the term 'grey marriage' spread into Belgium in the same period, and also fuels the climate of suspicion regarding migrants in the country. During my interviews with municipal councillors, they recalled the meeting they organized in the early 1990s to respond to reports of abuse by their colleagues. Many of them recounted the cases of young women coming into their office shortly after their wedding, crying because they now realized that their partner had only wanted to marry in order to obtain a residence permit. Civil registrar officers base their commitment to the fight against marriages of convenience and grey marriages on the basis of these so-called 'rescue narratives' (Bracke 2012), epitomized by stories of crying women who have been deceived by foreign partners. These tragic stories and their interpretation resulted in a change of legislation: preventive measures were added in 1999, and punitive ones in early 2006 (Foblets and Vanheule 2006: 264).

Preventive Measures and the Nation's Intimacy

Since 1999, the municipal councillor in charge of marriage ceremonies has been vested with a new power: he or she can postpone or refuse to officiate a wedding if they suspect a 'grey marriage' or what is popularly known as a 'marriage of convenience' – that is, a marriage contracted between two individuals who exchange money and intimacy for a residency permit. Legislative authorities hope this initiative will offer a response to a situation perceived of as problematic: the Ministry of Justice provided statistics revealing that during the previous ten years at least three thousand people had been proven to have contracted marriages of convenience (Foblets and Vanheule 2006: 265). The legislative change put emphasis on the active role of the municipal councillor in charge of marriages to prevent sham marriages. According to the article 146bis of the Belgian civil code introduced in 1999, 'there is no marriage, even if formal consent has been given in preparation for it, if it emerges that, from a combination of circumstances, the intention of at least one of the spouses is obviously not the creation of a lasting life-long community, but only the procurement of a residence permit, tied to the spousal status'. The law on marriages of convenience is accompanied by a memorandum detailing the elements that indicate that the marriage may not be based on the aim of creating a lasting life-long community. An administrative circular has been provided to help employees in their task of assessing sham marriages. Elements that may indicate a sham marriage include:

- The parties do not understand each other, or have difficulties in having a dialogue, or appeal to an interpreter
- The parties never met before the marriage
- One of the parties lives with somebody else in a long-term arrangement
- The parties do not know the name or the nationality of the other
- One of the future spouses does not know where the other one works
- There is an obvious difference between the statements of the two parties regarding the circumstances of their meeting
- A sum of money is promised to contract the marriage
- One or both is engaged in prostitution
- There is the intervention of an intermediary
- A significant difference in age

During interviews with civil registrars, I asked them what constitutes tangible signs of a sham marriage. They highlighted anecdotes of exceptional cases where potential partners did not share a common language, but also put great emphasis on a significant difference in age and a perceived difference of 'beauty'. The latter does not appear in the administrative circular, maybe because it is not politically correct and/or is difficult to define. However, this element of 'beauty' seems to be particularly important in guiding the decisions of the civil registrars.

In 2010, a scandal brought this issue to the headlines with the story of a Belgian man in his sixties and a 25-year-old woman from the Ivory Coast, whose marriage in the Ivory Coast was not recognized by Belgian authorities. The grounds were that the Belgian was 'in his sixties and paunchy'.[3] The 'paunchy' man responded in the media that love was not based on kilos. However, stark physical differences (of age and perceived beauty) are carefully scrutinized. When evaluating the sincerity of a marriage, such noticeable differences can make the marriage suspect, in the eyes of state agents. It was clear to me from interviews that municipal authorities actively scrutinize physical compatibility – based on ethnic, racial, class and gender components. Anne Lavanchy collected similar statements in her fieldwork with Swiss civil registrars. She described officials working on the replication of national likeness by holding on to an idealized vision of marriage as the search for sameness (Lavanchy 2013b: 77). For Helga Eggebø, compatibility – if the spouses are regarded as similar or different by immigration authorities – is a key dimension of determining whether a marriage is real or not (Eggebø 2012: 773).

In 2011, the public prosecutor in Brussels registered around eleven thousand cases suspected of being 'marriages of convenience' or grey marriage. This specific evaluation raises questions regarding identity and citizenship: who is and who is not part of the nation? Who is really a citizen?[4] Who belongs to the nation and who is excluded from it? These evaluations also question the ordinarily taken-for-granted dichotomy between private matters and public concerns (Eggebø 2012: 78), as narratives of intimacy are used to prove the (in)authenticity of conjugal life. Indeed, to pretend to live together, legally and in the same territory, the couple requesting to marry must submit to a whole process aimed at verifying and controlling their intimate life together. So, the ability of migrants or couples to cross national boundaries depends on state agents entering the intimate boundaries of the couples. Furthermore, the evaluation rests on the extent to which the official notions of love mesh with the couple's practices and narratives of love.

Tense Interactions

The political affiliation of my interviewees seems to be a determinant in their discourse, since the fight against marriages of convenience has long been a political discourse of the right. This is evident in the contrast between two archetypal municipalities where I conducted research – 'Steenzeel', which has a long history of right-wing government (the political party Mouvement Réformateur), and 'Cityville', a left-wing socialist municipality (Parti Socialiste). The discourse of the elected deputy mayors of the civil registrar's offices contrasted dramatically in these two municipalities. For the civil registrar officer of Steenzeel, the fight against marriages of convenience was a priority amongst his favorite campaign themes. He had a mission, a crusade, and frequently used the words 'cheaters', 'abuse' and 'invasion' when talking about migrants, and shared his fears about an uncontrolled future. He expressed himself regularly on this issue in the media. He was professionally involved in the 'fight', as he led all the interviews with suspected couples.[5]

In the view of the civil registrar officer of Steenzeel, his counterpart in Cityville had a more nuanced discourse. The latter positioned his view of migration with the migrant's motivations for coming to Belgium, and even confessed himself to having had a marriage of convenience with his first wife, from Portugal, when Portugal was not yet a member of the EU. In his daily work, he tried to distance himself from these processes. He never led interviews, which his employees resented. The staff felt he showed a lack of solidarity with them, and they denounced the fact that they were sometimes called on by him to defend a refusal decision in front of a couple. The staff felt that as an elected official he was just trying to curry votes by being lenient on marriage migrants. Questioning or not supporting their decisions demonstrated that he had no respect for their work.

I was expecting to observe heterogeneous practices according to the political party of each municipality, but the reality was totally different. Beyond political orientation, state agents' practices were relatively homogenous. One administrative employee justified this by explaining that 'politicians are only passing through the municipality, whereas the administrative staff are making a career here'. The ideology of the administrative staff, the particular hierarchical relations, and more specifically, the leadership of the departmental head were more crucial in managing the 'fight against convenience marriage'.

In Cityville, interviews were systematic. Every member of the staff perceived the two afternoons per week dedicated to this task (meaning that two couples are interviewed each week) as a chore. In the morning, a discussion occurs about who will be designated, and who will be on each team. It is a moment of disagreement, complaint, claims and counterclaims. When interviewing state agents individually, they all concur that doing such interviews should not be their job – they say it is a police task, and that they are not trained for it. This lack of training is possibly why they rely on stereotypes as a professional resource.

They always begin by interviewing the non-EU partner, asking when he/she arrived in Belgium, what was his/her migration route and the reason behind the decision to settle in Belgium. Then the state agents move on to investigate the circumstances of the encounter with his/her Belgian or EU partner. They insist on having a precise date and try to construct a diary with as much detail as possible. The agents try to establish what people share (phone number, email, Facebook) in order to communicate, and to establish the scenario of the encounter. A frequent question is: 'When did the relationship become serious?' Depending on the individual who is doing the interview, this question may be formulated differently, but always with great ambiguity: 'When did an emotional relationship begin?' This question is sometimes difficult to answer for partners because of its ambiguous nature.[6] Some interlocutors think they have to explain when they began to have a sexual relationship. In such cases the civil registrars back out, laughing: 'No, no we don't need to know that...!' But the information is recorded either way in the official document. They ask the partner the reason for choosing the other to live with, as well as 'What are his/her qualities and faults?' Next comes the reversed question of what qualities and faults the other would say about him/her – also sometimes very difficult to answer.

In this sense, interviewees are wise to confirm stereotypes. Another empirical example could be the one of a Brazilian illegal resident in Belgium being interviewed because he wanted to marry a Portuguese woman older than himself (by seven years). When asking him about his hobbies, he did not answer with 'football'. So both interviewers asked: 'You are not a fan of a Brazilian team?' He repeated that he was not a fan of football and had no interest in it. Both interviewers remarked, 'Oh it's strange, a Brazilian man who doesn't like football – very strange!' This response provoked a change in the atmosphere of the interaction. The previously relaxed tone of the communication transformed into more serious exchanges. I do not claim that this fact, per se, provokes the refusal of the marriage ceremony, but combined with others (like a difference in age, or discrepancies between the two versions of the encounter), it could lead to the confirmation of the initial suspicion.

They ask also about the daily schedule, work and habits of the partner. The migrant is asked if he/she works. The answer is often 'no' or 'little, sometimes', because the migrant knows that he/she is not legally authorized to work. Then the state agents move on with a question about who pays for the housing, food or gifts for their beloved – questions that could place an illegal migrant interviewee in a very uncomfortable position. The agents repeat that responses must be honest, and that they are not the police.[7] They ask about the families: who knows who, and the names of brothers and sisters, parents, children. They ask how the weekend was spent, and for a detailed description of daily life from the time they wake up to the time they go to bed at night. More details requested include: a description of the place where their partner lives, the color of the walls, the arrangement of the rooms; the financial means of each person; if the partner smokes or drinks alcohol; the wedding party they have in mind (or how the wedding took place, if the marriage is in process of being recognized in Belgium), who will be witnesses, and whether they have already bought the wedding dress and the wedding rings.

As each history is singular, civil servants do not employ the questionnaire in a rigid way, but basically try to know about particular events and facts that they can compare together after the interviews. When civil servants estimate they have enough information, the first partner is asked to read the document and sign it, and is then asked to leave the room. A state agent accompanies him/her, and then invites the other partner to enter, thus avoiding any exchange of information.

Now that the state agents have the first narrative before their eyes, the Belgian or EU partner is asked about the circumstances of the encounter. The state agents pursue the questioning by sounding out if their interviewee knows the aspirations and motivations of the non-EU partner, and this is also a way to prevent (or sometimes dissuade) him/her from going through with the marriage. 'Why is he/she choosing Belgium?' 'To have a better life, I suppose' responds a Belgian man. If people do not know or hesitate, the state agents regularly reply, 'But this person is your future husband/wife...' in such a way as to say that they need to be more precise and to collaborate. Answers such as, 'I don't know', 'I don't remember', hesitations, or worse still, 'It's not my business what happened before we met; I'm not curious', provoke exasperation and are perceived as bad faith or characteristic of an attempt to cheat. Hesitations that punctuate interactions during exchanges of memory recall such as 'I don't know', 'I'm not sure' or 'I don't remember exactly' are not willingly transcribed in the formal record of interview document. State agents then insist that the interviewee be able to produce concrete information. When a Portuguese woman cannot remember the date of her encounter two years ago, the municipal employee tries to help her: 'Was it cold or warm? Was it in the summer or winter?'; and when facing silence and confusion from the woman, she persists, showing her irritation: 'Did you wear a coat or not? You must remember!'

Some questions that had previously been asked have since been dropped. The question 'What are you going to do if your wedding is refused?' is no longer officially part of the questionnaire. However, some employees continue to ask it, because they find that in some cases answers such as 'I'll find another bride/groom' is proof of a sham engagement. This is because such answers are contradictory to the romantic idea of the unique other. This is also a way to emphasize the state agent's disapproval of their disregard for rules and authority.

Border Gatekeepers and the Game of Authenticity

The municipal councillors as well as the municipal agents are not formally trained in interviewing techniques as the police are, and nor are they informed about the different cultural dimensions of marriages. All these actors have to learn their job through on-the-job training and by practical experience in order to estimate the degree of authenticity of a proposed marriage. This training and learning 'favours the incorporation of implicit standards and separate physical and mental automatisms of the legal rules' (Spire 2008). The main idea shared by most state agents (and related services such as the police) is that migrants are a burden on the welfare state. Most state actors implicated in evaluating the sincerity of migrants' narratives see immigration as a real and growing 'plague'. This view of migration as a plague invading Europe (Martiniello 2001) often becomes a professional norm under the pressure and control of colleagues. In this sense, the discourse of the police is illustrative of this state of mind. When civil registrar agents have suspicions after their interviews with potential partners, they send a report to the public prosecutor, who, in turn, mandates the police to begin an inquiry, including a residence check and another interview at the police station. When I visited a police team specializing in the fight against sham marriage in 2013 – two policemen by the names of Jean and Michel – they explained their experience with migrants.

> Jean: You know, when I [entered the service] in 2004, I saw how illegal migrants were trying to find official status in order to stay in Belgium. ... And of all people who I see passing, I can say to you, Maïté, I don't see one with a hard-working spirit, not one. When I ask them why they want to come to Belgium, there is no one who says to me that he wants to work.

> Michel: When we ask what they do, they respond they have the CPAS.[8] I can say to you, Maïté, that in four years there is not one migrant who has been able to explain what the CPAS is – nobody knows what that means, and they don't care. As soon as we ask questions, the only thing they are able to say is, 'I have the right'.

> Jean: You know all this help from the CPAS, it is millions that leaves public funds every year. The leftists don't understand anything. I didn't see anyone a bit clever or a bit honest. When you ask them, 'What are your life plans?', no one speaks to me of working – no one.

This 'strong ideological cohesion' (Spire 2008) between some civil registrar offices (like that of Steenzeel) and the police and administrative employees transforms the fight against marriages of convenience into an effort to restrain migratory flows – a struggle against unwanted immigration.

In civil registrar offices, state agents try to ensure that the migrants they receive in their office will not be a burden on the welfare state. The interview at the civil registrar office can turn into a verification of the migrant's capacity to integrate. Some questions – that are not part of the official questionnaire – interrogate the idea of integration as a normative concept, such as: Which language do they speak at home? Which language will their children learn? For Muslim couples, will they send their children to a Catholic school? If not, why not? They are asked to give justifications for their answers. Will they learn French? Are they already taking French classes? Do they work? What do they do? And if they cannot find work in the sector of their choice, will they take something else? In this case, the expected answer is thus: 'Yes, I will take whatever I can find, even if my qualifications are higher'.

In this context, administrative employees explain how they sometimes manoeuvre to achieve their goal of restraining migratory flows: 'We play on delay', I heard. Another civil registrar in Steenzeel showed me a specific case of suspect cohabitation that he had examined. As he did not have any evidence to deny the request, he explained to me his administrative actions in these terms: 'I will send a report of a suspicious request for cohabitation to the Aliens Office and maybe they will delay giving him the residency permit'.

In numerous cases resembling the one above, the state agents adopt negative conceptions of the migrant as part of a professional posture, so as to reinforce the degradation and the stigma of the migrant. This somehow broader, hostile climate towards migrants creates conditions for both couples and state agents to engage in a kind of 'game of authenticity'. State agents try to find clues indicating a true romantic relationship – or the opposite – and interviewees try to respond to the state agents' expectations with appropriate responses.

Civil registrars cultivate meaning in their work, which is grounded in the characterization of the imaginary detective (even if they repeat in other contexts that they are not police). In their offices, they act as if they were inspectors or detectives, and this passion for the game of searching for signs and finding clues seems to constitute a source of pleasure. A young civil registrar in Steenzeel, called Fatima, referred to this game of authenticity when she described the way she flushes out the intentions of partners:

> I ask detailed questions because a woman remembers birthdays, the names of the brothers or sisters... Men less so, they are different. But when partners don't know and look at each other, stressed, I laugh and I say to them, 'Come on, you don't know that, it's strange...' It's a game.

This game-like dimension of the civil registrars' daily work must be considered as a way of making sense and providing meaning to the unsatisfying and difficult task they are assigned: defining the indefinable, measuring the immeasurable.

State agents use a lexicon that is borrowed from theatrical metaphor to describe potential partners' performance: civil registrars try to unveil the 'script' behind the testimonies; they denounce any obvious *mise-en-scene* of romantic love; and they try to baffle the partners. Some of them think that subtle details about the couple are what make it possible to distinguish a 'true' from a 'fake' relationship, while others think that too much detail given by partners is a sign of a made-up script learned by heart, and is thus suspect.

To distance themselves from the stigma of state categories, couples develop similar strategies across European countries. Helga Eggebø (2012) describes the active work of binational couples in Norway to distance themselves from stigmatized categories. Manuela Salcedo Robledo (2011) describes the strategies of binational couples in France when they try to justify the disinterested character of their union. Couples, she argues, answer the suspicious questioning by elaborating a speech, which opposes and answers that of the administration. To do so, they anchor their love story in a defensive rhetoric by anticipating the questions and by a multiplication of signs of normality – for example, by hanging photos of each other together on the wall. In Brussels, when I was talking with the police about the signs that confirm or disprove 'true love', one policewoman said: 'For example, when we enter an apartment and the first thing we see is a big photo of the partners on the hall wall, we know they put it there for us; it's already suspect'. Thus the challenge for couples consists in neither being too explicit or demonstrative about the authenticity of their romance, nor leaving the impression that the marriage is a practical or unemotional affair.

Exploring Others' Intimacies and Moral Dilemmas

This fieldwork is saturated with assumptions about intimacy: from the 'intimate conviction' asserted by state agents in charge of controlling potential partners of a marriage or a civil partnership, to the exploration of the intimate sphere of potential partners, as described above, which constitutes the concrete technique for distinguishing real from fake projects of marriages.

The 'intimate conviction' – a specific form of judgement traditionally associated with reason and conscience[9] – could be understood as an effective 'professional resource' (Lavanchy 2013b: 70) in administrative labour. When I was trying to understand the way state agents distinguish real from sham marriages, a civil registrar responded to me: 'As soon as they walk in the door, I can immediately feel if they are sincere, if it's a real couple or not'. Another woman told me: 'I cannot explain it, but I work a lot with my intuition'. Statements of this nature were frequent. Some interlocutors pay great attention to details while others do not, but in all cases, feelings and intuition seem to play a crucial role. The first impression is significant. All the work beforehand consists in rationalizing this very first physical and casual judgement. Another civil registrar, Karin, took me aside in her office to explain: 'You will see, first you will not be able to distinguish, you are still naive, but as you spend time with us, you will be able to feel it when you see the partners'. This feeling is thus a skill to develop. Nora, a colleague of Karin, adds and confirms: 'Yes, when I myself began this work, I was really naive. I thought every couple were true lovers but then, little by little, I began to see things otherwise'. As Hertz, Martin and Valli (2004) have shown in the case of Swiss agents in charge of evaluating the right of the unemployed to continue to benefit from welfare payments, emotion (under the form of trust, empathy and identification) is omnipresent in the discourse. Interaction between 'clients' and state agents is embedded in an 'emotional economy' that will guide the decisions of the agents. For these scholars, feelings become an implicit logic in the working of the welfare state. So, emotions are recognized as part of the daily activity of a state agent, and play a role in the general process of ordinary judgement.

In Cityville, the correct questions to ask of interviewees is the subject of perpetual debate between the administrative agents, who take their difficult task of distinguishing true love from false very seriously. During one lunchtime, a discussion took place amongst some of them, and Samantha, an administrative employee of Cityville in her twenties, gave her point of view to show that she can distance herself from the suspicion device:

> Well, we don't have to go through their intimate life. We are not police and everybody has the right to marry. And a couple who answers badly to questions may be a real couple. My father doesn't remember my birthday. I have three favorite colours and if you ask my boyfriend, I will say one and he will say another... I also have a lot of favorite meals...

Notwithstanding, she concluded by explaining her own approach: 'But I'm strict, you can ask my boss, she will tell you. If you ask me, even with marriages like that [she puts her thumb up], I can make you doubt. I doubt everything'.

Even if every agent can distance himself or herself from the method used to distinguish real from sham marriage, and even go as far as to call into question the reliability of the method, the weight of the suspicion device is tangible. It produces consequences manifest in the state of mind of those very agents. From this dubious perspective, everything and anything can be interpreted as suspect.

Such relativism can be seen in its extreme in the words of Gaston, a sixty-year-old employee in Steenzeel who feels at liberty to speak since he will soon be retiring. During an individual interview with him, I asked him if he faced moral dilemmas when interviewing couples – did he ever hesitate? He confessed that for him, the method they use in municipality is not reliable. He believed that the only thing that counts is the mood of the interviewer:

> Gaston: I am going to say this to you: if you do an interview, I do not know if you have already noticed it, whether it is with me or another person, when you want the person to fail the interview, you fail them, and when you want them to pass, they pass. You do not agree with this?
>
> M: Wait, you mean that...
>
> Gaston: When a person does not please you, if you want to crush it, well, you crush it. You ask really unpleasant questions. If it is a person who pleases you, and you want her to pass, well then, it will pass because you ask much easier and much more pleasant questions.
>
> M: I think I understand what you mean. There is a great deal of discretion?
>
> Gaston: All this depends on the mood of the person ... If we pissed you off all morning long, then well, you are going to put back everything on the person. That's it. (Laughter). It is like that.

Listening to Gaston's voice, we are far from the impersonal bureaucratic ethos. He obliges us to disabuse ourselves from the 'rationalist illusion of bureaucracy' (Wellner 2006).

Another character under suspicion during interviews is the translator. When it has been established during the first interaction that a person does not speak French well, a state agent asks him/her to come with a sworn translator. This person is treated with great deal of distrust for a number of reasons, the major one being that translators are perceived to have the potential to help people by making corroborating answers. And this possibility is strengthened in the eyes of municipal employees by the fact that they see a common background shared by the translator – a kind of linguistic, ethnic or community affinity. The interviewees could receive conscious or unconscious support in the question and answer session, and this perceived risk provokes tense situations. To prevent such practices, the agents continuously control the time the translator takes to formulate a question, and cut him/her off, reminding them to report exactly what the interviewee says, and not a word more.

Using Two Filters to Screen 'Acceptable' Intimacy

The bureaucratic perception of intimacy relies on an implicit idea of the 'correct or acceptable' form of shared intimacy, as assessed by two major criteria. First, the two versions of the partners' stories must match. If not, the state agent will send the file to the public prosecutor, who will proceed with an investigation through the police, and then send a notice again two months later. Nonetheless, it is the civil registrar officer who has the last word.[10] In their evaluation, state agents adopt a normative and rigid view of the fact that intimacy is something shared: the details must agree, and the way that each particular event is narrated must match. Yet the connection between language and intimacy is not so evident. There is no clear equivalence between intimate events, the intensity and quality of a relationship, and their formulation in words and sentences. Moreover, cultural settings also shape intimacy and the way we talk about it.

The second filter is what I call *bureaucratic feminism* constituted by particular ideas of freedom, equality and choice. Bureaucratic feminism is different from the feminist movement in the sense that it is a 'practical norm' (Olivier de Sardan 2008), an exploratory concept useful to investigate the dialogical dynamics between professionals' norms and the practical orientation of public agents in the decision-making process. This normative register of 'practical norms' opens – beyond easily identifiable professional norms or broader social norms – a large spectrum of 'subtle, invisible, implicit or underground social regulations' (ibid.: 13). This applied feminism is an implicit norm that informs the daily work of agents and has concrete effects and direct consequences in the lives of concerned people – the interviewees.

State agents try to establish if their interlocutors are resolutely modern, tied by modern forms of attachments, and if they can identify with them (Fernandez 2013). As Eva Illouz (2012) has noted: 'Modern men and women embraced freedom as the fundamental value and practice of their intimate life'. The capacity to base intimate relations on the mutual and free recognition of the value and worth of another person is the central element of the modernist project inherited from the Enlightenment's rupture with the 'genealogical society', as defined by Elizabeth Povinelli (2006: 5). Modernity is at the core in determining the desirability of migrants. To screen for modernity, state agents weigh the criteria of the choice of the partner, especially if women can exercise free choice, and also weigh the gender (in)equality within the couple. Women are the preferential subjects of attention, and state agents perceive them as victims or agents. Two ethnographic examples illustrate this bureaucratic feminism.

Example 1: Searching for Gender Equality

In the registrar offices, the question of the perceived gender equality of the couple is central. Civil registrars, who are mostly women, ask themselves if they should endorse couples seen as problematic according to a certain kind of feminist ideas.

When interviewing a 32-year-old Albanian woman, an administrative employee by the name of Martha asked her if she would work if she lived in Belgium. The Albanian woman responded that she would like to work in the care domain. When the same employee asked her husband, an Albanian man and political refugee in Belgium, an hour later if his future wife would work in Belgium, he responded with some pride in his voice: 'No, my wife will not work as my mother does, she never works'. When the couple left the office, the state employees began to share their feelings about what they had heard: the difference in aspirations about work, which the state agents perceived as the proof of gender inequality in the couple. The posture of the man 'prohibiting' his wife to work was seen as the mark of a kind of archaism and male dominance. The employee, wishing to justify the decision to refuse the marriage, concluded the discussion by this sentence: 'What would be the future of Brussels with such people?'

Later that same day, another civil registrar showed me a file she had examined in the previous week. It stated:

> When we asked the man to describe the qualities of the woman he planned to marry, he answered: 'She cooks well and she vacuums as well'. That appeared to us to not be the basis for a common life, and thus we made an appeal [against the marriage]; but the court did not agree with us because the partners had known each other for a long time.]

The real question at stake here is not the question of the dishonest request for a residence permit, but that the civil registrar is addressing the question of equality in the couple as an implicit criterion for admission into Belgium. In doing so, state employees assume that romantic love and gender equality should go hand in hand. Nevertheless, the idea that romantic love implies gender equality is not supported by empirical data (Holland and Eisenhart 1990; Mahony 1995; Rebhun 1999).

Paradoxically, the same state agents evoke gender differences in other contexts, such as when they show more tolerance towards men who forget the birth date of their future partner 'because men are like that'. So a gender bias is still present even if the 'inspectors of affect' put gender equality at the centre of their preoccupations. Another example is the disapproval of couples where the woman is older than the man, while the contrary is banal and provokes fewer suspicious reactions. According to the cultural background of the spouses, state employees weigh this difference in age differently. In practice, when the woman is older than the man, it is highly suspicious if one of the partners comes from a country of the Middle East because, as an employee explained to me, 'they don't approve of a man marrying an older woman', whereas the same kind of difference is not the object of great attention if the partner comes from a Latin American country, which are considered to be more liberal. An analysis in terms of intersectionality is useful here, connecting the conception of gender with nationality, and unveiling multiple lines of normativity.

Moral paradoxes are numerous in the field of policing migration. Nadine Fernandez (2013) highlights unexpected consequences of the policy of family reunification in Denmark. Those politics are articulated around the idea of the protection of personal freedom and gender equality. The fight against 'forced marriage' is one of the emblematic examples of such politics: 'But what if it is not the family, but the state (or states) that is (are) "forcing" the marriage', asks Fernandez (ibid.: 275), showing how native Danes who marry Cubans lack the autonomy to choose how they want to conduct their relationship. They are forced to marry in order to be together and continue their relationship.

Example 2: The Choice as a Moral Category

'Arranged' marriages provoke irritation among civil registrars because they are perceived as less egalitarian than companionate marriages[11] or marriage based on affective authenticity. In these spaces, the 'free' choice of the partner becomes a moral category. Arranged marriage is thus perceived as the formal opposite of free choice. These irritations must be placed in the broader context of the perceived threat that the norms of migrant groups have on the liberal values of Europe. Those marriages are perceived as immoral in various European contexts, a threat to numerous European nations (see Fernandez 2013 for the Danish case, and Eggebø 2012 for the Norwegian one).

Thus state officials see arranged marriages as equally problematic as marriages of convenience. During informal discussions with Emilia, a young municipal employee, she confessed her wish to forbid arranged marriages, in the same way as marriages of convenience are forbidden. Her reason was that she found these institutions archaic: 'Half of the inhabitants of this municipality are Moroccans. And it is true that in arranged marriages, people don't know each other very well; and, if you ask me, I would delay everybody and I would not authorize an arranged marriage'. This goal is shared by most state agents and has resulted in a form of distortion of the legislation on marriage of convenience by refusing arranged marriage on the grounds that parties are ignorant of each other, and/or the fact that union is the result of a rapid process. The structure of arranged marriages is thus at stake here.

Another employee confirmed this negative perception and complained about what she calls 'traditional' marriage:

> For the community we have here from the Maghreb, what do we make of the cultural context? Tradition demands that they marry without knowing each other. But don't we use tradition to mask marriages of convenience? And finally the people remain together only during the period of public investigation. We had the case of a couple last week. We asked the man, 'Why did you choose this girl?' He answered, 'She stands straight and she says her prayers'; and we insisted, 'Yes, but why her?' And he did not know how to answer any more. This man could get married to her just as he could get married to anybody else.

The last sentence describes the exact opposite of the romantic logic of love, according to which, in the multiplicity of potential partners, there is one and only one[12] (Gell 1996). In the romantic context, the choice of a partner has to do with maturing individuality (Hirsch and Wardlow 2006: 4–5); it is a crucial moment in the life of the individual, and must rest upon a deep self-examination or an intense revelation (Illouz 2012: 59).

Nevertheless, the marriage project has to rest on an intention of common life to be accepted by officials in Belgium. Love is not mentioned explicitly in the law, but a romantic conception of this idea seems to guide the evaluative itinerary of the agents. Eileen Muller Myrdhal (2010) and Helga Eggebø (2012) have shown how love also constitutes the appropriate basis for marriage in the Norwegian legislation and application. The prevention of sham marriages is thus bound with this very specific view of love and affect, which is shared by a majority of Belgians: '[A]ccording to romantic clichés, love is blind, love overwhelms, a life without love is not worth living, marriage should be for love alone, and anything less is worthless and a sham' (Lindholm 2006). An important construct of morality weighs on love and romance, which are considered sacred – 'the most influential mode of moral vision in our culture', as Roberto Unger put it (Unger 1984: 29; cited in Lindholm 2006) – and one cannot play, fraud or cheat with this. The state agents in charge of preventing marriages of convenience pay particular attention to the script of the lovers' encounter, which must be 'romantic' in essence. According to this logic, an encounter on the Internet will be more suspect than other ways of meeting. As Nicola Mai and Russell King argue, ideologies of romantic love 'play a key role in the construction of Europe (and the West) as spaces of emotional and civic superiority and in enforcing "common-sense-based" yet cripplingly restrictive migration policies' (Mai and King 2009: 300).

Indeed, as Kate Gavron (1996) has shown in the case of London-based Bengalis, this practice of arranged marriage – in the broader context of sexual morality – allows people to draw a demarcation line between 'Us' and 'Them'. In this context, Anglo-Saxons feel superior to the Asian community because, among other reasons, they perform marriages of 'love',[13] whereas Asians perform traditional marriages, which do not necessarily imply love.[14] Helena Wray documents the same tendency for Indian men who applied to move to Great Britain in the 1970s and 1980s, and were turned down because, according to state perspective, no 'love' was involved in arranged marriage (Wray 2006, 2011). The individual appropriation of romantic ideals could be seen as a prerequisite to migration to the West.

Furthermore, in numerous cases the clear distinction between 'arranged marriage' and 'love marriage' is difficult to maintain. Indeed, Victor De Munck (1996) has shown in his study of a Muslim community in Sri Lanka that the reality is not so clear cut: numerous arranged marriages are in fact generated primarily by 'romantic motivations'. Coralynn Davis makes a similar statement concerning South Asia, showing how, contrary to the one-sided perception of arranged marriage in Western media as emblematic of women's oppression, 'the cultural region is steeped in romantic and erotic narrative going back many hundreds of years' (Davis 2014: 593). More broadly, the two-tier and mutually exclusive opposition between love and self-interest, which structures the state practices preventing marriages of convenience, prevents us from seeing that all the affinity alliances – and more widely diverse relational forms such as the arranged marriage and marriages of love or friendship – rest on composite mixtures of affect and interests. Various authors studying love and friendship have illustrated this fact in touristic and sexual settings – see Sealing Cheng (2007) for the case of North Korea, Valerio Simoni (2012) for Cuba, and Linda-Anne Rebhun for Brazil (1999 and 2007). There is no such thing as a pure relationship; emotions, material conditions and personal interests intersect (Zelizer 2005; Thomas and Cole 2009).

Conclusion

The field of marriage migration in Belgium, as in other European countries, is marked by an over-regulation. Legal measures are produced, improved or changed every two years in order to stop or catch the 'border artists' (Beck 2006: 157). Actual debates about the phenomenon of the *bébés-papiers* – the conception of a child in order to guarantee a legal residence permit – demonstrate it. It is not a new phenomenon but it worries municipal bureaucrats. State authorities are filling all the possible border gaps with new control apparatus, introducing state surveillance to new areas of intimacy. The recent adoption of a punitive approach (Foblets and Vanheule 2006) related to marriages of convenience consolidates this trend towards an increasing criminalization of migration.

Yet, if state authorities want to be sure that people no longer use marriages of convenience to legally cross national Belgian boundaries, another kind of immigration policy is required: one that straightforwardly addresses the causes of migratory pressure on Europe (Foblets and Vanheule 2006). People of the Global South will continue to search for the material resources they lack at home – as everybody would – in order to achieve full personhood by caring for others, supporting their kin, and realizing their own desire for freedom (Cole and Groes 2016).

In Belgian migration policies, all areas of intimacy are gradually captured by state vigilance. This phenomenon has resulted in the transformation of the national territorial border into a moral boundary defining appropriate forms of intimate relationships and family life (Rytter 2012; Fernandez 2013). Trying to unveil the implicit and unarticulated hierarchies at stake when distinguishing 'true' from 'sham' marriage migration in Brussels, I argue that state employees' confrontation with marriage migrants and their partners is a story of (in)compatibility in its many forms. Bureaucrats treat couples differently according to their social and national belonging.

Two groups stand out. First, unions between a native Belgian citizen – or, to be more precise, a Belgian citizen with no recognized migratory past – and a non-EU citizen are screened according to administrative employees' perceptions of their compatibility. Bureaucratic judgements, their discretionary power about the perceived differences of beauty, age, class, nationality or religion of partners, are evaluated. In these cases, differences at the heart of the couple's intimate life constitute what could be reported as problematic. Homogamy is the implicit norm, and perceived dissimilarities in the couple seem to indicate the mark of simulated or interested affects from the migrant partner. If the Belgian citizen is perceived as ugly or old, and the young migrant from the Global South is seen as attractive, thus beauty and youth are exchanged for a residency permit so that the object of the relation is an interested transaction based on false affects, whether the Belgian is conscious of this or not.

In the second group, unions between a Belgian citizen of immigrant descent and a partner from his/her country of origin (or the country of ancestry) are gauged through their compatibility with Belgian national ideals. As shown above, through the lens of bureaucratic feminism, what is at stake in these cases is not the differences between partners, because in the eye of state agents they are the same, originating from the same culture (despite the fact that they have been socialized in different countries). Here the differences at stake are those that mark a rupture with national conjugal models. First, the choice of the partner from their own culture shows an evident lack of integration in Belgium. But more crucially, as shown, romantic love is the key concept defining those state encounters and thus playing a fundamental role as a criterion of 'Northcentric civility' (Mai and King 2009: 300). State agents' narratives of progress situate traditional gender norms in the past and therefore define them as incompatible with modern national ideals, reproducing an evolutionist division between an arranged marriage and a love relationship.

The work of suspicion is thus divided between these two types of couple configuration through which the state employees reproduce two commonsense divides: true love vs. interested love; and oppressive/genealogical society vs. free/autological society. This particular case study in Brussels, the capital of the European Union, questions the intimate borders of a West European nation and highlights a specific facet of the relationship between love and inequality. In this context, suspicion appears as the third term of this tumultuous relationship. More comparative analysis must be done in different settings where love and inequality intersect in order to deepen our anthropological understanding of this complex, historical and contingent relationship.

Maïté Maskens is lecturer at the Université Libre de Bruxelles where she works on love and its boundaries, focusing on the treatment of binational marriages by public authorities. Her work has been published in *Etnográfica*, the *Journal of the Anthropological Society of Oxford* and *HAU: Journal of Ethnographic Theory*. She is currently a guest editor of a special issue of *Migrations Sociétés*.

NOTES

1. I also conducted interviews with ten deputy town mayors of various Brussels civil registrar offices. My fieldwork also involved the examination of various types of stored data, meetings with specialized police, interviews with lawyers representing municipalities, and the examination of trial proceedings of a typical 'grey marriage'. The study was enriched by interviews with the founder of a non-governmental organization called 'Trapped Hearts', which defends the rights of the victims of such grey marriages, and also by interviews with Belgian citizens who had engaged in sham marriages.
2. According to Christian Groes, methodological conjugalism refers to 'the tendency to see marriage as the norm, the ideal and the natural end point for women from the global south who migrate with Europeans and settle in Europe' (2016: 174). But, as he shows in the case of Mozambican women, migrants do not always seek marriage; indeed numerous women resist marriage in order to achieve full personhood, and thus prefer to have work or a sponsor to guarantee their independence and search for freedom.
3. The article is available online: http://www.dhnet.be/infos/faits-divers/article/329585/yves-interdit-de-mariage-parce-qu-il-est-bedonnant.html.

4. Indeed, for numerous European citizens with a non-European partner, the experience of the administrative treatment they receive (with its share of violence, control or laughter) is the beginning of an in-between status, a 'fractured citizenship' (D'Aoust 2013). They feel they are 'lesser nationals than others', and this feeling could constitute the base of a political or associative engagement. See Ferran (2013) for an illustration of the French case, and Messinger and Digruber (2006) for a contextualization of the Austrian initiative 'Ehe ohne Grenzen' (marriage without borders), a project carried out by cross-border couples who wanted to draw attention to their difficult situation.
5. The methodological challenge I faced in this bureaucratic universe assigned with the task of regulating migration consisted in 'conducting fieldwork with those with whom you disagree' (Lavanchy 2013a). Another methodological challenge I faced was that of working with people entrusted with the power of the state to define and categorize (just as social scientists do!). I was accustomed to working with marginalized groups of people (Maskens 2013) whose lives and decisions had no direct consequences on others' lives.
6. There are no universal conventions on these topics, except in romantic movies, which take the first kiss as the visual beginning of a love story. However, in the non-fictive world, it could be more diverse: the first mouth kiss, a way of touching the other, the first sexual contact, one pronounced word, a silent decision, a sudden engagement, a special emotion, a religious engagement, etc.
7. This is an ambiguous turn of phrase, given that the document produced from the interview will be sent to the police in case of strong suspicion.
8. CPAS (Centre Public d'Action Sociale) is a state organization providing social assistance.
9. It was under the French Revolution that the legislature decided to call upon the intimate conviction of a judge.
10. Most of civil registrar officers confess that they usually follow the recommendation of the public prosecutor. According to Marie-Claire Foblets and Dirk Vanheule, when the decision is a refusal almost half of the couples lodge an appeal against the negative decision, and they often meet with success because judges apply stricter criteria regarding the evidence of a sham marriage (Foblets and Vanheule 2006: 267; see also D'Hondt and Foblets 2002).
11. Jennifer Hirsch and Holly Wardlow define companionate marriage as 'a project, the aim of which is individual fulfilment and satisfaction, rather than (or in addition to) social reproduction' (Hirsch and Wardlow 2006: 4).
12. The 'soulmate' – 'âme sœur' in French, or 'media naranja' in Spanish.
13. Alfred Gell remains sceptical with regard to the foundation of this feeling of superiority. For him, if the Bengalese arranged marriage is structurally predetermined, it rests on completely rational methods with the aim of maximizing the chances of both spouses in the life, whereas the British 'find [it] much more reasonable to trust the whims of young adults (where they are dulled by the media), who will decide themselves on their fate' (Gell 1996: 7).

14. Lindholm (2006) argues that affinity between romance and marriage is characteristic of Western thought (see also Myrdal 2010). Indeed, in numerous non-Western contexts, marriage is seen as a prerequisite for love, and not the opposite. Yet, in many places around the world, love is not traditionally the aim of marriage. It is an institution that has more to do with the politics of belonging, and is an economic or practical arrangement. Moreover, as Alfred Gell (1996) shows, there are many ethnographical testimonies that support the Indian idea, for example, that conjugal love grows with time. In the West, he argues, we could demonstrate the same things; spouses love each other more than at the beginning when partners spent a lot of time in feigning, following the normative injunctions of romance. But, as Hirsch and Wardlow have shown, globalization has increased the extent to which young people around the world 'are talking about the importance of affective bounds in creating marital ties' (Hirsch and Wardlow 2006: 1).

BIBLIOGRAPHY

Beck, U. 2006. *The Cosmopolitan Vision*. Cambridge: Polity Press.

Bracke, S. 2012. 'From "Saving Women" to "Saving Gays": Rescue Narratives and their Dis/continuities'. *European Journal of Women's Studies* 19: 237–52.

Cheng, S. 2007. 'Romancing the Club: Love Dynamics between Filipina Entertainers and GIs in U.S. Military Camp Towns in South Korea', in M. Padilla et al., *Love and Globalization: Transformation of Intimacy in the Contemporary World*. Nashville, TN: Vanderbilt University Press, pp. 226–51.

Cole J., and C. Groes. 2016. 'Introduction: Affective Circuits and Social Regeneration in African Migration', in J. Cole and C. Groes (eds), *Affective Circuits: African Migrations to Europe and the Pursuit of Social Regeneration*. Chicago, IL and London: The University of Chicago Press, pp. 169-196.

Cole, J. and L. Thomas. 2009. *Love in Africa*. Chicago, IL and London: The University of Chicago Press.

Davis, C. 2014. 'Transnational Marriage: Modern Imaginings, Relational Realignments, and Persistent Inequalities', *Ethnos*, 79 (5): 1–25.

D'Aoust, A.-M. 2013. 'In the Name of Love: Marriage Migration Governementality, and Technologies of Love'. *International Political Sociology* 7: 258–74.

De Munck, V. 1996. 'Love and Marriage in a Sri Lankan Muslim Community: Toward a Reevaluation of Dravidian Marriage Practices'. *American Ethnologist* 23: 698–716.

D'hondt S., and M. Foblets. 2002. 'De strijd tegen ontoelaatbare huwelijken: met welke middelen?'. *Tijdschrift voor Vreemdelingenrecht* 2: 115–149.

Eggebø, H. 2012. 'The Regulation of Marriage Migration to Norway'. PhD dissertation. Bergen: University of Bergen.

Ferran, N. 2013. 'Les Amoureux au ban public, genèse et contexte d'une mobilisation'. Presentation at Study Day (13 February) – L'amour et ses frontières: la régulation étatique des mariages transnationaux. Brussels: Université Libre de Bruxelles.

Fassin, D. et. al. 2013. 'Introduction: Au Coeur de l'Etat', in D. Fassin et. al., *Juger, réprimer, accompagner: Essai sur la morale de l'Etat*. Paris: Editions du Seuil, pp. 11-25.

Fernandez, N.T. 2013. 'Moral Boundaries and National Borders: Cuban Marriage Migration to Denmark'. *Identities: Global Studies in Cultural and Power* 20(3): 270-287.

Foblets, M.-C., and D. Vanheule. 2006. 'Marriages of Convenience in Belgium: The Punitive Approach Gains Ground in Migration Law'. *European Journal of Migration and Law* 8(3): 263-280.

Gavron, K. 1996. 'Du mariage arrangé au mariage d'amour: Nouvelles stratégies chez les Bengali d'East London'. *Terrain* 27: 15-26.

Gell, A. 1996. 'Amour, connaissance et dissimulation'. *Terrain* 27: 5-14.

Groes, C. 2016. 'Men Come and Go, Mothers Stay: Personhood and Resisting Marriage among Mozambican Women Migrating to Europe' in J. Cole and C. Groes (eds), *Affective Circuits: African Migrations to Europe and the Pursuit of Social Regeneration*. Chicago, IL and London: The University of Chicago Press, pp. 169-196.

Hertz, H., H. Martin and M. Valli. 2004. 'Le "feeling": une logique sous-jacente au fonctionnement de l'Etat providence'. *Aspects de la sécurité sociale* 1: 12-21.

Hirsch, J., and H. Wardlow. 2006. 'Introduction', in J. Hirsch and H. Wardlow (eds), *Modern Loves: The Anthropology of Romantic Courtship and Companionate Marriage*. Ann Arbor, MI: University of Michigan Press.

Holland, D., and M. Eisenhart. 1990. *Educated in Romance: Women, Achievement, and College Culture*. Chicago, IL: University of Chicago Press.

Illouz, E. 2012. *Pourquoi l'Amour Fait Mal? L'Expérience Amoureuse dans la Modernité*. Paris: Le Seuil.

Lavanchy, A. 2013a. 'Dissonant Alignments: The Ethics and Politics of Researching State Institutions'. *Current Sociology* 61(7): 1-16.

_____. 2013b. 'Par amour du même: La production de l'homogamie par les employés d'état civil en Suisse'. Presentation at Study Day (13 February) - L'amour et ses frontières: La régulation étatique des mariages transnationaux. Brussels: Université Libre de Bruxelles.

Lindholm, C. 2006. 'Romantic Love and Anthropology'. *Etnofoor* 10: 1-12.

Mai, N., and R. King. 2009. 'Love, Sexuality and Migration: Mapping the Issue(s)'. *Mobilities* 4(3): 295-307.

Maskens, M. 2013. *Cheminer avec Dieu: migrations et pentecôtismes à Bruxelles*. Bruxelles: Editions de l'Université Libre de Bruxelles.

Mahony, R. 1995. *Kidding Ourselves: Babies, Breadwinning, and Bargaining Power*. New York: Basic Books.

Martiniello, M. 2001. *La nouvelle Europe migratoire: Pour une politique proactive de l'immigration*. Brussels: Éditions Labor.

Messinger, I., and D. Digruber. 2006. 'Marriage of Residence in Austria'. *European Journal of Migration and Law* 8: 281-302.

Myrdahl, E.M. 2010. 'Legislating Love: Norwegian Family Reunification Law as a Racial Project'. *Social and Cultural Geography* 11(2): 103-116.

Neveu Kringelbach, H. 2013. 'Marriage Migration, Citizenship and the Policing of Intimacy in Contemporary France'. Conference 'Intimate Migration' (3–5 April). Copenhagen.

Olivier de Sardan, J.-P. 2008. 'A la recherche des normes pratiques de la gouvernance réelle en Afrique', Discussion Paper "Afrique: Pouvoir et politique", Overseas Development Institute, 5. Available at http://www.institutions-africa.org/filestream/20090109-discussion-paper-5-la-recherche-des-norms-pratiques-de-la-gouvernance-r-elle-en-afrique-jean-pierre-olivier-de-sardan-d-c-2008 (last accessed 17 January 2018).

Povinelli, Elisabeth. 2006. *The Empire of Love: Toward a Theory of Intimacy, Genealogy and Carnality*. Durham, NC: Duke University Press.

Rebhun, L.-A. 1999. *The Heart Is Unknown Country: Love in the Changing Economy of Northeast Brazil*. Stanford, CA: Stanford University Press.

_____. 2007. 'The Strange Marriage of Love and Interest : Economic Change and Emotional Intimacy in Northeast Brazil, Private and Public', in M. Padilla et al. (eds), *Love and Globalization: Transformation of Intimacy in the Contemporary World*. Nashville, TN: Vanderbilt University Press, pp. 107–19.

Rytter, M. 2012. 'Between Preferences: Marriage and Mobility among Danish Pakistani Youth', *Journal of the Royal Anthropological Institute* 18(3): 572–590.

Salcedo Robledo, M. 2011. 'Bleu, blanc, gris… la couleur des mariages', *L'Espace Politique* 13 | 2011-1 (placed online 3 May 2011).

Simoni, V. 2012. 'Love, Interest, and Morality in Touristic Cuba'. 54th International Congress of Americanists: 'Building Dialogues in the Americas'. Vienna, Austria, 15–20 July.

Spire, A. 2008. *Accueillir ou reconduire: Enquête sur les guichets de l'immigration*. Paris: Raisons d'agir.

Unger, R. 1984. *Passion: An Essay on Personality*. New York: Free Press.

Wellner, J.-M. 2006. 'Le travail administrative des petits bureaucrates: enjeux et transformations', in F. Dreyfus and J.-M. Eymeri (eds), *Science politique de l'administration: Une approche comparative*. Paris: Economica, pp. 253–68.

Wray, H. 2006. 'An Ideal Husband? Marriages of Convenience, Moral Gate-Keeping and Immigration to the UK'. *European Journal of Migration and Law* 8: 303–20.

_____. 2011. *Regulating Marriage Migration into the UK: A Stranger in the Home*. Farnham: Ashgate.

Zelizer, V. 2005. *La signification sociale de l'argent*. Paris: Seuil.

PART II

Circuits of Sex, Race and Gendered Bodies

CHAPTER
4

Survival within a Multi-circuited Maze
Latin American Sex Workers in Spain

Laura Oso

Introduction

A review of the literature developed in a previous publication (Oso 2016) has shown the growth of the sex industry on an international scale in recent decades, which has led to an increase in female migration and sexual tourism. Most of the literature on this subject has focused on the human trafficking of migrant women for sexual exploitation purposes, with the emphasis on their role as victims in the international sex industry (IOM 1995, 1996; Skrobanek, Boonpakdi and Janthakeero 1997; Stone and Vandenberg 1999; Kanti Paul and Abu Hasnath 2000; Farr 2005). Indeed, literature on prostitution and international migration has tended to place sex workers in a passive light (submitted and forced), rejecting the idea that they can be independent agents who use commercial sex for instrumental purposes (Agustín 2005).

In the late 1990s and early 2000s, the 'trafficking perspective' starts to be questioned. As Sophie Day (2009) points out, rather than addressing the issue of sex work, and in particular female employment and mobility, the trafficking perspective, quoted below, tends to bury it, making it invisible and leading to far more serious consequences. Major works that adopt this line include those by Laura Agustín (2005, 2007), Kamala Kempadoo

(2005) and Ronald Weitzer (2007), among others.[1] Although international bodies increasingly draw a distinction between voluntary and forced prostitution, Jo Doezema (1998) points out that the abuse of voluntary sex workers is rarely condemned. Consequently, a social dichotomy is emerging between voluntary/culpable prostitutes and coerced/innocent ones. The problem with this discourse is that women who are perceived to be victims are also considered to merit attention, whereas little political or scientific interest is paid to voluntary prostitutes and the abuses and exploitation they experience. The morality of this discourse dictates that the voluntary prostitute, who has transgressed a moral boundary, is perceived as 'getting no less than she deserves' in the sense of being harassed, exploited, imprisoned or deported (Doezema 1998). The trafficked migrant as a coerced prostitute, on the other hand, is considered more sympathetically as deserving assistance and care from the state and NGOs. As pointed out in a previous review of the literature, 'although there are indeed terrible cases of migrant women who have been duped and traded against their will, numerous studies confirm that large numbers of migrant women in the European sex industry are aware that they will being selling sex (see, for instance, Mai 2001; Oso Casas 2003; Piscitelli 2008; Spanger 2010; Plambech 2014)' (Oso 2016: 1).

On the other hand, and moving away from the trafficking approach, other authors have pointed out the economic role played by the sex market in terms of the financial gain generated among various sectors of the population and in national and international economies, highlighting how the sex industry is linked to migratory flows within the framework of global capitalism (Lim 1998; Ehrenreich and Hochschild 2003; Sassen 2003; Bernstein 2008; Cabezas 2009). Lin Lean Lim considers prostitution as an economic activity, condemning the profits and income generated by the sex industry amongst certain sectors of the population for domestic economies as well as the international economy (Lim 1998). Saskia Sassen points to the way in which the alternative global circuits that migrants join, which she chooses to term the 'counter-geographies of globalization', generate considerable financial resources. As a result, women are not only central to the survival of their families and communities, but also of certain companies and even governments (Sassen 2003). A number of authors have also referred to the series of dependent microeconomic relations, debt and assistance for families and intermediaries, which have emerged within the framework of migratory networks, articulated through the earnings generated by sex work (Cole and Groes 2016).

In this chapter I will examine the case of women mainly from Colombia and Brazil who, as a strategy for social mobility, decide to travel to Spain, aware that they will be working as prostitutes, regardless of their means of entry (autonomously or by small-trade debt). I argue that the migratory projects (the goals and dreams underpinning the determination to migrate) are very similar to those of women who migrate in order to work in other sectors, such as domestic service. In both cases the driving force behind migration is typically the need to support a family or a desire for upward social mobility (Oso Casas 2001, 2003). Nevertheless, migrant women who decide to work in the sex industry and whose migration strategy is to pursue social mobility are no less exempt from abuse and exploitation by third parties. A trafficking discourse that points exclusively to pimps, prostitution rings and mafias as the 'baddies' overlooks the responsibilities of other social actors (such as governments, politicians, business people, police, lawyers, clients) with regard to the exploitation and poor working and living conditions of sex workers.

The main objective of this chapter is to highlight that Latin America women in Spain, as the main providers for families in their homeland and in transnational households, can opt for sex work as a social mobility strategy; however, this decision leaves them to deal with a multi-circuited maze that perpetuates social and gender inequalities in the framework of global capitalism. The 'maze' concept refers to a complicated system of paths or passages that people try to find their way through. I refer to this concept in order to show the intersection between agency and barriers. Migrant women have agency as they take strategies of action in order to improve their social mobility; they opt for migration and sex work as part of this social mobility strategy, and they embark on a path, just as when entering a maze. Nevertheless, their action strategies will clash with what I termed the 'interwoven circuits'. I use the maze concept because it is the idea of the intersection of these circuits that I wish to highlight. Nevertheless, instead of being mere victims or becoming trapped by these circuits, they opt for action strategies in order to try to find their way through. They can be stuck in a passage, but will try to find the way out by adopting certain action strategies. The idea of the maze conjures up an image of an actor struggling to get out, and therefore implies action, but it also helps us to understand the idea of the barriers that migrant sex workers encounter on their path to social mobility. It is this tension between action and barriers that I wish to highlight in this chapter.

The empirical analysis led me to identify how this maze is constituted by the intersection of four circuits, identified as follows: (1) the transnational migratory circuit; (2) the sex worker circuit; (3) the transnational household circuit; and (4) the informal circuit (as undocumented migrants and informal sex workers with no rights).[2] This chapter analyses the structure of and connection between these circuits, their impact on the working and living conditions of migrant sex workers, and their repercussions in terms of social mobility. It also considers the way migrant women react to such circumstances, and how they struggle to survive and achieve their social mobility strategies.

The text therefore aims to contribute to the debate in literature in two ways. Firstly, it highlights the fact that Latin American sex workers in Spain have agency. By agency I am referring to the capacity of individual 'agents' to construct and reconstruct their worlds.[3] The term is used in order to show how migrant women develop strategies of social mobility that include migration and sex work. The chapter therefore questions the approach of victimization, centred on the figure of the woman who has been tricked into sex work. Secondly, it draws attention to the financial gains the sex industry generates for many social actors, who, in addition to the actual traffickers themselves, are responsible for creating many of the barriers that migrant sex workers encounter and have to overcome in their attempts to achieve their strategies and dreams of social mobility. Many of these barriers are associated with the informal circuit and imposed financial interests (of a range of social actors) that migrant sex workers face. Indeed, the lack of social protection (either as citizens or workers) pushes many migrant women to depend on third parties (club owners, etc.), thus drastically reducing their possibilities of working independently, and often leading to situations of abuse and exploitation. In this sense, this chapter falls within the scope of other studies, which, as Martha Cecilia Ruiz explains, 'stress that women in commercial sexual activities are situated in the continuums of oppression and agency, control and resistance, constraints and opportunities; this position recognizes the ambivalent and contradictory contexts in which women experience and negotiate sexuality' (Ruiz 2014: 14–15). The text questions the approach based exclusively on the victimization of sex workers, trying to assess how structures of different kinds of inequality affect the agency of migrant women.

The theoretical framework of analysis follows an approach that is intended to articulate the role of the social actor, as well as structure in explaining migration.[4] The chapter wants to show up how the multi-circuit maze is the result of structural determinants but also of the clash of interests between different social actors, and how migrant women's agency is shaped by the intersection of the four interwoven circuits.

The analysis will be based on the results of a qualitative fieldwork carried out with 50 Latin American sex workers in Galicia (north-west Spain) (34 Colombians, 6 Brazilians, 6 Ecuadorians, 2 Dominicans, 1 Argentinean and 1 Venezuelan), as well as with 6 business owners, 11 clients of brothels and in-call flats, and 15 key informants in contact with sex workers, such as NGO workers and doctors (a total of 82 people were contacted during the fieldwork) in the framework of a PhD thesis (Oso Casas 2001), and the updating of qualitative data carried out in 2014 (6 interviews with sex workers and key informants). The level of education of the women sex workers interviewed was medium (secondary education, vocational training, some years of study at university). In many cases women sex workers were separated, divorced or single women who migrated to Spain leaving their children in the country of origin. Only in two of the cases had the migrant been tricked in her country of origin and was unaware of the fact that she would be working as a prostitute following migration to Spain. The remaining (48) respondents, regardless of their means of entry, further details of which will be provided later on (women in debt who arrived via small-trade channels or who emigrated autonomously), were either fully aware of the type of work they would be doing in Spain before making the decision to migrate, or else entered the sex sector after arriving in the country (Oso Casas 2003).[5]

In the following section I analyse the way in which migration is configured as a social mobility strategy, focusing on the migratory projects and types of sex work carried out by my informants in Spain.

Latin American Migration of Sex Workers in Spain: A Social Mobility Strategy

As I have shown in previous publications (Oso Casas 2003), for the majority of the informants, the decision to migrate to Spain is attributable to reasons similar to those of many female migrant workers in other sectors of employment such as domestic service: the search for financial stability for the migrant and her family, achieved by saving the considerable amount of money needed to buy a house or set up a small business.

The research reveals the presence of two main types of migratory projects among migrant female sex workers in Galicia, as elsewhere: family projects and individual projects (Oso Casas 2001, 2003). The family project tends to be repeated amongst married, widowed, separated or divorced female migrants, as well as single mothers who have left their husbands/partners and/or children behind in the country of origin and whose social mobility strategy centres on saving up enough to return to their home country. However, there are also cases of family regrouping, whereby the members settle in Spain. Individual strategies are adopted by single women with no dependent family members in their country of origin and who are seeking to 'better themselves' by means of the migratory process (Oso Casas 2001, Oso, 2016).

These family and individual strategies often fail to be reflected in their absolute sense. Indeed, combinations of both types of strategy are also common. Many single women with individual social mobility projects also share the objective of contributing to the social and economic improvement of their family members (parents, brothers and sisters) in their country of origin. Likewise, a number of the married, separated, divorced or single-mother women we interviewed also included an individual element into their family strategy: in some cases, the decision to migrate was conditioned by conflict with their partners over a quest for economic independence and a greater say in family decisions, whilst others combined the family project of providing their brothers and sisters with study opportunities with objectives such as of building their own homes (Oso Casas 2001).

Individual or family social mobility strategies targeting the country of origin tend to be associated with an additional, savings-based strategy. In this case, 'women see migration as a "temporary sacrifice" that consists of earning as much money as possible in the shortest possible time … in order to be able to return to their countries of origin, where supposedly they will reap the benefits of their planned social mobility' (Oso 2016: 9). The savings strategy consists mainly of sex work whilst living in clubs or brothels. In Galicia, brothels are mainly located on main roads or on the outskirts of cities, and vary in size. Some are small businesses with just a few women (3–5), whilst others are medium sized and have a larger number of 'girls'. The largest bars may employ up to fifty women. They are generally open from 5 or 6 in the evening to 3 or 4 in the morning. Earnings are normally shared out between the club owner and the sex workers, according to a percentage or a daily rate. The large clubs usually offer accommodation (rooms) and board for the days the woman works. However, some small- and medium-sized businesses also have rooms in the club itself or rented apartments in the surrounding towns. The women pay a daily rate for board and lodging. The club provides a series of advantages for the women migrants with a migratory project based on saving and return. Firstly, it enables them to make a considerable amount of money in a relatively short time, thereby making it easier for them to save. Secondly, it provides them with board and lodging, and eliminates the cost and difficulty of renting a flat (which requires valid documents and permits) and the need to buy food and other necessities. However, there are also numerous drawbacks in terms of the harsh working conditions, as will be seen in greater detail later.

> Living in a club is cheaper, because you pay a fixed amount for your board and lodging. If you live outside you have to pay rent on a flat, as well as for your food and transport, and it works out more expensive … When you live in a club, you spend most of your time in the bar, so you save more. My sister and I get up and go straight to work, and we go to bed as soon as we get back. We don't get up until it's time to go to work, as that way we don't spend any money and the time seems to

> go quicker. When we lived in the flat we had a lot of expenses; you had to pay for this and that, and because there was a shop opposite where we were living, we were always popping out to buy something. So in the end you hardly save at all. But living in the club is different; you know you've got your food and everything, so you save more. (Colombian woman working in a club in Galicia. This testimony also appears in Oso 2016: 9)

As discussed in previous publications, 'women with a social mobility strategy targeting the host social space, whose objective is to regroup their family and settle in Spain', either by means of an individual or family strategy, 'tend to be less obsessed with the idea of saving and therefore deploy labour and residential strategies aimed at improving their living conditions' (Oso 2016: 9). One such strategy is based on renting flats that they share with several other women, providing them with their own personal space and limiting their time in the clubs to their working hours only.

> I talked to María to see if she would rent me out a room. We come here to rest and at 6.30 they pick us up and take us to the club. She rented a flat and offered me the chance to share the cost with her. Living in a flat is better. In the club you get robbed, there is lots of gossip and conflict, the girls don't get on, you have to keep your mouth shut and there are lots of problems. You are exposed to all sorts of malicious comments, it's horrible, not like being in your own flat... In a club you have to get up at a certain time, pay fines, and do the cleaning. The girls that live in a club can get fined, but you can't if you live in a flat. (Colombian woman working in a club in Galicia)

Another strategy aimed at improving the quality of life for those women migrants who are willing to save less consists of moving from a club to what is known as a *piso de contactos* (in-call flat). *Pisos de contactos* are usually small businesses run by a *dueña* (madam) who pays all the expenses. They are rented flats, situated in discrete areas, where various girls go to work several hours a day or to spend certain periods of time. There may be from three to thirty women in these apartments. The clients contact the apartment through advertisements in the local press or on the Internet. The flats work on a percentage basis and, unlike the clubs, they function twenty-four hours a day. As in the clubs, the women rotate from flat to flat depending on the amount of work available, reflecting the sex worker circuit, which will be discussed below. Some combine this work with other types of employment; they go to the flat either in the morning or the afternoon, and at fixed times, in order to avoid arousing suspicion in their social environment. The number of women leading this kind of 'double life' in flats is far higher than in the clubs. Some women receive their clients in their own homes, which gives them a greater degree of autonomy, but which also brings a greater risk to their personal security. As I have discussed in previous studies, discretion is the main advantage of in-call flats: there are no police raids (which do occur in the clubs, as will be seen later on), and there is greater peace of mind and increased autonomy. Furthermore, the 'standard' of clients in these apartments is usually better: the men generally treat the women better, they are looking for discretion and, as my informants report, they rarely arrive drunk – unlike in the clubs. However, earnings in general are lower than for those who work in clubs, and so less can be saved (Oso Casas 2001, 2010).

Some women start off by working in clubs before moving to an in-call flat, as they consider the working conditions to be better:

> In a club you have to flirt with the guys; there's lots of chatting involved. In a flat, you introduce yourself and the client takes his pick; that makes a big difference. I prefer working in a club because you don't end up so exhausted; the work is more relaxing and you don't have to stay up all night. In the clubs you are always at risk: I once got into a fight with a girl, the police arrested me and I was held in custody for 24 hours. It's less tiring in a flat, although in a club you can earn more money because there's more work. (Colombian woman working in an in-call flat)

However, many of the social mobility strategies of my informants came up against a series of structural determining obstacles and/or factors, as well as the strategies of other social actors who seek to take advantage of the sex industry. These difficulties often prevent them from realizing their dreams of individual or family social mobility. The obstacles that female migrants featured in my study encounter are determined by their incursion into what I have termed the 'multi-circuited maze' or the articulation between four circuits, as referred to earlier: (1) the transnational migratory circuit; (2) the sex worker circuit; (3) the transnational household circuit, and (4) the informal circuit. I will now go on to consider how these circuits work, and how they hinder the social mobility strategies of sex workers in Spain.

The Multi-circuited Maze

The Transnational Migratory Circuit

My fieldwork in Spain revealed the existence both of small-scale trade in migrants and an autonomous migration by women. Although around half of the respondents arrived in Spain after taking out a loan, they did so within a system of small-scale trade, sustained fundamentally by social networks constructed among migrants themselves (as I will explain later) rather than by mafias. Only two using this small-trade system were tricked into travelling to Spain without knowing the work they would be doing. The rest were fully aware that they would be working in the sex industry. The other half of our respondents migrated independently, funding the process with savings accumulated in their own country, by mortgaging a property, or by obtaining a loan (from a bank, private credit provider, friend, or family member). Unlike those opting to migrate under a small-trade scheme, the autonomous women typically work independently and are not subjected to trickery, coercion or direct pressure from third parties (Oso 2003).[6] As Christina, a Columbian woman who migrated autonomously, told me:

> In Colombia I belonged to the upper-middle class and I didn't fancy the idea of working in someone's house. A girl told me how to go about doing this sort of work. I arrived in Madrid; my sister gave me money for the trip and my expenses. Then the girl who was my contact arrived and we went to Pontevedra. I came entirely of my own accord, nobody tricked me into coming and no one has ever hit me or anything like that. I look after myself; I have a private insurance policy as well as Social Security. I've never had any trouble working in flats. There are girls who need lots of money because they have to repay a debt. I made the decision to get into this of my own free will and I've made sure I look after myself. I'm not proud of what I do but I look at it as a job. It's a quick way of earning money.

My fieldwork has revealed that in the early years of Latin American immigration to Spain, sex trafficking was more organized and networks were more structured. However, growing numbers of migrant women in Spain eventually led to the development of migratory networks that fed further migrant inflows to Spain, with relatives and friends helping to bring other migrants over. According to several of the respondents, it is normal practice for migrants already settled in Spain – and with some degree of legal stability – to help to meet the migration expenses of relatives, friends or acquaintances in the country of origin, and provide them with the funds necessary to pay for their flight or prove to the Spanish authorities that they have adequate funds to enter the country as a tourist. These settled migrants also provide the mandatory letter of invitation required to get a visa, and information on work contacts in Spain. The amount of the debt assumed by the respondents tends to vary depending on the social networks used. When relatives or friends lend them the money it is often interest-free or at a low rate of interest, whereas lending from other, more distant contacts often entails high interest rates. This kind of deception, which is in line with the official definition of trafficking, lies not so much in hiding the fact that the women will have to work as sex workers when they arrive in Spain, but is more related to the extremely high interest rates and 'fees' for travel assistance, which typically far exceed the actual cost, and often also oblige them to pay extraordinarily high rents and other charges (Oso Casas 2001, 2003). As Jennifer, a Colombian woman who came to Galicia to work in a club via a small network, tells us:

> A friend told me that if I wanted to come over, she knew a girl who could help me. In Colombia it's really hard to find work and I wanted to get out of the country, so I said to myself that I would take whatever was going. Back in Colombia you sign a bill for seven million pesos, and you're told that you'll be able to pay it back with a month's work. You know what you're letting yourself in for. And if anyone says otherwise then they're lying. How can a woman with children not know what she'll be doing over here? When you arrive, you get a shock, because the work is terrible and you can't possibly pay off the debt in a month. Talking to other girls you realize that the debt is higher than the girl actually paid to bring you over. I want to pay her back, because by bringing you over she's taking a risk too; maybe you never pay her back or you get stopped at the border, but it seems a lot of money to me. I don't owe the club owner anything – I owe the girl who brought me over.

Working and living conditions are tougher for women who have to pay off debts, as they frequently have to remain in the club or *piso de contactos* they were originally assigned to until the debt has been repaid. Moreover, the owners of these establishments sometimes take advantage of the indebted migrants by not providing good working conditions. Some also tend to form a paternalist and dominant relationship with these women. The women in debt in my study felt that they are constantly under surveillance (to ensure they do not leave before repaying their debt), and they are often under pressure to work at a pace that ensures maximum earnings in the shortest possible time. This leads to longer or more intensive working days and fewer rest days. Furthermore, the financial pressure to repay the debt as soon as possible also often leads women to put their health at risk – for example, by working during menstruation, using sponges as contraceptives, or not using condoms (Oso Casas 2001, 2003). Juliana, a Colombian woman, sheds light on the way club owners exploit newly arrived women with a debt to repay:

> In the club I was first sent to, we had to pay a daily fee for board and lodging there. We had to make our own food and wash our own clothes. In other parts of the country it's the club that is responsible for making your food, washing your clothes and cleaning. But we had to

do it all ourselves, and to make matters worse, we had to pay a daily fee. You would get fined for everything; if you took too long, they would fine you. If you did anything wrong, you would always get a fine. If we were going out, we would always have to sneak out without anyone realizing.

In this sense, newly arrived female migrants – especially those with a debt to repay, even though they were aware that they would be working in the sex industry – added to the number of workers who were fuelling the worst segments of sex work in Spain, generating considerable amounts of money for a number of social actors. It can thus be seen how the first circuit in our maze, referring to the mobility of people, is configured by the female migration that has fed the Spanish sex industry for the last two decades. This circuit is also boosted by restrictive Spanish immigration legislation. The border closure policy leads to a series of alternative devices that provide access for those women who are prepared to pay large sums of money to enter Spain and work in the sex industry. We will now consider how this circuit is articulated with sex worker mobility.

The Sex Worker Circuit

The traditional figure of the prostitute in Spain has changed in recent decades. As indicated by Sequeiros (1996), in a wealthy economy that belongs to the select group of advanced societies, the notion of novelty has acquired a new importance and has come to be seen as a value in itself. The 'traditional prostitute' – a Spanish woman who was the lover and friend of long-term clients – has given way to the foreigner, who responds to the clients' demands for constant renewal. The relationship between the sex worker and her client has thus become both less personal and more dependent on marketplace dynamics (Sequeiros 1996). In a market characterized by steady influxes of 'exotic' women and ongoing renewal, a sex worker circuit is configured by the mobility of sex workers feeding the sex market in Spain. The high turnover among sex workers, reflected in a high degree of intrasectorial mobility, is attributable to a number of factors.

Firstly, and as the informants reveal, the sex market demands the constant renewal of sex workers, based on the notions of novelty and variety, requiring a constant supply of 'new girls' (Oso Casas 2001, 2010). New arrivals are guaranteed initial success in brothels or in-call flats. Although the number of clients a woman may have in a single day varies greatly, the possibility of having more clients increases considerably in the case of new arrivals. Consequently, women are forced to move on when they fail to maintain a satisfactory number of clients.

Secondly, police raids or possible police raids on brothels affect mobility, and information is frequently exchanged on the sex worker grapevine in relation to when and where the next police raids might take place. In Spain, prostitution is not illegal but instead is outside the law. In other words, it is not prohibited, but neither is it regulated. The police cannot arrest someone for practising sex work. Police raids are aimed at checking documents and arresting undocumented migrants, not prostitutes. Since prostitution is not a crime, Spanish and migrant women with the proper documentation cannot be arrested by police during a raid on a brothel. Undocumented women thus tend to keep moving from one brothel to another to avoid arrest. These women rotate from one business to another, according to the opportunities available; however, it is true that deciding which club to move to also depends on police raids. Women choose their destination not only according to the amount of work available, but also the length of time since the police last visited each business. Indeed, police raids are the main disadvantage of hostess bars, as the women risk deportation or a serious reduction in their chances of legalizing their situation in another employment sector in the future once they have a police record and an expulsion order.

The principal driving force for the mobility of workers is the rotation system, known as *plazas* ('places'), which has operated over the last few decades in clubs and in-call flats. The term *'plaza'* comes from the fact that the women contact the club, asking for a 'place' for a certain number of days, guaranteeing that she will work for twenty-one consecutive days (reflecting availability in accordance with the menstrual cycle), without a day off. In a *plaza*, the club charges the woman a certain amount of money (generally the price of the first service with a client) for each day she works and the rest she keeps for herself. Two or three women sometimes work together as a team and accompany and protect each other during temporary stays in brothels and in-call flats.

Ongoing rotation under the *plaza* system – in both brothels and in-call flats – occurs on a local, regional, national and transnational level. Thus, the women in our fieldwork could choose to take up *plazas* in Spain, either remaining in the same city or geographical area in the rural context, or moving to another part of the region (local and regional rotation, respectively). An alternative option was to go to another part of Spain (national rotation), for example, from Palma de Mallorca to Malaga, then Madrid, Asturias, and so on. Another type of rotation, which emerged mainly as a result of the economic crisis in Spain, is on an international level (France, Germany, etc.). Greater mobility means higher earnings, so women who only move between brothels and flats in the same region will earn less money than women who move throughout Spain or abroad. This geographically mobile system ensures greater earnings and savings for migrant women. However, it also has a number of drawbacks, such as the unsettled sensation caused by moving from place to place, the fatigue resulting from non-stop work (high client turnover, no rest days, irregular eating patterns, etc.) and the lack of autonomy (as they do not have their own space to live in).

Sex worker mobility responds to the sex market characterized by steady inflows and ongoing renewal. The *plazas* system is fed, in fact, by supplies of migrant women, and particularly those who have no family or permanent place of residence in Spain. Women within the migratory circuit and who are under pressure to repay debts usually opt for the most ambitious rotation options, namely national rotation. Working all over Spain ensures maximum earnings in the shortest possible time; the downside, however, is substantial working and living costs, as discussed earlier. As can be observed, the sex worker circuit is largely sustained and articulated by the migratory circuit. Although many migrants eventually manage to settle in Spain and improve their working and living conditions, the migratory circuit essentially supplies a steady flow of 'new arrivals' to join the other sex workers in each location.

The Transnational Household Circuit

Migration for sex workers who have other roles as mothers, daughters, sisters and wives, however, is also shaped by the expectations of loved ones. As indicated earlier, greater social and employment precariousness affects indebted migrant women: they have to work harder to repay loans; they have to accept poorer working conditions that may endanger their health; and they suffer the pressures of creditors. However, women with significant financial burdens in their countries of origin – the heads of transnational households – also experience greater employment precariousness. The pressure to save and transfer as much money as possible leads such women to choose to work in *plazas*, living either in a brothel or in-call flat. They earn more, but, as we have seen, they also work in poorer conditions and are under greater pressure from the owners. Since they are willing to sacrifice everything for their families, they tolerate a greater degree of abuse and exploitation. They also typically run greater health risks, driven by the need to transfer large sums of money to their home country on a regular basis. Their possibilities of improving their quality of life in Spain by renting a place to live and/or working independently are limited by the fact that the cost would reduce the amount of money available for transfers to their families (Oso Casas 2010).

As the breadwinner in a transnational household, there is also pressure on the migrant woman not just to send money to ensure basic survival but also to satisfy the consumer aspirations of her family. Thus, some of the respondents in our study spoke in colloquial terms of their little *macarras*, this time referring not to a parasitic pimp, but to demanding children, brothers, sisters, and other family members asking for money to buy branded clothes or footwear, skateboards, or other products that reflect social success and standing. As one of the respondents tellingly said, 'Today I have to get a client so I can buy Christmas presents'. Sex work is not simply a strategy for ensuring survival or accumulating savings; it also fuels consumerism and satisfies demands in transnational households. Moreover, the desire for goods may originate in Spain from the migrant herself, or in her country of origin from the beneficiaries of money transfers from Spain. Consequently, social pressure to consume also constitutes a force that drives migrant women to seek work in the sex industry in developed countries. As Lorene, one of the Colombian informants explained:

> I have two brothers and a daughter. I don't have a father, and my mother had a car crash and is in a wheelchair or walks with crutches. They're always asking me for money. My younger brother is the worst: now he wants a PlayStation, and the other one wants a motorbike. They think money grows on trees here. They don't realize what I have to go through to earn it. They don't know how I earn a living. My mum does, but my brothers don't. I feel like telling them, just to get them to stop asking me for money. I wish a man would appear for me to fuck! I need the money. (Testimony already quoted in Oso 2016: 9)

As shown, the transnational household circuit generates a series of financial obligations for migrant women that represent one of the main barriers to improving their own living and working conditions. Indeed, those women under less pressure to send money back home tend to implement more strategies designed to improve their living and working conditions than those who have to 'make more sacrifices' in order to send money back to their countries of origin. The transnational household circuit feeds into and is inextricably associated with the sex worker circuit. Indeed, the financial pressure exerted by families is one of the main reasons why women who have paid off their debts do not leave the *plazas* system but continue working in the brothels and in-call flats in Spain, which are also their only home.

The Informal Circuit

The informal circuit represents another barrier that prevents migrant sex workers in Spain from improving their living and working conditions. The fact that the status of the majority of sex workers remains undocumented for a considerable period hugely benefits many social actors in Spain, who profit directly from the significant flows of goods and money.[7]

Two major barriers confronting migrant sex workers in Spain are Spanish immigration policies and the existing legislation regulating sex work. The former is responsible for generating a pool of informal workers, whilst the latter has created a legal limbo for prostitution: although not illegal, it is neither recognized nor regulated as a profession. The regulation of prostitution and immigration has merged to form what I term the 'informal circuit', which is further shaped by the factors described below.

Firstly, police raids to arrest undocumented migrants, affecting brothels in particular, are a major factor in creating feelings of insecurity among sex workers, who live in constant fear of arrest. As we have already pointed out, police pressure is one of the key reasons for the ongoing rotation of workers, which in turn has a negative impact on the working and living conditions of migrant women.

Secondly, these women have no rights as citizens or workers, making it more difficult for them to work independently and operate their own businesses. The absence of legal protection also means that migrant women have no choice but to rely for protection on those who view them as a source of profit, namely the owners of the brothels and the in-call flats. The ways in which owners or managers of brothels make money from sex workers include taking a percentage of payments from clients for sexual services and drinks, charging a daily fee for accommodation and food, and imposing fines – for example, for using a room for longer than paid for by the client, for dating clients outside work, or for arriving late for work.

The fact that migrant women are undocumented also makes them afraid to leave brothels and in-call flats, and this isolates them. As a hold over the women, owners or managers of brothels and flats often threaten to report them to the authorities. Owners or managers take advantage of the isolation and fears of undocumented migrants, not only by demanding greater productivity, but also by selling them products and services. An example is the public telephones that are installed in the brothels so the women can call home; however, these telephones consume coins so quickly that some of the women in our survey referred to them as *teléfonos macarras* (parasite telephones). Other individuals such as street vendors often take advantage of the isolation of these women to sell them products or services, such as clothes, jewellery, perfume or cosmetics, often at exorbitant prices. These street vendors are often themselves migrants who set up informal businesses that sell, for example, Latin American food dishes to women in brothels. There is also a network of doctors who travel to brothels to conduct gynaecological examinations for which they typically charge far higher prices than normal. Some clients also threaten undocumented migrants in order to obtain special services that some women may not wish to perform (for example, anal sex). Lawyers also take advantage of the undocumented situation of the migrants working in the sex industry by charging exorbitant sums of money in return for helping them to regularize their administrative situation and obtain a residence permit. Finally, Spanish men can also benefit, by arranging a *matrimonio blanco* (a 'sham marriage'; a fraudulent marriage in return for money), or registering a domestic partnership (in recent years Spain has contemplated the granting of residence permits by registering a domestic partnership with a Spanish citizen, regulated by a series of terms and conditions).

It would therefore appear that a whole series of social actors are eager to take advantage of the migrants' undocumented situation. The informal circuit cannot be divorced from the sex worker circuit, and by leaving undocumented sex workers in a poorer negotiating position, this situation benefits brothel owners and managers, as well as doctors, lawyers, street sellers, and others who can take advantage of these women. The informal circuit thus enhances the movement of goods and money in and around the sex industry.

The combination of a restrictive migratory policy and the prostitution policy in Spain that fails to provide social or labour protection for sex workers, considerably limits their chances of securing recognition of their rights. For a female migrant working in recognized sectors (domestic service, the hotel and restaurant trade, etc.), obtaining work and residence permits is already difficult, but for those in the sex industry the road to regularizing their legal situation is paved with many more difficulties. The informal circuit therefore becomes more maze-like, creating numerous social actors who take advantage of migrants for their own personal gain. Furthermore, the fact that it is impossible to legally channel flows of migrant sex workers leads to the small trade in migrants, discussed at the start of this chapter. Sex workers have consequently to migrate using intermediaries who see them as a means to personal gain and profit. The undocumented situation feeds the sex worker circuit, and particularly the *plaza* system – the most demanding kind of prostitution, given the ongoing rotation between brothels and in-call flats. Informality in sex work also feeds the migratory circuit, often leading to small trade and migrant debt. Workers in other (legal) sectors, such as domestic service, have far greater opportunities for regularizing (by obtaining official documentation) their situation in Spain.

The Multi-circuited Maze: A Mechanism that Clashes with Migratory Projects and Social Mobility Strategies

This chapter has shown how female migrants provide a steady supply of sex workers to Spain. These women offer services in a market that functions on the basis of a continuous rotation of workers. In the *plaza* system, the rotation principle ensures that sex workers are constantly on the move on a local, regional, national and even international level. The *plaza* system functions in the two main locations where sexual services are provided, namely clubs and *pisos de contactos* (in-call flats). Thus, the mobility of migrants, which I refer to as the transnational migratory circuit, sustains the mobility of individuals in the sex worker circuit.

In contrast to the view that is generally held of the woman migrant exploited for sexual purposes, I have stressed the fact that migrant women usually opt to work in the sex industry as a strategy for social mobility. In this sense, I argue that migrant women have agency, as sex work in this case is driven by a desire for social mobility and economic betterment for the women and their families. Nonetheless, the fact that these women choose to work in the sex industry does not necessarily mean that they do not suffer any abuse or exploitation by third parties. These women have to deal with the multi-circuited maze, which is sustained not only by the constantly mobile sex worker and migratory circuits, but also by the transnational household circuit and the informal circuit. The transnational household circuit imposes a series of financial obligations on the migrant women, pushing them to save and transfer money to their families in the home country. This financial pressure is one of the main reasons why women continue to choose to work in the *plaza* system, once they have paid off the debts they incurred in order to travel to Spain, which shapes their working conditions. Likewise, there is a pool of people who supply the informal circuit, either as undocumented migrants or as sex workers with no labour rights. This informal circuit, in turn, feeds the sex worker and migratory circuits. Although many of the Latin American women who migrate to Spain may have chosen sex work, and may even have done so in response to social mobility strategies (agency), they still have to deal with the multi-circuited maze in which their aspirations for social mobility clash with the interests of different social actors such as government authorities, clients, madams, lawyers, and even their own families.

This chapter has shown how female migrant sex workers have agency, as they take active decisions in order to implement their social mobility strategies within the framework of the sex industry. Indeed, they can choose between working in clubs, flats, living separately, doing *plazas*, and so on. Nevertheless, the analysis has also highlighted how the multi-circuited maze affects women's agency. Indeed, migrant sex workers encounter many barriers, mainly due to their undocumented status and the lack of legal protection for informal sex workers in Spain. Furthermore, the barriers they encounter are determined not only by the numerous economic interests generated by the sex industry, but also by the financial demands of the family that stays in the country of origin, asking for remittances, to the extent that the women's interests clash with those of numerous social actors. In this sense, even if they have agency, the articulation of interests of different social actors together with the undocumented and informal situation can affect the women's agency. Indeed, the intersection of the women's strategies of social mobility and the barriers they encounter in the multi-circuited maze can lead to social mobility paths stagnating, or even cause deterioration in the living conditions of the key actors in the migration project.

Laura Oso is a senior lecturer at the Faculty of Sociology of the Universidade da Coruña. She is the coordinator of ESOMI (The International Migration Sociology Team). She was awarded a PhD in sociology by the Université de Paris I-Panthéon Sorbonne (2002). Her research work has centred mainly on the study of gender and migration, and specifically the insertion of immigrant women into the labour market (domestic service, sex work, ethnic entrepreneurship). She has also co-edited the 2013 book *The International Handbook on Gender, Migration and Transnationalism: Global and Development Perspectives* (Edward Elgar Publishing) with N. Ribas-Mateos.

NOTES

1. The focus of literature about sex work and migration on trafficking has already been mentioned in a previous. review of the literature (Oso 2016).
2. A first idea of the development of these circuits was developed in an earlier analysis (Oso Casas 2006).
3. https://en.wikipedia.org/wiki/Structure_and_agency.
4. Beyond the traditional analytical approaches that focus on analysing migration from the point of view of the rational decisions of the individual (the neoclassical perspective) or the macro-structural factors behind migration (the structural approach), from the 1980s onwards, new perspectives refer to macro- and micro-determining factors when explaining migratory processes (Massey et al. 1987).
5. Even if only two of my informants were unaware that they would be working in the sex industry, this does not imply that they were not associated with small-trade networks, subjected to situations of abuse and exploitation, as we shall see later on. However, my interest lies in highlighting the fact that regardless of the means of entry into Spain, the female migrants interviewed took the decision to leave their

countries to work in the sex industry as part of a strategy of social mobility (Oso Casas 2003).
6. Studies conducted in other parts of Spain report similar conclusions with regard to Latin American immigration (Agustín 2001; Piscitelli 2008; López Riopedre 2010).
7. The way of entrance to Spain of the women sex workers interviewed during the fieldwork was as tourists on a three-month visa, remaining undocumented after the visa expires. Two thirds of my informants had regularized their legal situation at the time of the fieldwork.

REFERENCES

Agustín, L. 2001. 'Mujeres migrantes ocupadas en servicios sexuales' in Colectivo Ioé (ed.), *Mujer, inmigración y trabajo*. Madrid: IMSERSO, pp. 647–716.

———. 2005. 'Migrants in the Mistress's House: Other Voices in the Trafficking Debate'. *Social Politics* 12(1): 96–117.

———. 2007. *Sex at the Margins: Migration, Labour Markets and the Rescue Industry*. London: Zed Books.

Bernstein, E. 2008. 'Sexual Commerce and the Global Flow of Bodies, Desires, and Social Policies'. *Sexuality Research and Social Policy* 5(4), Special Issue.

Cabezas, A. 2009. *Economies of Desire: Sex and Tourism in Cuba and the Dominican Republic*. Philadelphia, PA: Temple University Press.

Cole, J., and C. Groes (eds). 2016. *Affective Circuits: African Migrations to Europe and the Pursuit of Social Regeneration*. Chicago, IL: University of Chicago Press.

Day, S. 2009. 'Renewing the War on Prostitution: The Specters of "Trafficking" and "Slavery"'. *Anthropology Today* 25(3): 1–3.

Doezema, J. 1998. 'Forced to Choose: Beyond the Voluntary v. Forced Prostitution Dichotomy', in K. Kempadoo and J. Doezema (eds), *Global Sex Workers: Rights, Resistance and Redefinition*. New York: Routledge, pp. 34–50.

Ehrenreich, B., and A.R. Hochschild (eds). 2003. *Global Woman: Nannies, Maids, and Sex Workers in the New Economy*. New York: Macmillan.

Farr, K. 2005. *Sex Trafficking: The Global Market in Women and Children*. New York: Worth Publishers.

International Organization for Migration (IOM). 1995. *Trafficking and Prostitution: The Growing Sexual Exploitation of Migrant Women from Central and Eastern Europe*. Budapest: Migration Information Programme.

———. 1996. *Trafficking in Women from the Dominican Republic for Sexual Exploitation*. Budapest: Migration Information Programme.

Kanti Paul, B., and S. Abu Hasnath. 2000. 'Trafficking in Bangladeshi Women and Girls'. *Geographical Review* 90(2): 268–76.

Kempadoo, K. (ed.). 2005. *Trafficking and Prostitution Reconsidered: New Perspectives on Migration, Sex, Work, and Human Rights*. Boulder, CO: Paradigm Publishers.

Lin Lean Lim. 1998. *The Sex Sector: The Economic and Social Bases of Prostitution in Southeast Asia*. Geneva: L'Organisation Internationale du Travail (OIT).

López Riopedre, J. 2010. 'Inmigracion colombiana y brasileña y prostitución femenina en la ciudad de Lugo: historias de vida de mujeres que ejercen la prostitución en pisos de contactos'. PhD thesis. Madrid: Departamento de Sociología I, Facultad de Ciencias Políticas y Sociología, UNED.

Mai, N. 2001. 'Transforming Traditions: A Critical Analysis of the Trafficking and Exploitation of Albanian Girls in Italy', in R. King (ed.), *The Mediterranean Passage: Migration and New Cultural Encounters in Southern Europe*. Liverpool: Liverpool University Press, pp. 258–78.

Massey D.S., et al. 1987. *Return to Aztlan: The Social Process of International Migration from Western Mexico*. Berkeley, CA: University of California Press.

Oso Casas, L. 2001. 'Domestiques, concierges et prostituées: migration et mobilité sociale des femmes immigrées, espagnoles à Paris, équatoriennes et colombiennes en Espagne'. PhD thesis. Paris: IEDES – Université de Paris I-Panthéon Sorbonne (Director: Prof. Bruno Lautier).

———. 2003. 'Colombian and Ecuadorian Women's Migratory Strategies', in J. Freedman and N.K. Poku, *Gender and Insecurity: Migrant Women in Europe*. Aldershot: Ashgate.

———. 2006. 'Prostitution et immigration des femmes latino-américaines en Espagne'. *Cahiers du Genre* 40: 91–115.

———. 2010. 'Money, Sex, Love and the Family: Economic and Sentimental Strategies of Latin-American Sex Workers in Spain'. *Journal of Ethnic and Migration Studies* 36(1): 47–65.

Oso, L. 2016. 'Transnational Social Mobility Strategies and Quality of Work among Latin-American Women Sex Workers in Spain'. *Sociological Research Online* 21(4).

Piscitelli, A. 2008. 'Entre as "mafias" e a "ajuda": a construcçao de cohecimento sobre tráfico de pessoas'. *Cuadernos Pagu* 31: 9–28.

Plambech, S. 2014. 'Between Victims and Criminals: Nigerian Migrant Sex Workers and the Politics of Rescue'. *Social Politics: International Studies in Gender, State and Society* 22(2): 382–402.

Ruiz, M.C. 2014. 'Bodies, Borders and Boundaries: Erotic Transactions and Intra-regional Migrations in Southern Ecuador'. PHD dissertation. Amsterdam: Vrije Universiteit.

Sassen, S. 2003. 'The Feminisation of Survival: Alternative Global Circuits', in M. Morokvasic-Müller, U. Erel and K. Shinozaki (eds), *Crossing Borders and Shifting Boundaries. Vol. I. On the Move*. Opladen: Leske+budrich, pp. 59–77.

Sequeiros, J.L. 1996. *Estudio sobre a prostitución no sur de Galicia*. Santiago: Consellería de Familia, Muller e Xuventude.

Skrobanek, S., N. Boonpakdi and C. Janthakeero. 1997. *The Traffic in Women: Human Realities of the International Sex Trade*. London: Zed Books.

Spanger, M. 2010. 'Destabilising Sex Work and Intimacy? Gender Performances of Female Thai Migrants Selling Sex in Denmark'. PhD thesis. Roskilde, Denmark: Roskilde Universitet.

Stone, A., and M. Vandenberg. 1999. 'How the Sex Trade Becomes a Slave Trade: The Trafficking of Women to Israel'. *Middle East Report* 211. *Trafficking and Transiting: New Perspectives on Labor Migration*, pp. 36–38.

Weitzer, R. 2007. 'The Social Construction of Sex Trafficking: Ideology and Institutionalisation of a Moral Crusade'. *Politics and Society* 35(3): 447–75.

CHAPTER
5

Mobility through the Sexual Economy
Exchanging Sexual Capital for Respectability in Mozambican Women's Marriage Migration to Europe

Christian Groes

Introduction

This is what 26-year-old Maria (a pseudonym) said during an interview about her experiences of moving to France with her ex-husband Gilles, whom she had met a few years earlier in Maputo, the capital of Mozambique: 'I wanted to shop in the most beautiful malls, but I ended up doing the dishes ... When I saw that pretty white man next to me in the bar I never dreamt that I should one day be his "maid". Come on, I was his beautiful African princess'.

The quote above illustrates the gap between Maria's dreams of living a life of luxury in Europe and the burdensome role of housewife she ended up assuming before their breakup and her return home. Maria's story points to common challenges related to reconfigurations of class and gender when a particular category of women in Maputo called *curtidoras* marry and move to Europe with their husbands – in particular, how the respect they get from their charm and beauty when they meet their partners in Maputo sometimes becomes devalued in Europe, but how they are sometimes able to convert their attractiveness into more stable forms of respectability. *Curtidoras*, a local notion meaning 'women who enjoy life' are women who look for white men in downtown Maputo and engage in transactional sex with them and sometimes marry and move with them to Europe. Unlike sex workers, who work the unsafe streets at night and primarily cater to local men, *curtidoras* do not see themselves as workers who have clients, but as lovers or girlfriends. They do not have fixed 'working hours' or 'prices' for their company, nor do they have employers or pimps (Groes-Green 2013). They mix 'having fun', friendship, drinking and dancing with receiving gifts and having sex with white men, but are open towards liaisons becoming more serious. They do not accept certain kinds of behaviour, such as men asking them 'how much they cost'. Those who do not treat them with respect are simply held at bay or taught a lesson. A self-imposed respectability code is common, which makes *curtidoras* choose staying alone or together in a bar over 'going home with the wrong person', even if this means losing money. Nevertheless, having money and being able and willing to spend it on them – through gifts, cash, dinners or travel – is a condition for wanting to engage with men; therefore, not being relatively affluent or generous is seen as another reason for rejecting men. As one of the *curtidoras* said, 'as a young and beautiful lady I'm worth more than a simple smile or a drink in the bar', illustrating an awareness of the potential of their looks, age and charm.

Transnational intimacies, interracial desire and dreams of a better life have become vehicles for migration from poorer postcolonial settings to wealthier countries in the Global North. Numerous studies show how, in the Global South, women's desires for white men often overlap with desires for social and geographical mobility. Such matchmaking on the global stage takes place at sex tourist resorts, in postcolonial capitals and towns, and on Internet sites where women can meet affluent partners (Constable 2003; Brennan 2004; Cabezas 2004; Kempadoo 2004; Kim 2006; de Sousa e Santos 2009; Cole 2010; Hoefinger 2013). Recent studies of interracial romance in the global sexual economy have paved the way for an understanding of the complex desires, power relations and motives involved in what has been broadly described as marriage migration, which in some cases is not easily separable from sexual migration, love migration or sex worker migration (e.g. Constable 2003; Brennan 2004; Piscitelli 2008 Palriwala and Uberoi 2008; Mai and King 2009; Fernandez 2010; Oso Casas 2010; Plambech 2010).

There is still a dearth of literature describing the transformation of a pre-migration lifestyle of transactional sex among women in the Global South to a post-migration life of marriage with men in Western contexts. By addressing the use and meaning of erotic power and sexual capital among Mozambican women, and the degrees to which these pave the way for class mobility, this chapter adds to an understanding of the relationship between sexual economies and migration to the Global North. This analysis builds on Bourdieu's ([1979] 1986; 1987) conception of class as part of a complex social system within which a person's options are decided by access to economic capital (money and labour) as well as to cultural capital (education and knowledge), symbolic capital (taste and consumption) and social capital (social network and kin), but adding to this the notions of erotic power (Groes-Green 2013) and sexual capital (Martin and George 2006; Groes-Green 2009; see also Hakim 2011 for erotic capital). As Skeggs (1997) reminds us, class cannot be severed from gender or sexuality, and for many poor women the quest for social mobility and status may equally become a search for 'respectability'. Thus defined, social class was highly significant in Mozambican women's stories of success or failure when moving to Europe. Yet as the material reveals, the desire for social mobility is rarely spoken about as related to class or access to money, but often in terms of 'respect', 'generosity' and a desire for 'white men'.

The second factor, which seems to have a profound impact on the women's capacity for spatial and social mobility, is kin support. Kinship has received much attention in studies of marriage migration, especially since kin obligations often motivate migration and because kin are key recipients of remittances and a cardinal point in global care chains (Plambech 2010). Yet, kinship has to a lesser degree been examined as a key resource in women's ability to build viable relationships vis-à-vis Western men when they migrate. As a result, little has been written about kin as an absent or present 'power base' when women move with a partner to Europe. This study fills that gap by demonstrating how young women who search for white partners in Maputo, often with the aim of migrating to Europe, largely draw on advice in matters of seduction and intimate economies from kin at home (see also Groes-Green 2013) and how the presence or absence of kin support once they arrive in Europe has deep-seated ramifications for the migrants.

Finally, this chapter adds to the study of marriage migrations from Africa to Europe, a phenomenon that has hitherto received limited attention. In existing literature on marriage migration to Western contexts, scholars' attention has been skewed towards marriage constellations between white 'sex tourists' or 'love tourists' and local 'sex workers' or 'mail order brides'. What makes interracial matchmaking in Maputo different from that portrayed in studies of sex tourist resorts in Latin America, the Caribbean and South East Asia, as well as in Kenya and Gambia (Brennan 2004: Cabezas 2004; Kim 2006; Piscitelli 2008; Oso Casas 2010; Meiu 2011), is that the city's sexual economy as a stepping stone for migration rarely involves sex tourists or sex workers. The men that they marry are not sex tourists but expatriates from Northern Europe with a relatively high status and income.

Methodology and Fieldwork in a Transnational Sexual Economy

The study is based on extended fieldwork carried out during various field visits to Maputo, Mozambique between 2007 and the end of 2012, during which time I conducted interviews and carried out participant observation among twenty-six women with experiences of living in Europe. I also conducted informal interviews with kin and partners. Some of the women had returned to Maputo to visit their families, while others had returned because their relationships in Europe had not succeeded. I interviewed seven of these women while they were living in Europe – Portugal, Sweden, England and Denmark – choosing these countries because it was easier to establish contact with migrants there. In 2012, I conducted formal interviews with eighteen of the women, but over the years several informal interviews were carried out in informants' homes and in restaurants and other public places. Since then I have had regular contact with informants, visiting them in Denmark and Portugal or communicating with them through social media. I conducted the interviews in Portuguese and to a lesser extent in Changana and Ronga, the mother tongues of many informants. The migrant informants I interviewed were identified and recruited in places where they went looking for white men, including bars, restaurants and shopping malls, and among informants known from my earlier studies in Maputo's transnational landscape. I used the snowball sampling method, asking women who had been to Europe to help me to find other informants with migratory experiences. Participant observation consisted of 'hanging out' with the young women in local malls, restaurants, bars and nightclubs where they meet foreign men, as well as in their neighbourhoods.

Although there are no exact statistics on the number of women migrating from Mozambique to Europe with their partners, informants told stories of numerous female acquaintances who had travelled there. The women in this study had migrated to Portugal (seven), Germany (four), Scandinavia (four), Italy (three), France (three), England (two), Spain (one), Holland (one) and Ireland (one). These countries are representative of young women's main destinations when they move from Maputo to Europe. The women were between 21 and 30 years old when migrating, and their partners were on average 15 years older, varying from 29 to 56 years old. All the women lived in Europe for at least six months and about half of them lived there for more than two years. One-third of them had children with the European partner or with a Mozambican ex-boyfriend. The majority left the children with their kin when migrating but sent money home to support their offspring. Three migrants became pregnant with their partner while in Europe. Five of the women came from educated families with respectable jobs and stable incomes higher than average, while the rest hailed from poor urban or suburban backgrounds where families have limited incomes and little schooling. All migrants had been to secondary school, which is common in Mozambique, and four of them had also been to college. About half of them had work experience as hotel receptionists, waitresses, shops assistants or street vendors, or had assisted kin in the *machamba* (small garden or field). However, after finding a European sponsor who could support them, they hoped to never have to return to such jobs again. Many had concurrent and casual partners besides the man with whom they had migrated. Before moving to Europe most of them had reduced their number of partners, and sixteen of them married their European partner or lived with them. The more fortunate women received between one and two thousand dollars a month in allowances from a stable partner, while others were only paid between two and three hundred dollars a month, and sometimes less. The amount of money that they convinced men to pay depended on whether or not they were married and lived together, had children or were more casual lovers, but it also depended on the partner's income and his feelings for the woman. The couples themselves, and women's kin, generally did not see this payment as 'prostitution', most likely because local gender norms demand that men support women with money or gifts – a logic also evident in the bridewealth custom (*lobolo*). Although women dating white men are easily scorned and stereotyped as 'whores' (*putas*) by the broader public, such liaisons become more acceptable when couples are married or live together. As a social group, *curtidoras* often distinguish themselves from women they call 'prostitutes' (*prostitutas*), 'tramps' (*vagabundas*) or 'whores' (*putas*), as well as from poor female peers who do not have a *patrocinador*. Prostitutes working in brothels or on the street, they said, 'cannot choose who they want to be with'. By contrast, they described themselves as 'classy women' who love the excitement of nightlife and men, and who see what they do as a lifestyle choice, not, they said, as a consequence of 'need or greed'. At the same time, they distanced themselves from female acquaintances without a male provider – scorning them for not being smart or attractive enough to seduce a man who will support them with money. Despite their tendency to identify themselves in opposition to other social categories of women, I noticed no clear-cut boundaries between categories. In fact, some informants traversed multiple categories, shifting between being a sex worker, being a *curtidora*, and staying out of the sexual economy to study or be with a boyfriend.

Interracial Affairs: European Men and Local Women in Maputo's Sexual Economy

The aspects that distinguish Maputo from better-known transnational settings where mixed couples meet and marriage migrations develop is its large expatriate community, the informality of the sexual economy and the involvement of kin in the women's endeavours. Europeans there are, for the most part, expatriates or what scholars call mobile professionals and 'privileged migrants' (Fetcher and Walsh 2010), whereas sex tourists and visitors coming solely to meet a potential wife are very rare. During fieldwork I also met some European expat women who had transactional relationships with local men, but this was less common.

In the wake of neoliberal reforms in the country since the 1980s, the Mozambican capital saw an influx of Westerners constituting an ever-expanding expatriate community investing or working in businesses, development organizations, NGOs and the UN. Although there are also a significant number of American, South African, Indian, Chinese and Brazilian expatriates in Maputo, most expatriates come from Europe. The Portuguese community is by far the largest, while others hail from Germany, France, Spain, Italy, England and Scandinavia in their thousands. Many men stay there for more than six months and often they stay for several years until ending their contracts or finding a new job elsewhere. About half of the men in the study were married back home or had their European wife or girlfriend with them, and the other half were single. Together with the growing local middle class, these expatriates have paved the way for new forms of urban social life and nightlife in bars, discotheques, restaurants, parks, hotels, beach clubs and art centres.

The dark side of this globalization of neoliberal reforms is the extremely high number of unemployed local youths in Maputo, and a society in which new generations have few options in life. The high hopes following the end of the devastating civil war from 1974 to 1992 soon turned into despair as privatizations of national companies and market reforms primarily served the interests of the middles classes and the political elite, and increased social inequality (Hanlon and Smart 2008). Against the background of deepening poverty and unemployment, the formation of a transnational space for romantic and sexual-economic exchanges became one of the only avenues for social mobility for young women. In this space, they can find a well-heeled partner who will take care of them and provide them with money and gifts, and maybe the opportunity to migrate abroad. For many Mozambicans, Europe remains a beacon of social opportunity and financial security. The women also see liaisons with white men as a way to ensure the well-being and reproduction of their families. Being provided for by a white man, they dream of Europe as a place where money is more accessible and where one can make a good life materialize in gifts like mobile phones, fancy handbags and expensive cocktails. Yet, these liaisons cannot easily be reduced to 'prostitution'. As also reported from other Southern African settings, these intimate exchanges cut across a gamut of relationships, often overlapping, ranging from casual affairs and sex-for-money to genuine romance and marriage (Leclerc-Madlala 2003; Cole 2010; Hunter 2015).

Sexual Capital and the Role of Kin in Marriage Migration to Europe

I use the notions of erotic power and sexual capital as a way of understanding the role of female powers of seduction, appearances and kin's assistance in the process of using eroticism to find and get together with expat men. Notions such as transactional sex and sexual capital have been used to address sexual economies around the world and exchanges of intimacy and money or materialities that cannot easily be reduced to what, in a Western conception, is regarded as 'prostitution' (Hunter 2002; Leclerc-Madlala 2003; Cole 2010). Applying the notion of sexual capital means to acknowledge the importance of degrees of attractiveness related to looks, charm, bodily appearance, notions of beauty and the ability to dress up or appear according to local ideals for attraction. As Martin and George (2006) argue, we should address sexual stratification as a field with many available forms of capital, in the Bourdieuian sense. Sexual capital is unevenly distributed and is valued differently by different actors of various genders, social positions, ethnicities and so on (Groes-Green 2009). 'There is no reason to assume that the degree of consensus regarding standards of desirability is a constant across time and space: in contrast to the universalism of the market approach, we may conclude that a field analysis is unwarranted due to underlying disorganization in preferences' (Martin and George 2006). Thus, sexual capital can, under certain circumstances, be converted to symbolic, cultural, social and economic capital, but it must be understood in contexts of systems of differentiation of class, age, gender and ethnicity, and the power mechanisms related to these, both locally and globally. With regard to Mozambican migrants, sexual capital is clearly very unevenly distributed and has different connotations in different destination countries and social situations.

It is important to pay attention to the mobility between different forms of capital, alongside the spatial and social mobility related to this. As I have argued elsewhere, the significance of kin, for example, must be addressed in order to understand the meaning and use of sexuality and eroticism in the transnational setting of Maputo (Groes-Green 2013, 2014). During fieldwork I noticed a strong emotional tie between female relatives, which did not seem to exist between male and female kin to the same extent. The majority of *curtidoras* said that they felt indebted to their female seniors, especially within the household and with regard to spiritual issues, whereas male seniors were regarded as marginal in domestic affairs. Fathers and brothers were expected to play a role in the public sphere, but had little say when it came to child rearing, cooking, or festive arrangements. In these poor suburban settings, mothers rarely seemed economically dependent on their husbands, firstly because few of the men had a steady job and income, and secondly because most of the household income came from women's own work as informal traders or tending their *machambas* (small gardens). In this sense, the households were mostly female headed – if not always publicly, then de facto within the communities (see also da Costa 2005). Most *curtidoras* live with or often visit kin and family members in the city. Thus, I realized that in order to properly understand the significance of sexual capital, and how this is developed among *curtidoras*, it must be analysed within female spaces and through exchanges between female relatives. Female kin, I found, have a central role in developing erotic power and assisting *curtidoras* in their seduction of men. From a girl's first menstruation and until marriage it is common for aunts and sisters to teach her ways of controlling a man through sexual, emotional and spiritual practices – what *curtidoras* referred to as 'putting men in a bottle' (Groes-Green 2013).

The involvement of kin in finding a white man and perhaps moving with him to Europe is also rooted in machangana/maronga (the two biggest ethnic groups in Maputo) notions of reciprocity, obligations and redistribution within the kin unit. The help that female kin give through advice on sexual issues, love and monetary negotiations is returned with money and gifts that *curtidoras* give their mothers, who then distribute it to the extended family (Groes-Green 2013). *Curtidoras* are well aware of their value as attractive women, and so were their kin, who helped them to maintain and improve their magnetic qualities. Their power to extract money from men was closely associated with their ability to 'appear', and as a consequence, to be seen and wanted by men. An aunt explained how she took a niece to a *curandeira* (traditional healer) to learn how to use herbs and cooked roots. The woman taught the niece how to cut them, apply them to her skin, and put them in her mouth or apply tiny bits to her lipstick before meeting a man. 'At first sight he will be enchanted and unable to take his eyes off her', the aunt told me. Combined with more profane beautification practices like putting on hair extensions and fashionable clothes, this was believed to have a powerful effect to attract men. Female kin also taught how to use certain body movements and flirtation skills when approaching men of interest. In cosmological terms, the exchanges of erotic skills that can be used to generate an income and security for the family also serve to satisfy ancestral spirits, who are seen as masters of life and death and from whom elders derive their authority and knowledge. Elders are seen as living representatives of ancestral spirits who have generative powers to assist in the birth of new family members as well as in the production of value, money and happiness. And generally, the erotic skills that are transferred from generation to generation are believed to be rooted in the ancestral world of mostly female spirits. Meanwhile, brothers, fathers and uncles take on the role of protectors against violence and exploitation: whenever a white partner becomes abusive, family members are often swift in rebuking the man or removing the daughter. Thus, erotic power as well as sexual capital, which can sometimes be converted to other forms of capital, is developed throughout the life of *curtidoras*, and becomes the primary asset facilitating their mobility out of poverty, and towards a new life in Europe.

The collective erotic power of kin and *curtidoras*, transmitted to younger women in order to gain control over the liaisons with men, enable *curtidoras* to not only ensure their families a comfortable life and themselves a valued place within the family, but it also earns them enough economic capital to 'move up' socially and establish themselves as part of the local middle class. When referring to their achieved status they often evoke the notions of *respeito* (respect) and *ser uma pessoa* (being a person). 'Being a person' is equal to being respected, seen, listened to and also obeyed by others with less status. For example, 'being a person' also encompasses being able to employ people or having the power to make others work for them. I often heard them using their new-won status to command the hairdresser, the taxi driver and the waiter in a restaurant – something they would never have done or been able to do before becoming rich, and showing off their wealth. For some of them, the most significant marker of middle-class status derived from employing a maid. Whether they lived alone or with their partner, the maid was the most conspicuous indicator of social mobility. Thus, being able to convert sexual capital into having a relationship with a man who could give them status and money was the single most important condition for social mobility. To understand this, I also examined the mobility of power and capital that was transmitted from one person to another – in this case, sexual capital transmitted from kin to *curtidoras*, and economic and cultural capital from expat men to *curtidoras* – and finally how migrants were able to reciprocate to kin by assisting them financially. Yet, as we shall see, these exchanges were complicated by the changing mobility of capital. When the women become spatially mobile and move to Europe, the use and distribution of capital is different, and sexual capital may become less valued.

Whiteness, Masculinities and Class Properties

The women in the study referred to white men as *mulungus* or *valungu* ('whites' in local languages Ronga/Changana) or *brancos* ('whites' in Portuguese). These expressions were used synonymously with notions such as *patrocinadores*, meaning sponsors who support the lives of younger lovers. As described by scholars, many poor women in transnational 'sexscapes' view white men as a source of gifts, luxury, and financial support, as well as providing the possibility of moving to rich countries in the Western world (Brennan 2004; de Sousa e Santos 2009; Cole 2010). However, the women also often highlighted another *mulungus* dimension: 'educated behaviour' (*bom comportamento*). Most informants insisted that they preferred *mulungus* not only because they were rich and well connected, but also because they possessed desirable qualities like education, status and generosity. In line with Bourdieu, I argue that what *curtidoras* see as 'educated behaviour' is just as much an indicator of middle-class positions as the men's incomes and jobs. The meanings of class are formed by economic and cultural capital; this becomes evident when comparing stories about Europeans and locals. Thus, 'Europeans' become an emblem of respectability. They are seen by *curtidoras* as people who are not only able to support them financially but also educate them in good behaviour, charm, and stylish appearance. This includes how to dress, dine and be social among other middle-class or upper-class citizens, whether local or foreign. It involves learning English or other languages, and knowing more about Western music, fashion, food, literature and art. These are all classic elements of cultural and symbolic capital in the system of distinction that not only characterize the modern ranking of classes through classification in Europe (Bourdieu 1987) but also in cosmopolitan settings in, for example, Africa and on other continents (see also Friedman 1994).

'A Sweet White Prince': The Ideal Husband and Differences between Mulungus and 'Blacks'

When women talk about white men or explain what an ideal husband should be like they rarely speak of a romantic 'love that conquers all' where money and status are irrelevant, nor do they reduce love to a question of finance. As Melisa, a 25-year-old woman said, 'I'm going to find a *mulungu*, and he is going to take me there [to Europe]. He will save me – from poverty, Africa, all this suffering. He will be my sweet prince, and care for me. I am sure he will take me to the prettiest places'.

In general terms the migrants described their partners as gentler, more romantic and more generous than Mozambican men. They did not see their love for these men merely as an effect of their affluence per se, but rather it was their 'educated behaviour', which quite often implied the extent to which the men shared their wealth with them. For example, some emphasized how Europeans give them a lot of money to spend on clothes, hair and make-up, and invite them to fancy restaurants where, they said, 'black men will never take us'. These and other offerings were seen as expressions of generosity and sacrifice – and as signs of love or respect. Besides paying for clothes and other consumer goods, some *mulungus* also help them to pay for school fees, rent or medicine for a sick family member. Because of the lengths that some of the men would go to in order to help the women's family members, many women were convinced of their partners' good qualities as husbands and fathers, and equally important this help made it easier for them to convince their kin that these men were worth having a relationship with, or even marrying. By contrast, they talked of Mozambican men in stereotypical terms, such as lazy, selfish and chauvinistic towards women. *Curtidoras* recounted having unpleasant experiences with Mozambican men, controlling their whereabouts, being violent and not contributing to the relationship. Of course, the picture is more nuanced than this, and it is important to remember that the great majority of women outside the sexual economy did not see white men as more attractive than Mozambicans. There were also stories of love and desire for 'black men' among *curtidoras*, but the moral in these stories was that these men were young and had not yet settled in life, not having completed an education or found an income. The older age of expatriate partners combined with their whiteness and good behaviour were seen as signs of wealth, status and mobility.

As these stories illustrate, notions of race, masculinity and age are underlying class divisions that position European expatriate men as superior to local men. So, it seems, we should not take *curtidoras*' judgements of local men at face value when they are described as unwilling to take women out, or selfish, or bad fathers. Racial, cultural and gendered stereotypes about 'European' and 'African' men in fact hide the significance of class, education, knowledge and material conditions. As de Sousa e Santos (2009) argues, with reference to her work on poor Cuban women's love for Europeans, white men are juxtaposed to black Cuban men, who are seen as having weak masculinities because they cannot perform as breadwinners like Europeans can. Similarly, it is impossible for most disenfranchised young Mozambican men to invite their female peers out for dinner at a nice restaurant, buy them fashionable clothes or be heads of households. The absence of work and education in Maputo gives young impoverished men a sense of a 'loss of masculinity', in particular when compared with middle-class men in the city (Groes-Green 2009, 2012).

Going to Europe: Exchanging Sexual Capital for Respectability

As described above, in Maputo many *curtidoras* have relative access to middle-class positions by drawing on their sexual capital – in the sense of getting respect, admiration and authority. Their social mobility is experienced as 'becoming a person' and having money to employ a maid, as well as being able to support their family. In the following I present cases that illustrate the variety of women's migratory trajectories. For most migrants who accomplish their dream of going to a European country, the contrast between life with a partner in Maputo and the everyday realities in Europe can be stark. The women in the study generally described their arrival in a European country as exciting and adventurous – telling stories about cities filled with beautiful buildings and cars, the cleanliness of streets, and the variety of food, drinks and clothes. Many described it as a happy and romantic moment when their partners took them shopping for the first time or took them to a nice restaurant. In many cases, disappointment set in after a short while and relationships were put to the test. Nevertheless, since some couples do make it in Europe, the question is which criteria tend to decide the outcomes of such African–European migrations. Drawing on fieldwork among and interviews with female migrants moving with their men to Portugal and Denmark, I realized how the meaning and use of sexual capital quickly transforms when settling in these countries. The precondition for making it in Europe and experiencing a well-functioning relationship seemed to be rooted in, on the one hand, the ability to transform sexual capital into other forms of capital, and on the other, on the extent to which the men maintained the qualities that the women had originally found attractive, such as their generosity, both socially and economically, and their willingness to let the women sustain themselves and their kin.

Down the Social Ladder: From Respected Wife to Mistreated Maid

Adriana was twenty-three years old when she met Pedro in a bar in Maputo. She fell for his promises to take her to Portugal and live there with him. Pedro, who was thirty-one, had a short contract as blue-collar worker with a mining company, but was trying to find work in the big city so that he could stay. His income was low compared to other expatriates, including the residing Portuguese businessmen. One day, Pedro was fired and ended up living more like a tourist on the three months of salary he had received. Nevertheless, he still enjoyed the great nightlife there and the luxurious restaurants and beach bars, where he met Adriana. She found him fascinating and was so happy that they got married in one of the city's most beautiful churches, despite not being sure how things would play out because of his unstable job situation.

They had been married for four months when they moved to his hometown in Portugal in 2010 because he could not find work in Maputo. With no money they had nowhere else to stay than with his parents. Adriana did not manage to find work, partly, she believed, due to racism, and partly because Pedro did not like her walking around alone on the streets. As most other *curtidoras*, she dreamt of finding a job that could make her more independent and settling down as 'a respected adult', as one put it. Instead, she felt alone and under Pedro's control and surveillance. Also, her contact with the family back home had waned and she had no money to send home as Pedro could not pay her the allowance he used to in Maputo. Since she was unemployed, Pedro and his parents told her it was her duty to keep the house clean, and her in-laws asked her to cook and bring them food and drinks. The transformation from being a *curtidora* and later a respected wife with money at her disposal in Maputo to becoming a housewife or a 'maid', as Adriana described it, was a recurring theme in some migrants' stories. When they had lived in Mozambique, none of the women did housework and most of them could afford to have their own maid, paid for by themselves or by their European partner. Housework was something they had distanced themselves from – a tiresome task that they had often been forced to perform when they were children in poor suburban homes. Now they saw themselves as independent women who had moved up in society, and gained a new status. For this reason, they saw this new role as a sign of their partner's loss of respect for them, and it gave them a sense of failure. The relative gender equality the couple had enjoyed in Maputo was inverted. Now Pedro seemed 'just as traditional as Mozambican men', as Adriana put it. Another fundamental change in Adriana's life was the way in which she could no longer go out at night and potentially have relationships with other men. As many other *curtidoras*, the lifestyle she had practised in Maputo had entailed going out and achieving recognition and respect from others by showing off her good looks, fashionable clothes and her ability to spend money on her friends and relatives. Furthermore, in Maputo Pedro had not checked her whereabouts as much as in Portugal, and had let her go out and even stay out until late. Occasionally, Adriana had experienced a sense of recognition and power from still being able to flirt with and seduce high-class men. In Portugal, by contrast, with the gradual social isolation from the surrounding society and the concomitant lack of recognition and independence, as well as her lack of contact with her family, Adriana ended up having a life that, in her own words, consisted of 'sleep, housework and watching TV'. In the end she could not stand her situation any longer, and chose to leave Portugal and her husband and return to Maputo, where she settled down and lived with her child and her aunt. She kept having white lovers, but insisted that she never wanted to return to Europe. Instead she used the money she got from men to save up for her future. She dreamt of buying a house for herself and opening a beauty shop. This is an example of how, for some women, the ability to convert sexual capital into respectability seemed easier in Maputo than it had been in Portugal and other European countries.

Such stories are similar to what Denise Brennan found among informal female sex workers in the Dominican Republic marrying their partners and going with them to Germany. Arriving in Germany they almost immediately stepped into a traditional female role as homemaker and saw their social life disappear in a relationship of dependency, which contradicted the image they had had of being independent women with status and 'a good life' in Europe – more so, because they had in fact been heads of households back home and used to generate incomes as well as control how these were managed in the domestic sphere. The sources of authority and independence disappeared in Germany if they became dependent on their husbands for money. If the husband's economic situation worsened, they not only lacked money, opportunities and agency, but they also experienced downward social mobility (Brennan 2004: 193).

'Beauty Queen' in the Tourism Sector: Converting Sexual Capital to Model Jobs and Education

Twenty-six-year-old Sasha had been married to José for a year when they decided to move to Lisbon in his home country Portugal, bringing her seven-year-old son. José, who was twenty years older, owned a four-star hotel in Maputo and now wanted to open a hotel back home. When they moved to Portugal Sasha and José had to marry again in order for her to get a temporary residence permit. In her attempt to climb up the social ladder and gain respect, she wanted to use her beauty to get jobs as a bartender and as a model. Through the colleagues and customers she met working as a bartender, exploiting her social and sexual capital, she met influential people who knew what it would take to enter the university and study tourism, another dream of hers. They helped her to apply for a scholarship and get access to tourism studies at the University of Lisbon. Sasha now had the opportunity to finish the tourism studies that she had started long ago in Maputo, but had never had the money to complete. José also encouraged her to take modelling jobs while she was studying. Before long, she was making commercials for clothing and soft drinks companies. These jobs were well paid and made her relatively independent of José financially, although he still transferred allowances to her bank account. When she got her master's degree two years later she had the qualifications needed to one day go back to Mozambique and be employed in the public or business sectors. In Mozambique, she had been relatively independent of her white lovers, but even in Lisbon she was able to maintain a financial freedom that was ensured both by her ability to use her social network to find jobs and by José's encouragements and continued payment of allowances without making demands. Thus, she was able to provide for her children and her kin back home while pursuing her own career. After she completed her education they decided to live half of the year in Portugal, the other half in Mozambique. She dreamt about using her skills in Mozambique, and finally she got a job there in the Ministry of Tourism.

While language barriers and a lack of knowledge about a country can worsen conditions for some migrants, this is less of a problem for those who migrate to Portugal instead of for example Sweden or England. Speaking Portuguese fluently and knowing a lot about the country from school and television give Mozambican migrants like Sasha an advantage in Portugal. What this story shows is that the class position of both the local woman and the white man impacts on the outcome. By coming from a middle-class background and being well off, as well as being protective of Sasha's son and paying for his admittance to Lisbon's best private school, José was able to provide for Sasha and gain her family's trust and respect. Similar to Brennan's findings (2004: 193), this case shows how a migrant whose decision-making authority has been increased, and who finds wage labour and social networks independently of her husband, has better odds of finding her own feet and tolerating misfortunes.

Uneven Paths to Respectability: Getting Divorced, Deported and Coming Back to Work

Daimy, a twenty-four-year-old nurse, walked down the hospital hall as she bumped into forty-two-year-old Erik, her Swedish husband to be. He invited her to the most expensive restaurant in Maputo and later took her on a trip to visit South Africa. He was on a three-year contract in Mozambique working for the UN, and earning a very high salary. When his contract finished they decided to get married and move to his home country. She left her five-year-old daughter with her aunts and uncle because Erik did not approve of taking her with them to Sweden. After they settled down in Sweden he no longer earned as much as he had done in Maputo, and was depressed. Daimy told me how Erik, who had been kind to her in Maputo and had allowed her to go out with friends at night, started becoming more aggressive and controlling. He did not want her to work, saying that she did not have to since he could support her, and he asked her not to go out at night because she might find another man. He started controlling the minutes she spent on the phone talking to her family, saying that she was using up all his money. To make matters worse, he continued refusing to bring her daughter to Sweden. In the end, after a violent incident, she decided to leave him. She phoned the police, who helped her to find refuge in a shelter for victims of domestic violence. She hired a solicitor to fight for her right to stay in the country, since to obtain legal residence one must have been married for several years. As with many of the other migrants going to Europe, the awareness that getting divorced will lead to being deported made Daimy put up with loneliness and suffering for much longer than she would have done in Maputo. Six months after she had been sent back to Mozambique, the Swedish embassy contacted her to inform her that she had been deported unjustly, since a new law now granted migrant victims of domestic violence the right to stay in the country. Coming back to Sweden, this time with her child, she returned to a job as a care worker in the same retirement home where she had worked after the divorce. At the time of the interview, done in Sweden, she was looking forward to meeting 'the right one', ideally an educated man of her own age, with a nice job and income. As Daimy confessed, 'being in Sweden is hard without my family, but I can take it, as long as I have work and money to spend – and now that I can go out freely, I meet new friends and sweet guys'. She enjoyed being free to go out with her friends, who also helped to take care of her daughter, and she continued sending remittances home.

This story exemplifies how the generosity that men show in Mozambique sometimes disappears once back in Europe. Some men demand that the wife pitches in financially, although they know that it is hard for them to get a job. In other cases, the man asks their Mozambican partner to remain in the house. Both tendencies seem to be a result of the husband's changing economic and occupational situation, as well as the absence of the wife's family who thus cannot give the migrant woman the moral support and social advice she had been used to. Yet, in other cases, being able to establish a new social network in the destination country, obtaining work and not living in fear of deportation can pave the way for a life in Europe where migrants feel safe and respected, while continuing to support kin back home.

A Generous Man, an Investing Wife: A High Life of Spending and Finding 'an Insurance Policy'

Sadia, twenty-eight years of age, encountered her husband in a casino bar in downtown Maputo. Andy was a fifty-six-year-old investment banker living in Maputo for three months each year to check up on investments, while also enjoying the city's vibrant Latin-African lifestyle. One year after they met he asked her to come to visit him in London. She went there and stayed in his big house in a rich neighbourhood. When she became pregnant, her two sisters were invited to England to be with her before and after she gave birth. After coming to London her allowance was raised to a higher level than before – she now had the equivalent of three thousand US dollars every month that she could spend as she wished. Furthermore, while he was working – often twelve hours a day – she was free to move around town, shopping, dining and going to the cinema. She quickly found friends among other African migrants, and her spending power ensured her admiration from others and enabled her to live up to fashion ideals in the city. She also began taking courses in fashion design, but as she admits, the ambition was not to work but to meet new people, be inspired and learn new things. Her frequent visits back home also enabled her to maintain a close relationship to her kin and to remain respected in the community. She also saved up some of the money to buy land and a house outside Maputo – an 'insurance policy', she called it – and a place she could return to if the marriage with Andy did not work out. Like many other *curtidoras*, Sadia never wanted an 'ordinary job' as a waitress, hairdresser or maid, although these are jobs that her family members and friends in Maputo would gratefully accept. Neither did she dream of becoming a housewife 'working in her own house', as she said. *Curtidoras*, including Sadia, preferred 'stylish' and 'respectable' jobs with good salaries. If they were unable to find a good job, they hoped to keep getting allowances from the husband so they would be able to build a future for themselves, their kin and their children. Another reason why some of the migrants talked about the importance of an 'insurance policy' was their awareness that their youthful beauty and attractiveness would gradually fade as they get older. As their sexual capital would diminish with time and age, it was important to accrue enough money or property to survive and live well in case the husbands left them or no longer wanted to take care of them. Some migrants were remarkably aware that their worth and attractiveness in the eyes of their husbands was at least partly due to their looks or charms, and that the current love or attachment might disappear as they lost the power of beauty.

As shown, some of the expat men ended up having lower salaries and less purchasing power when they returned to Europe, and as a consequence less money to offer as allowances. Others were so affluent that they could maintain the same level of support and ensure the Mozambican partner had the same degree of economic independence that she had had before migrating. Yet, being rich does not necessarily mean being 'generous'. Some men stopped giving allowances, not because they had less money but, according to the women, because they wanted to limit their movement around town, either out of jealousy or the fear they might lose them. Thus, these women's mobility was decreased, both in terms of spatial movement, social networks and movement or exchange of capital(s). In her study of Brazilian women moving to Italy with their husbands or to visit lovers, Piscitelli (2008) shows how they usually become more dependent after they migrate. Some of her informants believed they achieve better standards of living, but lament how their contact with other Brazilians is restricted and how they are not allowed to have family members visiting them. Those who found jobs had better possibilities for tolerating life there. As she argues, migrants' possibilities for action are limited within the conjugal framework. It becomes clear that the men are not as egalitarian in the household as they thought, nor as rich as they imagined, nor as humble as they believed (ibid.; see also Groes 2016). As she comments, the fact that these men are working class and from the provinces also turns out to be a disappointment to the women, as these men had middle-class positions when they met them in Brazil.

In her study of Thai–Danish marriages in Denmark, Plambech (2010) shows how Thai women often arrive in Denmark through social networks of other Thai women. This social network or diaspora also helps them to find work and gives them social support, and hence replaces the family as a 'power base' in relation to their husbands. Although they leave their own children and family back home, they also become able to wire back money to kin, ensuring that over time they become part of the middle class in Thailand even if they are working class in Denmark. The same applies to migrants from Mozambique: they pursue a middle-class status, if not in the host country then at least back in Mozambique. Yet, to reap the fruits of their labour or allowances in Europe they must be able and allowed to return home occasionally, to feel respected and to experience that they have actually moved up in status – that they have 'become a person'.

Conclusion

Among *curtidoras* in Maputo migrating with expatriates to Europe, sexual capital was decisive in their ability to seduce men and enter into marriages. Social class mobility, status and female independence, as well as kinship, were also significant factors. In fact, stories of the desirable white man often hide a deeper truth about a partner's class privilege and financial capabilities. The women linked attractive masculinities to whiteness, wealth, generosity, education, good behaviour and sometimes age, and some found a way to exchange sexual capital for social mobility, often in alliance with kin from whom they received support in the generation of erotic power.

What most *curtidoras* strive for, whether in Maputo or Europe, is a middle-class position where they feel 'respected'. Back home this is within their reach due to a combination of access to rich expatriate men willing to support them, the ability to move up in society, being respected as middle-class people with fashionable clothes, cars and conspicuous consumption, having a maid, and benefiting from sustained kin support vis-à-vis partners. By going to Europe they risk having their privileges reduced or reconfigured. For this reason, some migrants realize that unless certain criteria are met, it might be preferable to stay in Maputo with a husband or a series of lovers.

In order to avoid reproducing stereotypes that 'marriage migration' is doomed to fail or that abuse is necessarily a part of relationships between rich white European men and poorer black women, we should perhaps pay more attention to women's stories of respectability, obligations towards families and dreams of social mobility. This chapter's findings go against conclusions that economic inequality between partners necessarily destroys a relationship. It is not imbalances in income or class inequality itself that unravel the migratory project, it is the extent to which the husband is able and willing to provide his wife with money and help her to find work or education, and the wife's agency in convincing him to do so or in being able to convert sexual capital to other forms of viable capital. Being with a relatively poor European man with few financial and social resources, for example, might impede the options, agency and mobility of them both. Controversially maybe, the further up the social ladder the husband is the more likely he will support his wife and help her to get ahead, although this is not always the case. Rather than blaming 'sad migration stories' on economic inequality within the couple or on racial, cultural or national differences, we should scrutinize the degree to which migrants have access to money, mobility, education, work and citizenship, as well as explore their support from kin and social networks – all of which are stepping stones on their journey up the social ladder where they hope to find 'respect'.

Acknowledgements

I wish to thank my research assistant Desiree Paz Hillman for her assistance in identifying patterns in the interview data, and for constructive discussions in the early phase of the writing process.

Christian Groes, an anthropologist, is associate professor and head of studies at Cultural Encounters, Roskilde University, Denmark. He has co-edited two books: *Affective Circuits: African Migration to Europe and the Pursuit of Social Regeneration* (University of Chicago Press, 2016) with Professor Jennifer Cole; and *Studying Intimate Matters: Engaging Methodological Challenges in Studies on Gender, Sexuality and Reproductive Health in Sub-Saharan Africa* (Fountain

Publishers, Kampala, 2011) with Barbara Ann Barrett. He has published articles in the journals *American Ethnologist, Journal of the Royal Anthropological Institute, Anthropological Theory* and *Men and Masculinities*, and several book chapters. In 2008 he was a PhD research fellow at Columbia University, and in 2012 he received the Young Elite Researcher Prize from the Danish Council for Independent Research.

REFERENCES

Bourdieu, P. (1979) 1986. *Distinction: A Social Critique of the Judgement of Taste*. London: Routledge.

———. 1987. 'What Makes a Social Class? On the Theoretical and Practical Existence of Groups'. *Berkeley Journal of Sociology* 32: 1-17.

Brennan, D. 2004. *What's Love Got To Do With It?* Durham, NC: Duke University Press.

Cabezas, A.L. 2004. 'Between Love and Money: Sex, Tourism, and Citizenship in Cuba and theDominican Republic'. *Signs* 29(4): 987-1015.

Cole, J. 2010. *Sex and Salvation*. Chicago, IL: University of Chicago Press.

Constable, N. 2003. *Romance on a Global Stage*. Berkeley, CA: University of California Press.

Costa, A.B. da. 2005. 'Genero e poder nas famílias da periferia de Maputo'. *Lusotopie* 12(1-2): 203-16.

Farrer, J. 2002. *Opening Up: Youth Sex Culture and Market Reform in Shanghai*. Chicago, IL: University of Chicago Press.

Fernandez, N. 2010. *Revolutionizing Romance: Interracial Couples in Contemporary Cuba*. New Brunswick, NJ: Rutgers University Press.

Fetcher, A.-M., and K. Walsh. 2010. 'Examining "Expatriate" Continuities: Postcolonial Approaches to Mobile Professionals'. *Journal of Ethnic and Migration Studies* 36(8): 1197-1210.

Friedman, J. 1994. 'The Political Economy of Elegance: An African Cult of Beauty', in J. Friedman(ed.), *Consumption and Identity*. Amsterdam: Harwood Academic Publishers, pp. 120-34.

Groes, C. 2016. 'Men Come and Go, Mothers Stay: Personhood and Resisting Marriage among Mozambican Women Migrating to Europe', in J. Cole and C. Groes (eds), *Affective Circuits: African Migrations to Europe and the Pursuit of Social Regeneration*. Chicago, IL: University of Chicago Press, pp. 169-197.

Groes-Green, C. 2009. 'Hegemonic and Subordinated Masculinities: Class, Violence and Sexual Performance among Young Mozambican Men'. *Nordic Journal of African Studies* 18(4): 286-304.

———. 2012. 'Philogynous Masculinities: Contextualizing Alternative Manhood in Mozambique'. *Men and Masculinities* 15(2): 91-111.

———. 2013. '"To Put Men in a Bottle": Eroticism, Kinship, Female Power and Transactional Sex in Maputo, Mozambique'. *American Ethnologist* 40(1): 102-17.

_____. 2014. 'Journeys of Patronage: Moral Economies of Transactional Sex, Kinship and Female Migration from Mozambique to Europe'. *Journal of the Royal Anthropological Institute* 20(2): 237–55.
Hakim, C. 2011. *Honey Money: The Power of Erotic Capital*. London: Allen Lane.
Hanlon, J., and T. Smart. 2008. *Do Bicycles Equal Development in Mozambique?* Woodbridge, Suffolk: Boydell and Brewer.
Hoefinger, H. 2013. *Sex, Love and Money in Cambodia: Professional Girlfriends and Transactional Relationships*. New York: Routledge.
Hunter, M. 2002. 'The Materiality of Everyday Sex: Thinking beyond "Prostitution"'. *African Studies* 61(1): 99–120.
_____. 2015. 'The Political Economy of Concurrent Partners: Toward a History of Sex-Love-Gift Connections in the Time of AIDS'. *Review of African Political Economy* 42(145): 362–75.
Kempadoo, K. 2004. *Sexing the Caribbean: Gender, Race and Sexual Labor*. London: Routledge.
Kim, N.Y. 2006. '"Patriarchy is so Third World": Korean Immigrant Women and "Migrating" White Western Masculinity'. *Social Problems* 53(4): 519–36.
Leclerc-Madlala, S. 2003. 'Transactional Sex and the Pursuit of Modernity', *Social Dynamics* 29(2): 213–33.
Mai, N., and R. King. 2009. 'Love, Sexuality and Migration: Mapping the Issue(s)'. *Mobilities* 4(3):295–307.
Martin, J.L., and M. George. 2006. 'Theories of Sexual Stratification: Toward an Analytics of the Sexual Field and a Theory of Sexual Capital'. *Sociological Theory* 24(2): 107–32.
Meiu, G.P. 2011. 'On Difference, Desire and the Aesthetics of the Unexpected: The White Maasai in Kenyan Tourism', in J. Skinner and D. Theodossopoulos (eds), *Great Expectations: Imagination and Anticipation in Tourism*. New York: Berghahn Books, pp. 96–115.
Oso Casas, L. 2010. 'Money, Sex, Love and the Family: Economic and Affective Strategies of Latin American Sex Workers in Spain'. *Journal of Ethnic and Migration Studies* 36(1): 47–65.
Palriwala, R., and P. Uberoi. 2008. *Marriage, Migration and Gender*. London: Sage Publications.
Piscitelli, A. 2008. 'Tropical Sex in a European Country: Brazilian Women's Migration to Italy in the Frame of International Sex Tourism'. *Estudos Feministas* 4. http://socialsciences.scielo.org/pdf/s_ref/v4nse/scs_a03.pdf.
Plambech, S. 2010. 'From Thailand with Love: Transnational Marriage Migration in the Global Care Economy', in Tiantian Zheng (ed.), *Sex Trafficking, Human Rights, and Social Justice*. London: Routledge, pp. 47–61.
Skeggs, B. 1997. *Formations of Class and Gender: Becoming Respectable*. London: Sage.
Sousa e Santos, D. de. 2009. 'Reading beyond the Love Lines: Examining Cuban Jineteras' Discourses of Love for Europeans'. *Mobilities* 4(3): 407–26.

CHAPTER
6

Fluid Sexualities beyond Sex Work and Marriage
Thai Migrants' Racialized Gender Performance in Copenhagen

Marlene Spanger

Introduction

The nexus of commercialized sex and intimacy has become an urgent issue within migration studies. In particular, the aspects of intimacy or emotions challenge the predominating discourse within migration studies of sex work that compartmentalize marriage and sex work. At an early stage in my research,[1] I realized that intimate exchanges between female Thai migrants and Danish men take place in a space between sex work and marriage, as has been noted by other scholars also (e.g. Faier 2007; Cheng 2010). Thus, the relationships existing between the Danish men and the Thai migrant sex workers are somewhat fluid, since sex work, friendship, marriage, love and patronage are not rigidly compartmentalized. For instance, the brothels and the bars do not just function as workplaces for the women, but also as spaces of leisure; places where they hang out and meet potential boyfriends and husbands.

The scholarly field of commercial sex work tends to compartmentalize the sex worker identity from other identities outside the space of sex work (Doezema 2001; Chapkis 2003; Read 2013) – for instance, the identity of wives. As a consequence, other aspects of identity are silenced. The silence is created through the radical feminist discourse that articulates women who sell sexual services as a product of unequal economic and social structures caused by a patriarchal society (Pateman 1988; Barry 1995; Jeffreys 2010). This articulation springs from a dichotomous logic between the sex worker and the prostitute, often accompanied by images of the female prostitute as the vulnerable victim, as opposed to the more assertive sex worker. In particular, migrant women within the sex industry often suffer from the prostitutes' stigma connecting with the discourse of female victimhood (Cheng 2010: 9). This epistemological stance leaves little space for investigating how women who sell sexual services may also at the same time be wives, lovers and mothers. The objective of this chapter is to demonstrate how we can rethink the logic of compartmentalizing sex work and marriage. I argue that the logic of the boundary between the fields of sex work and cross-border marriage is an obstacle if we want to analyse complex migratory trajectories related to commercialized sex. In order to analyse this complexity, in terms of blurred boundaries between commercial sex and intimacy, I ask: how do the Thai migrants perform racialized femininities through commercialized sex, money, sexual desire and love within the global nightscape of Copenhagen? Thus, I address how the gendered subject positions of sex workers, lovers and wives somehow entangle within commercial sex. More precisely, I analyse the ways in which migrants from less affluent societies, for instance Thailand, establish entangling subject positions in affluent receiving societies, such as Denmark, which reflects a transgression of this compartmentalization. Moreover, the process of how the Thai migrants become gendered subjects focusing on their negotiation of femininities stems from the discourse of heterosexuality and the colonial discourse of 'the racialized other'.

This chapter focuses on how brothels, go-go bars and ordinary bars can be perceived as what Farrer calls 'global nightscapes as sexual contact zones', in which the Thai migrants perform multiple femininities that relate to the intertwining of erotic and labour subjectivities. 'Global nightscapes' are local urban spaces that serve as sites for transnational flows (Farrer 2011: 748). In this case, the global nightscape in Copenhagen is organized into nightlife genres such as ordinary bars, go-go bars and brothels. In particular, I draw on Judith Butler's theory on heterosexuality and gender supplemented with critical theory on racialization (Butler 1990, 1997; Berg 2008; Myong 2008). I analyse how the female Thai migrants perform multiple femininities through the process of what Butler terms *becoming* a subject, which signifies processes of power that subordinate the individual. At the same time, power provides for the existence of the subject since power forms the subject. Butler terms this process *subjection*: 'consist[ing] in this fundamental dependency on a discourse we never choose but that, paradoxically, initiates and sustains our agency' (Butler 1997: 2).[2] Not only gender constitutes the process of subjection. Myong (2008) and Berg (2008) stress that racialization is a constant process of 'doing race'. Like gender, racialization is a complex historically sediment process that classifies and sets boundaries (Myong 2008: 199). Within the global nightscape, images of 'the gendered racialized other' are reproduced, destabilized, subverted, rejected and/or celebrated by the migrants and the patrons, which we will experience in the narratives of Lucy and Nook who work in a go-go bar, and Sheela who visits an ordinary bar.

The chapter starts by briefly describing the methodology followed by a section that describes the space in which the encounter between the Thai migrants and the Danish men takes place. Thirdly, based on the concepts 'the fluidity of sexuality' and 'love' as a cultural construct, the following sections offer examples that demonstrate in different ways how the migrants shape, encourage and regulate intimacy in terms of linking love, money, sexual desire and consumption through their racial gender performances in the global nightscape. Finally, I suggest how the Thai migrant's subjectivities in Copenhagen's nightscape unfold in fluid spaces beyond the dichotomy of sex work and marriage.

Methodology

My fieldwork consists of interviews with fourteen Thais selling sex, informal conversations and participant observations. Due to the difficulties in establishing contact with the female Thai migrant sex workers, I chose two entrances: making contact with them through social work and contacting massage parlours and bars directly, together with a research assistant. My strategy was to create multiple perspectives by establishing various entrances and perspectives that create the basis for analysing contradictions, transformations and ruptures. Here building confidence as well as reflections about gatekeeping became central elements in the premises for getting access. Inspired by the ethnographic fieldwork of Nencel (2001) on women selling sex in Lima, I structured my participant observations in a day and night rhythm. During the daytime from September 2005 to April 2006, I followed a social worker of a social counselling programme directed towards Thai migrant sex workers in Denmark. I carried out observations. I participated in the meetings between the social worker and the female Thais in different situations: at the police station, at a shelter for battered women, at the hospital, at the homes of the female Thais, and at the office of the counselling programme. I also experienced situations that were more informal when the social worker and I went out for lunch with some of the Thai migrant sex workers. Both in relation to the tasks of the counselling programme and by myself, I visited brothels during the day. At night during the same period and independently of the municipal programme, I conducted participant observations together with my research assistant, visiting go-go bars and an ordinary Thai bar, as well as participating in different events within the Thai migrant community. I visited places and events that female Thai migrant sex workers visit or participate in (Thai concerts, annual Thai festivals arranged by one of the temples, a Thai supermarket, Thai clubs and a Buddhist temple) while I followed a counselling project. These multiple entrances gave me opportunities to meet Thai migrant sex workers in different everyday situations and settings, which resulted in different narratives. In combination, the female Thais' narratives drew a complex picture of their everyday lives.

Setting the Scene: The Brothel and the Go-go Bar as Venues for Love

The female Thai migrant sex workers form a particular social group within the Thai population in Denmark. In 2017 the population is the nineteenth largest ethnic population in Denmark (Statistic Denmark 2017a).[3] The Thai sex workers are not an isolated group within this Thai migrant community in Denmark. For instance, during my fieldwork I found that some Thai migrant sex workers are recognized as respectable members of that community. Through their business within the sex work industry (e.g. ownership of go-go bars) they acquire high social status due to their ability to make money and thus to take care of their families.

In 2006, the total number of Thai migrants in Denmark was 7,438 consisting of 6,060 females and 1,378 males. In 2010 it went up to 7,847 females and 1,808 males, and in 2017 to 10,519 females and 2,709 males.[4] Thus, the number of Thai migrants in Denmark is growing. In 2006, number of males was highest in the 'under 19' age group, whereas for females the 30–39 age group was highest. Similar demographic development existed in 2010 and 2017 (Statistics Denmark 2017a).[5] Most likely, these Thai males are the sons of the Thai female migrants who bring their sons to Denmark. Of the Thai migrant population in Denmark, 88 per cent have obtained work and residence permits through family reunification, which includes marriage to a Danish citizen (Statistics Denmark 2016: 25; Statistics Denmark 2017b).[6] The same pattern is in evidence among the Thai migrant sex workers. All my interviewees were or had been married to a Danish citizen. Thus, the Thai migrant community is characterized by female Thais married to Danish men. Inter-ethnic marriage is not widespread in the Thai community.

The employment of Thai migrants in the Danish labour market is significantly lower than for citizens born in Denmark (Bjerre, Mortensen and Drescher 2016). Moreover, between 2008 and 2015, the majority of both men and women in the 25-50 age group were employed within the unskilled labour market in Denmark. In the same period, only five women (two in 2013, two in 2014, and one in 2015) were employed within the skilled labour market, and six female migrants were self-employed (Statistics Denmark 2017c). Some Thai migrants are self-employed within the Danish service sector, such as restaurants, bars, groceries and other shops. Presumably, the majority work within the service sector or at different kinds of factories and plants. We do not know the educational background of the Thai population in Denmark, but it is assumed that the majority of the Thai migrants moving to Denmark do not have an education or are not able to obtain a profession based on their educational experiences. Moreover, no Thai migrants in Denmark obtained residence and work permits based on their professional background.

None of the Thai migrant sex workers I talked to had had an education, either in Thailand or Denmark. The majority had attended primary school in Thailand but few had passed a high school examination. Besides selling sexual services, which is not defined as a profession in Denmark, they combine their earnings from the sex industry with temporary unskilled work – for instance in restaurants and bars, fish plants and in the cleaning industry. Moreover, the migrants are documented migrants in Denmark. They all are or have been married to Danish men. All Thai migrant sex workers, except the transgendered (m-t-f), have children living in Denmark or in Thailand (see Dahl and Spanger 2010 about Thai migrant sex workers and motherhood).

During my fieldwork I noticed how a range of sexual, intimate and social liaisons established between the women and their patrons went beyond the migrant's sale of sexual services. Regardless of the genres of sexual contact zones in Copenhagen, the articulation of romantic love through sexual services and money exists in many of the narratives of the female Thai migrants. For instance, besides earning money through their work in brothels, this site also becomes a sexual contact zone for meeting future husbands or boyfriends. The brothels in which the Thai migrants work are mostly open both night and day, offering a number of different time-limited sexual services for fixed prices. Usually, the brothels are not just work places defined by sexual commerce; they are also gathering points at which female Thai migrant sex workers frequently stay overnight and socialize during quiet periods, eating and playing cards together in the private room. In general, sex clients are not permitted to enter the private room. However, this rule is often transgressed when intimate sexual and social relations between Thai sex workers and Danish patrons are established that go beyond the sale of sexual services. Thus, the private room serves as a space where they can meet and hang out. Friends pass by for a visit; these may be both other female Thais and male Danish friends. Thus, occasionally, the Danish husbands and boyfriends are somehow connected to the milieu revolving around the Thai brothels in Copenhagen as patrons, friends and/or some kind of helpers. Being a patron does not necessarily exclude the men as boyfriends or husbands. Sometimes the female Thai migrants who work in the go-go bars and/or in the brothels fall in love with their patrons. Groes-Green (2014) describes similar trends in his analysis of how the migration of Mozambican women to Europe is realized through the patronage of European men, which involves money, sex and intimacy.

Dina, a Thai migrant, told me that one of her patrons from the brothel had fallen in love with her, and this became apparent to her through his offers. When I talked to Dina she had just left her Danish husband with whom she had been together for approximately four years. Assisted by the social authorities she was able to find a new flat for herself and her child. Dina told me that he wanted to help her to pay off her consumer loan, and he also offered for her and her daughter to move into his home. He proposed these financial offers shortly (one month) after they had met. Dina regarded his offers as a sign of his affection and of how he was crazy for her and loved her. Another Thai, Malai, who also worked at a brothel, told me about her affection for one of her sex clients: 'I was crazy, crazy, crazy with him, but he was not crazy with me. [I said to him] I give you three free hours!' However, the sex client refused her offer. In this example, during the exchange of sexual services and money, affection develops and suddenly the distinction between commerce and affection is blurry. Malai's services become a sign of affection and not just a service for sale. The transaction of money and sex revolves around the interracial heterosexual couple.

Approaching the Entanglement of Commercial Sex and Intimacy

Turning towards the literature of cross-border marriages, sex work and marriage are frequently perceived as incompatible. If the issue of sex work is brought into the scholarly field of migration, the link between sex work and cross-border marriage is predominantly understood within a socio-economic logic. For instance, marriage between sex workers and their sex clients is often perceived as a conscious survival strategy on the part of the sex workers (Ruenkaew 2002; Brennan 2003; Mix and Piper 2003; Kristvik

2005; Cabezas 2004, 2006). Brennan argues that the cross-border marriages of Dominican sex workers with the sex tourists is a stepping stone for the Dominicans to enter the United States or Europe. Yet, she places little emphasis on understanding how the aspects of intimacy between couples affect their identity formation. In this regard, there is a risk that the sex workers' identity becomes compartmentalized from other identities such as wives or lovers. Thus, the literature of cross-border marriage and sex work does not capture the highly complex narratives of migrants who marry as part of migration, but at the same time sell their sexual services and fall in love with or feel desire towards their clients. Often, marriage and intimate relations are perceived as diametrically opposed to sex work, which is regarded as a cynical and emotion-free trade. As my study shows, understanding female Thais migrating to Denmark requires a transgression of the research fields of sex work and cross-border marriage. The sale of sexual services by the Thai migrants in Denmark is not just an isolated act compartmentalized from other liaisons such as marriage and love. Rather, their sales of sexual services are entangled with other intimate relations such as love, sexual desire and friendship.

Informed by a burgeoning literature that studies the very links between cross-border marriages, sex work, love, intimacy and sexuality (Suzuki 2004; Faier 2007; Piscitelli 2008; Oso Casas 2010; Cheng 2010; Farrer 2011; Groes-Green 2014), I argue that new analytical tools can be developed in order to move beyond this division. My aim is to investigate how the migrants create complex subjectivities in a society that compartmentalizes sex work and marriage. These studies analyse the link between sexual monetary transactions, intimacy and love. Seen through the lens of 'flexible sexual economies', Groes-Green (2014) investigates how love, desire and sexual economy characterizes the trajectories of young female Mozambican women's migration to Europe through intimate relations with European men. Focusing on the link between sexual economic exchange, intimacy and love, Cheng's (2010) study covers Filipina migrants' liaisons with US soldiers stationed in Korea. She suggests that these women are perceived as both erotic subjects and labour subjects in migration, which opens up for analysing the 'fluidity of their sexuality' across different contexts (ibid.: 28). In a similar vein, I argue that Thai women in Denmark are both erotic subjects and labour subjects. This view enables me to analyse how their sexuality is relevant not only in the space of marriage outside of the sex industry, but is fluid as they interlink their erotic and labour subjectivities within the nightscapes of Copenhagen.

In particular, approaching love from a poststructuralist perspective is a burgeoning trend within the literature of the sex industry.[7] Inspired by Faier's study of how love is made meaningful in cross-border marriages between

Japanese men and Filipina migrant women working as hostesses in Japan, I approach love as discursively constructed, through which migrants articulate subjectivity in transnational power relations. In this understanding, love is a social practice that is negotiated (Cheng 2007: 228; Faier 2007: 149). Thus, love is ascribed multiple meanings, depending on the particular context. Faier (2007: 154–55) notes that the migrants challenge the stigma associated with such transnational marriages by articulating their jobs in terms of love, showing gratitude towards their Japanese husbands for supporting their families in the Philippines and identifying themselves as 'cosmopolitan, modern women'. Similarly, Sheela, the transgendered woman in Copenhagen, tells stories about affairs, flirts, money and her nightlife that reflect how she perceives of herself as a cosmopolitan independent modern woman, while at the same time playing with the idea of being a desirable object of white men's racial fantasies of 'the exotic woman'. Applying love grounded in discourse allows me to develop a complex analysis of the migrants selling sex in Denmark, considering how love affairs are articulated in terms of emotions, romance, money, gifts and care, as well as the notions of 'the good husband' and the nuclear family. Practising and negotiating love through the racialized gender performance, these migrants merge erotic and labour subjectivities. For instance, having just filed for a divorce from her Danish husband, Dina met a new Danish boyfriend through the brothel, who became her true love. Despite approaching the migrants as subjects with agency (Spanger 2012), I agree with Cheng (2010: 30–31) that love does not erase power differentials between the partners, just as it does not erase powers of global neoliberal economies. However, breaking with the silence of women selling sexual services as erotic subjects creates a space for analysing how ambiguities and complexities create the subjectivities of these Thai migrants. Thus, a deconstruction of this compartmentalization is possible by approaching love as a social construct (Faier 2007) as well as bringing in the idea of 'the fluidity of sexuality' (Cheng 2010). By asking what happens when sexual desire and intimacy are brought into play within the studies of sexual-economic exchange, it might prompt an analysis of Thai migrants living in Denmark and married to or having intimate relationships with white Danish men.

In different ways, these migrants are employed in the sex industry either as dancers or hostesses at go-go bars, or as prostitutes at brothels. The Thai migrant sex workers include female-born individuals, transgendered individuals (m-t-f) and cross-dressers (m-t-f). This performance of different kinds of femininity within the discourse of heterosexuality highly accentuates the global nightscape of Copenhagen. Moreover, this gender diversity results in multiple interpretations of femininity among the migrants, and plays a central role in how they establish complex intimate relations in the midst of the sex industry, which demonstrates the possibilities for creating the fluid sexualities that blur the boundaries between the labour subject and the erotic subject. Such blurred boundaries reflect how it is not a question of performing as sex worker, lover or friend, but how the subject positions entangle.

Flirtation and Seduction within the Global Nightscape of Copenhagen

During my fieldwork, I spent some time in an ordinary Thai bar in which the boundaries of sexual intimacy are fluid. The bar is a gathering point for female Thai migrants and Danish men. The guests drop by for a beer after work or visit the bar at the weekend when they go out at night. Besides being a venue for a night on the town, the bar is also a site for selling sex. According to some of the female Thais, the bar's Danish male customers and a former bartender, the sale of sexual services takes place in secret. For instance, chatting over a beer and flirting in the bar sometimes lead to the men taking the women home or to a hotel where they pay for sex. Thus, the boundaries between sexual services, sexual desire, intimacy and money are fluid and are not necessarily attached to specific places. Rather, this implies that the site for intimacy encompasses both the space of sex work and the space of leisure. The liaison between the white Danish man and the brown Thai woman is the predominant racialized gender pattern, whereas the absence of adult male Thais and white Danish women is widespread in the Thai migrant's global nightscape in Copenhagen, regardless of whether the genre of space is brothels, go-go bars, the ordinary bars, or festivals organized by Thai migrants.

The go-go bars present a different picture; here the hostesses and dancers earn money by selling sex to the guests in addition to their fixed salary from their job in the bar. When a patron buys a bottle of champagne, the hostesses and dancers are allowed to leave the bar with him. One dancer told me that her main income came from selling sex. Thus, the sale of sexual services is formalized and is a crucial theme of visiting a go-go bar. Still, acting out femininity through acts of seduction and flirting is central. As Nook, a go-go dancer and hostess told me:

> It is not necessary to wriggle. It is not necessary to just lie down on the bed with legs apart. It is not like that. All who work have their skills. It depends on how you speak, on your style and charm, how you play up to them. It is what you say that determines the sum of money. It is the words that decide!

Wearing dresses that signify glamour and using body language closely connected to gender, body, sexual desire and practices all constitutes a female subject that meets the idealized heterosexually desirable object within the global nightscape of Copenhagen. With the combination of her (female) body, dress, flirtation, sexual desire and practices addressed to men, Nook lives up to the cultural norms of citing 'correct' heterosexual femininity. This particular type of femininity does not only define the female sex worker subject. Nevertheless, Nook refers to the encounter with the guests as a professional skill. Other female Thais talk about a sexual desire for Danish men that does not necessarily exclude or include financial support from the men. Hence, the boundaries between their work life in the brothels or bars and their leisure time are rather fluid. Both the circumstances under which they demand monetary remuneration for intimacy and how much remuneration they demand are varied and cannot always be predicted. Such exchanges depend on a combination of factors such as emotions, desire, space, negotiations and interests or expectations. Thus, the sale of sexual services may be described as the gradual and ambiguous movement between bodily services of a more or less intimate or sexual nature.

The bar is a venue for the white male's fantasies of Asian women as 'the erotic other'. Such images spring from colonial discourses. Within this historical discourse, the Asian woman was 'sexualized as pretty, passive and infantilized'. Andreassen (2011) argues that the former characterization of the Asian woman as a doll was a way of dehumanizing them. The sexualization of the Asian woman is still at play both in the space of sex work and in the nightlife of the Thai migrant community in Denmark. However, the image has slightly changed. Ahmed (2004) stresses that certain histories are reopened in the process of how the particular body is construed. Thus, the body is not a neutral site. In the case of female Thais selling sexual services, their bodies carry the past through which a colonial discourse of race and sexuality establishes gender hierarchies (Myong 2008). Bishop and Robinson (1998) draw a line from the sexualized images reproduced within sex tourism to the late eighteenth-century images of the Orient as a space of an abundance of sexuality, sexual opportunities and available women. In the narratives of beauty being sexy, the importance of looking good, fashion and being desirable objects in the eyes of men are all important issues to the Thai migrants, and this reflects how they negotiate the 'right' femininity attached to 'the erotic other' in terms of the images of 'the Thai woman'. Becoming an 'erotic other' occurs through the agency of the female Thai migrants in terms of how they perform gender, race and sexuality as 'the hot sexy Thai woman' and 'the good housewife' in the global nightscape of Copenhagen, as well as in how Thai migrants and Danish men negotiate and use their narratives about fluid sexualities.

Some of the Danish men visiting the Thai bar are looking for Thai women, or at least women from Asia in general. Often the men have previously been acquainted with female Thais, either in Denmark or through their journeys to Thailand. Among Danish men, a fetish for Thainess related to the female Thai is quite common, as one of the men told me: 'Marlene, I am crazy with everything that is Thai: Buddhism, Thai ceremonies, Thai food, Thai houses, Thai dance, Thai massage...'. He explained that the best part of Thai culture is Thai massage. In the same breath, he emphasized that he is not a sex tourist, but he is indeed attracted to Thai women. Such a sexualized celebration of the female Asian, and especially Thai, body is distinctive among the Danish men who are a part of the Thai migrant community. The men in the bar are aware that selling sexual services is not an isolated activity within the migrant community. Thus, a compartmentalizing of the female Thai migrants into groups – 'prostitutes' and 'non-prostitutes' – does not exist. However, this does not mean that the sale of sexual services is accepted or acknowledged among the Thai migrants or the Danish men. According to Peter, a male guest in the bar, 'the Thai woman' represents the traditional femininity of being loyal towards their husband and of regarding domestic work as a natural female responsibility. He said that, unlike the Danish woman, the Thai woman has not been 'spoiled' by women's liberation, which he accused of destroying 'the good marriage'. On the one hand, he assumed that Thai migrant women represent the ideal femininity as described above. On the other hand, he had been rather disillusioned by his bad experiences with female Thai migrants, and distinguished between loose women and women of virtue. In particular, he had experienced that Thai women are not interested in his affection and love for them, but only in his money. Another male guest, Simon, disagreed with Peter's distinction of female Thai migrants as either loose women or women of virtue. Instead, Simon emphasized that it is not a question of whether or not they sell sex, smoke, or offer themselves to men on the first night. Such Thai women might also be perceived as decent women; but their images and fantasies of 'the female Thai' is what the male guests all had in common.

Furthermore, I argue that 'the erotic other', which is discursively constituted, is not only produced in the gaze of the white man as representing Westernized male fantasies about the 'sexually available Thai woman', which then leads to a reproduction of the stereotypically sexualized subject position, as indicated by Bishop and Robinson (1998) and Davidson and Sanchez Taylor (1999). Rather, such a subject position is negotiated and reiterated through the gender performativity of the female Thai migrants within the sex industry. When seen through the lens of performance offered by Butler (1990, 1997), it becomes more evident how sexual desire, romantic love and economy are deeply entangled and situated, as we will see in the following.

Seducing Patrons: Displacement of Global Nightscapes

Lucy and her future husband met at a tourist resort in Thailand; here liaisons formed between tourists and locals are often ambiguous and diffuse, as other scholars have previously demonstrated (Ryan and Hall 2001; Kempadoo 2001; Cabezas 2004). Typically, the liaison lasts from one night to a week or more, and given that the encounter takes place in coffee shops, restaurants, on the beach and in bars, the patron and the Thai do not perceive it as sex work. Such sites do not signify prostitution. Despite the encounter taking place in the known sex-tourism destination of Pattaya, there are similarities to Copenhagen's nightscape that the Thai migrant navigates in. The images of 'the erotic other' and the entanglement of money, sex and intimacy characterize both spaces. I argue that Farrer's (2011) term 'global nightscape' succeeds in capturing 'the fluidity of the Thai migrant's sexuality, demonstrating how love, sexual desire and sex-economy are all linked. Brennan (2004), Cheng (2010) and Farrer (2011) are all inspired by the groundbreaking suffix '-scapes' offered by Appadurai (1996: 33). In different ways they refine the '-scape' circulating around the spaces of the consumption of sex, tourism and sex-economy exchanges conceptualizing the sites as global sexscapes, touristscapes or global nightscapes in which the encounters take place. In order to understand how identities and culture are produced through locally lived experiences in a deterritorialized world, Appadurai investigates how the transnational flows of both materialization and ideas in a modern global world take place through the concept of ethnoscape. The concept of global nightscape is relevant, since it refers to how cities, in this case Copenhagen, may be approached as ethnosexual contact zones produced in a tension between a particular local site and global flows of racial images of sex, masculinities and femininities (Farrer 2011: 748). Thus, global nightscapes are both spaces of consumption and an outcome of the culture of global cities having been produced by transnational mobile elites (ibid.: 761). Slightly differently, I argue that not only do global elites produce the culture of the global city, but class stratification intersects with race and gender in the case of the Thai migrants in Copenhagen. Even if they do not represent the global elite, they represent a mobile group of migrants who challenge the predominant narratives of the 'victimized Third World woman' or 'the modern slave' that exist within the Danish policy discourse on prostitution (Spanger 2011). Simultaneously, the white male fantasies of 'the erotic other' are negotiated and replayed within the global nightscape of Copenhagen.

Following Farrer (2011: 748), the global nightscape is shaped by the tension between the similarities across local sites. On the other hand, nightscapes are not identical across global cities. Rather, the global nightscape is what Farrer refers to as 'heterogeneous sites of sexual and racial stratifications'. In the Copenhagen nightscape, local encounters between female Thai migrants and male Danish patrons take place in various genres of sexual contact zones (brothels, go-go bars and ordinary bars) that establish racialized gendered hierarchies. Take the case of Lucy:

> In the beginning, when I had just arrived at Pattaya [a tourist resort], then I waited at a restaurant. I had a friend who worked as a go-go dancer, and she said to me: 'Lucy, you will get more out of it if you work with me'.
>
> I loved him ... He was my first love, the Dane and I. In the beginning he said to me that I should stop working. He said: 'I will send remittances to you'. So I stopped. I stayed at home and he sent remittances. I tell you I got 5,000 baht a month and I agreed to stop working – can you then see that I loved him! Only 1,000 Danish crowns a month ... A Danish woman had just broken his heart and then he went to Thailand, but just for vacation. It wasn't to be intimate with a woman either. It was a coincidence ... Well, at home [in Thailand] you don't have to look for love. It comes to you.
>
> *Interpreter (addressed to Lucy)*: So, you had not decided to ... [unclear] ... farang?
>
> *Lucy*: I wasn't, because I had decided finding a ... He invited me [to Denmark]. He loved me!

In line with Faier's interpretation of love, a complex understanding of sex work, love and marriage emerges in Lucy's situation. In her study, Faier suggests that love has enabled Filipina migrants to claim 'a sense of humanity in the face of their work in the hostess bars' (Faier 2007: 157). This is similar to what happens among female Thais in Denmark. Linking her bar job and her bar life with love is one way for Lucy to legitimize her marriage to her Danish patron, and this bears witness to the complexity of their encounter. First of all, Lucy closely relates love and money. In her case story, money is considered a sign of affection, and love is two-sided. She regards the remittances as a sign of the Danish man's commitment and, in addition, she proves her devotion to him by giving up her job as a dancer, which pays more than the monthly DKK 1,000 she receives from him in Denmark. Second of all, she describes her encounter with the Danish man as a romantic one. Emphasizing how they fell in love by accident, and how it was not premeditated, was probably a way for her to perform the role of a 'respectable woman' when I followed her during my fieldwork. Lucy was aware of the reasons for this male tourist's visit to the nightlife in Pattaya, and clarified this by saying: 'Is she [Marlene] aware of what a *farang* who goes to Thailand and goes to Pattaya is? Is she aware of what kind of a place Pattaya is?' *Farang* is the Thai word for a foreigner of European origin, and it can be used as an insult. Presumably, when Lucy used the word, she was referring to white 'First World men' looking for Thai women who sell sex. Thus, perceiving their encounter in the go-go bar as a romantic love story that resulted in marriage was a way for Lucy to challenge the stereotypes of the 'First World man' and the 'Third World woman'. Suzuki (2004) demonstrates that these binary stereotypes constitute inadequate representations of Filipina–Japanese marriages. Likewise, similar stereotypes cannot fully represent the relations between female Thais and Danish men. When talking about her job as a dancer in Thailand, Lucy ascribed a central role to love in her story. This breaks with the stereotype of the victimized 'Third World woman'. Likewise, Lee Ann, another female Thai migrant sex worker I interviewed, assured me that she loves her Danish husband whom she met in Thailand; she swore that she never worked in a go-go bar in Thailand. The women add love in the form of emotional involvement to the equation as a way of counterbalancing the stigma of the 'fallen woman' – a woman whose subject position is predominantly that of a sex worker. Seduction and flirtation are central elements that characterize Copenhagen's nightscape in which the Thai migrants move.

'I am sexy... and the Danish men are very sexy': The Desire for White Danish Men

It is Friday night and the bar is crammed, mainly with Danish men but also female Thais. Their clothing is casual; the men wear T-shirts or shirts and jeans, and the women wear tank tops with jeans or skirts. The light in the bar is dimmed and a mix of disco music and loud voices pervade the room. The atmosphere is intense, saturated by flirtation and the high party spirit among the guests. In this case, spare time, work and pleasure are inadequate categories used to comprehend the kind of liaisons that are played out between the female Thai migrants and the Danish men. Rather, some of the connections made at the bar may be viewed as fluid sexual liaisons in which sexual pleasure, attractive femininity and economy are entangled. Sheela is one example of this. That night was the first time I met Sheela.

Dressed in an evening tank top, a short pink skirt with a large slit, and glittering gold stiletto heels that accentuated her long legs, she made a grand entry that made the guests around her aware of her presence. Sheela is nearly two metres tall, slim, and her red-brown hair is long and straight. In a loud and slightly rusty voice, and using large energetic gesticulations, she explains that she has just lost DKK 50,000 (approx. € 6,650) playing cards for four hours. She continues with a shrug, and emphasizes that her boyfriend paid. She orders a red bull at the bar before she walks, accompanied by two men, to a sofa at the other end of the room. For Sheela, visiting the bar means having a fun time, and this includes playing up to the male guests, being sexually attractive and having sex with them.

> *Sheela*: I really like Denmark, in particular the Danish men who are really sexy…
>
> *Marlene*: How would you describe a fun time at the bar?
>
> *Sheela*: A fun time in the bar… my favourite bar is [the bar described above] … fantasy-girls is something the guys want to try out. Not because I say that I am good looking but you have to be feminine, hot and sexy, that is what the boys like. When I go out, all the hot boys tell me that I am attractive.
>
> *Marlene*: Are you able to get what you want [to attract the men]?
>
> *Sheela*: Approximately 90 per cent of the time, when I go out at night.
>
> *Marlene*: Please define, what do mean that you 'sometimes' get what you want? What do you look for?
>
> *Sheela*: I like sex. We boys are always happy. If you ask a woman who works in a bar whether she is a happy hooker, if she says yes she lies. If you ask lady boys if they are happy with their lives they will say yes – that they are very happy with their lives. I am happy and regret nothing.

Sheela's nightlife of visiting bars and having a fun time is very closely linked to sexual liaisons and the seduction of men. The narratives of Sheela reflect that the entanglement of sexual pleasure, happiness and money is realistic due to her configuration of gender that relies on the components of social gender, body, sexual practices and sexual desire. As a transgender (m-t-f), Sheela's gender performativity opens up for both the subversion and reproduction of the heterosexual discourse that constitutes the ideal norms of 'a woman' in regards to sexual practices, sexual desire and money. On the one hand, when Sheela refers to herself as a boy by stating 'We boys…', she does not refer to her social gender. Instead, she refers to her bodily parts (genitals) and the biological component (male hormones etc.). Following the logic of Sheela, the male body parts and biology conditions her sexual appetite as something natural. At the same time, she confirms that money and sexual pleasure does not fit with the ideal of the biological woman. On the other hand, she subverts the very same matrix by the ways in which she reiterates femininity.

> *Marlene*: Are the men aware that you are a lady boy?
>
> *Sheela*: I tell everybody I meet. Sometimes at Hayley Bar (an ordinary bar) thirty or forty men pay attention to me. I tell them all that I am not a woman. They do not care and tell me that I am feminine and sexy. Sometimes they are shy and tell me that they cannot believe that I am not a woman – in my bed they never say no.
>
> *Marlene*: You dress like a woman...
>
> *Sheela* [interject]: ...and feel as a woman...
>
> *Marlene*: ...yes, and feel as a woman. Have you had any surgeries?
>
> *Sheela* [laughing]: only my breasts... that is all. Most Asian lady boys use too much silicone in order to look like a woman, but I do not. Everything you see is real.
>
> *Marlene*: And your genitals are they just as a man's?
>
> *Sheela*: Yes, and that is exactly also what the guys like.
>
> *Later on, Sheela tells me*: I am fond of the beach and sunbathe. I think some of the Thai women in Denmark are little bit ridiculous, because they want a white skin and they have this cream [that contains whitening]. They are very preoccupied with their skin and they want to be white. But every time when I return to Denmark [from a vacation in Thailand] I think that I am a little bit too brown. There are so many white people in this country, so you get lots of attention with your dark or brown skin.

As a transgendered Thai, Sheela performs heterosexual femininity based on the configuration of social gender (dress, make-up, gestures, feelings, body language, etc.), some of her bodily parts (breasts) and sexual desire (heterosexual men). With her Asian look, brown skin, long legs, slim body, high cheekbones and long straight black hair highlighted by her provocative clothing, make-up and stilettos, she represents the ideal sexualized exotic woman. For Sheela, being exotic is a balancing act between being positioned as a female Thai migrant, a global citizen and an independent woman. She uses her brown body to get attention from white men and for dissociating herself from the other female Thai migrants and their desire for the white female body, even using whitening cream in an attempt to obtain this. On the other hand, she does not want her skin to be too dark. Sheela subverts the heterosexual matrix by performing racialized femininity through her appearance in terms of her skin, dress, gestures, speech and parts of her body. Thus, her femininity is defined by the configuration that the social gender follows sexual desire (for heterosexual men), and partly by her body. The sexual practices and her male genitals do not enter into this configuration. Rather, this configuration subverts the heterosexual matrix. Seducing white heterosexual men by performing racialized femininity while having male genitals as well as breasts relates to the subject position of what Sheela calls a 'fantasy girl'. This confirms the images of 'the erotic other' based on the logic of 'Thai women as sexually available', or as Davidson and Sanchez Taylor (1999: 43) identify among sex tourists: '[S]ex is more "natural" in Third World countries, [and] prostitution is not really prostitution, but a "way of life"'.

Conclusion

In this chapter I have demonstrated how marriage and sex work are rather difficult to compartmentalize if we want to understand the complex migratory trajectories of the Thai migrants selling sexual services. In particular, my ethnographic study shows how their performances of gendered subject positions (wives, lovers and sex workers) take place through an entanglement of commercial sex, money, sexual desire and love.
Through their different bodily and sexual practices, the female Thai migrants challenge, subvert or confirm the ideal female subject within this Westernized heterosexual discourse that constitutes the global nightscape of Copenhagen. In particular, the heterosexual racialized gender stratification – 'the brown Third World woman's sexual liaison with 'the First World white man' – permeates this global nightscape in which the female Thai migrants move. Within this nightscape, the subject positions of the white woman and the Asian man are absent. Be it the bar or brothel in Copenhagen or the go-go bar in Pattaya, these genres of sexual contact zones create spaces for the women to link sexual consumption, money, sexual desire and love through ways of performing racialized femininity. This challenges the idea of clear boundaries between sex work and intimate relationships. Rather, a sexual flexibility or 'fluidity of sexuality' creates opportunities for an entanglement of the labour subject and the erotic subject in terms of the migrants' subject positions of sex worker, lover and wife. Thus, a combination of applying Butler's gender theory (1990, 1997) and Farrer's (2011) concept of 'global nightscapes' offers analytical tools for

a complex analysis of how the Thai migrants' sex sale intersects with their everyday lives away from the sex work.

Marlene Spanger is associate professor at the Department of Culture and Global Studies at Aalborg University, Denmark. She co-chaired the 'Sex, Money and Society' Working Group in the COST Action IS1209 'Comparing European Prostitution Policies: Understanding Scales and Cultures of Governance (ProsPol)' from 2012 to 2017. Spanger co-edited with May-Len Skilbrei the books *Prostitution Research in Context: Methodology, Representation and Power* (Routledge 2017) and *Understanding Sex for Sale: Meanings and Moralities of Sexual Commerce* (Routledge 2018). She has published articles in the journals *Critical Social Policy* & *Gender, Place & Culture*, and *Nordic Journal of Feminist and Gender Studies*.

NOTES

1. This chapter is based on the empirical material from my PhD dissertation (Spanger 2010).
2. The subject is produced within an ambivalent process of power, compulsion and reproduction conditioned by the discourse of heterosexuality that constitutes and dissolves the very same subject. Ambivalence is the premise of becoming a subject which is captured by the tension between the dichotomy of what Butler calls 'already there and the yet-to-come' (Butler 1997: 18). This ambivalent process implies that the agency of the subject is signified by racialized gender performance: reiterations of norms, bodily practices, gestures, appearance and words (Butler 1990: 173). According to Butler, the question is not whether or not the subject repeats the norms, practices etc., because these are always repeated (ibid.: 185). Instead, the question is *how* the subject repeats these, and this is linked to the subject's agency (ibid.: 33). Consequently, the subject is not able to stand outside the norms (ibid.: 17).
3. The size of the Thai population is similar to the Norwegian or the Swedish populations in Denmark, as neighbouring nation states. Thus, the size of the Thai population in Denmark is significant.
4. These numbers encompass Thai migrants born in Thailand, but living in Denmark (which means registered as citizens in Denmark) – both Thais who have changed Thai citizenship into Danish citizenship and Thais who have maintained their Thai citizenship (Statistics Denmark 2017a).
5. The size of the Thai population in Denmark based on figures from Statistic Denmark is precise, since the state registers all citizens who migrate to Denmark through a personal civil registration system.
6. In Denmark, family reunification only encompasses children and spouses/partners and not elderly parents or other family members (New to Denmark 2017).

7. See e.g. Zelizer 2006, Cheng 2010, Casas 2010 and Groes-Green 2014 on analysing how money, sex and intimate relations intermingle and arguing that different meanings are ascribed to money, depending on the sexual and intimate relations in question, which include both marriage and sex work. Zelizer (2006) argues that in such relations love is constructed through a negotiation of the meanings of money and sexual and intimate relations.

REFERENCES

Ahmed, S. 2004. 'Collective Feelings: Or, the Impressions Left by Others'. *Theory, Culture & Society* 21(2): 25–42.

Andreassen, R. 2011. *'Representations of Sexuality and Race at Danish Exhibitions of Exotic People at the Turn of the Twentieth Century'*. *NORA – Nordic Journal of Feminist and Gender Research* 20(2): 126–47.

Appadurai, A. 1996. *Modernity at Large: Cultural Dimensions of Globalisation*. Minneapolis, MN and London: University of Minnesota Press.

Barry, K. 1995. *The Prostitution of Sexuality: The Global Exploitation of Women*. New York: NYU Press.

Berg, A.-J. 2008 'Silence and Articulation – Whiteness, Racialization and Feminist Memory Work'. *NORA – Nordic Journal of Feminist and Gender Research* 16(4): 213–27.

Bishop, R., and L. Robinson. 1998. *Night Market: Sexual Cultures and the Thai Economic Miracle*. London: Routledge.

Bjerre, J., L.H. Mortensen and M. Drescher. 2016. *Ikke-vestlige indvandrere på arbejdsmarkedet i Danmark, Norge og Sverige: Hvordan klarer Danmark sig?* Copenhagen: DST Analyse no. 25. Retrieved 29 July 2017 from: http://www.dst.dk/Site/Dst/Udgivelser/nyt/GetAnalyse.aspx?cid=28102.

Brennan, D. 2003. 'Selling Sex for Visas: Sex Tourism as a Stepping-Stone to International Migration', in B. Ehrenreich and A.R. Hochschild (eds), *Global Woman: Nannies, Maids and Sex Workers in the New Economy*. London: Granta Books, pp. 154–68.

Butler, J. 1990. *Gender Trouble: Feminism and the Subversion of Identity*. London: Routledge.

―――. 1997. *The Psychic Life of Power: Theories in Subjection*. Stanford, CA: Stanford University Press.

Cabezas, A.L. 2004. 'Between Love and Money: Sex, Tourism, and Citizenship in Cuba and the Dominican Republic'. *Signs* 29(4): 987–1015.

―――. 2006. 'The Eroticization of Labor in Cuba's All-Inclusive Resorts: Performing Race, Class and Gender in the New Tourist Economy'. *Social Identities* 12(5): 507–21.

Chapkis, W. 2003. 'Trafficking, Migration, and the Law: Protecting Innocents, Punishing Immigrants'. *Gender and Society* 17(6): 923–37.

Cheng, S. 2007. 'Romancing the Club: Love Dynamics between Filippa Entertainers and GIs in U.S. Military Camp Towns in South Korea', in M. Padilla, J.S. Hirsch, M. Munoz-Laboy, R.G. Parker and R. Sember (eds), *Love and Globalization: Transformations of Intimacy in the Contemporary World*. Nashville, TN: Vanderbilt University Press, pp. 226–251.

Cheng, S. 2010. *On the Move for Love: Migrant Entertainers and the U.S. Military in South Korea.* Philadelphia: University of Pennsylvania Press.

Dahl, H.M., and M. Spanger. 2010. 'Sex Workers' Transnational and Local Motherhood: Presence and/or Absence?', in A.L. Widding Isaksen (ed.), *Global Care Work: Gender and Migration in Nordic Societies.* Lund: Nordic Academic Press, pp. 117–36.

Davidson, J.O., and J. Sanchez Taylor. 1999. 'Fantasy Islands: Exploring the Demand for Sex Tourism', in K. Kempadoo (ed.), *Sun, Sex and Gold: Tourism and Sex Work in the Caribbean.* Boulder, CO: Rowman & Littlefield, pp. 37–54.

Doezema, J. 2001. 'Ouch! Western Feminists' "Wounded Attachment" to the "Third-World Prostitute"'. *Feminist Review* 67: 16–38.

Faier, L. 2007. 'Filipina Migrants in Rural Japan and Their Professions of Love'. *American Ethnologist* 34(1): 148–62.

Farrer, J. 2011. 'Global Nightscapes in Shanghai as Ethnosexual Contact Zones'. *The Journal of Ethnic and Migration Studies* 37(5): 747–64.

Groes-Green, C. 2014. 'Journeys of Patronage: Moral Economies of Transactional Sex, Kinship, and Female Migration from Mozambique to Europe'. *Journal of the Royal Anthropological Institute* 20: 237–55.

Jeffreys, S. 2010. *The Industrial Vagina: The Political Economy of the Global Sex Trade.* London: Routledge.

Kempadoo, K. 2001. 'Freelancers, Temporary Wives and Beach Boys: Researching Sex Work in the Caribbean'. *Feminist Review* 67: 39–62.

Kristvik, E. 2005. *Sterke hovud og sterke hjarte: Thailandske kvinner på den norske sexmarknaden.* Oslo: Seksjon for medisinsk antropologi, Institutt for allmenn- og samfunnsmedisin.

Mix, P.R., and N. Piper. 2003. 'Does Marriage "Liberate" Women from Sex Work? Thai Women in Germany', in N. Piper and M. Roces (eds), *Wife or Worker? Asian Women and Migration.* Oxford: Rowman & Littlefield, pp. 53–73.

Myong, L. 2008. 'Hvid avantgardemaskulinitet og fantasien om den raciale Anden', in J. Koefoed and Staunæs (eds), *Magtballader: 14 fortællinger om magt, modstand og menneskers tilblivelse.* Copenhagen: Danmarks Pædagogiske Universitetsforlag, pp. 197–220.

Nencel, L. 2001. *Ethnography and Prostitution in Peru.* London: Pluto Press.

New to Denmark. 2017. 'Family Reunification'. Retrieved 29 July 2017 from: https://www.nyidanmark.dk/da-dk/Ophold/familiesammenfoering/

Oso Casas, L. 2010. 'Money, Sex, Love and the Family: Economic and Affective Strategies of Latin American Sex Workers in Spain'. *Journal of Ethnic and Migration Studies* 36(1): 47–65.

Pateman, C. 1988. *The Sexual Contract.* Cambridge and Oxford: Polity Press.

Piscitelli, A. 2008. 'Transits: Brazilian Women Migration in the Context of the Transnationalization of Sex and Marriage Markets.' *Horizontes Antropológicos* 4(se): 11–30.

Read, K. 2013. 'Queering the Brothel: Identity Construction and Performance in Carson City, Nevada'. *Sexualities* 16(3/4): 467–86.

Ruenkaew, P. 2002. 'The Transnational Prostitution of Thai Women to Germany: A Variety of Transnational Labour Migration', in S. Thorbek and B. Pattanaik (eds), *Transnational Prostitution: Changing Global Patterns*. London: Zed Books, pp. 69–85.

Ryan, C., and M.C. Hall. 2001. *Sex Tourism: Marginal People and Liminalities*. London: Routledge.

Spanger, M. 2010. 'Destabilising Sex Work and Intimacy? Gender Performances of Female Thai Migrants Selling Sex in Denmark'. PhD dissertation. Roskilde: Roskilde University.

_____. 2011. 'Human Trafficking as Lever for Feminist Voices? Transformations of the Danish Policy Field of Prostitution'. *Critical Social Policy* 31(4): 496–517.

Statistics Denmark. 2009. www.statistikbanken.dk/BEF3. Retrieved 16 February 2009.

_____. 2016. Indvanderere i Danmark. Danmarks Statistik, November.

_____. 2017a. www.statistikbanken.dk/BEF5. Retrieved 28 July 2017.

_____. 2017b. www.statistikbanken.dk/VAN8. Retrieved 28 July 2017.

_____. 2017c. www.statistikbanken.dk/DB07. Retrieved 28 July 2017.

Suzuki, N. 2004. 'Inside the Home: Power and Negotiation in Filipina–Japanese Marriages'. *Women's Studies* 33: 481–506.

Zelizer, V. 2006. 'Money, Power, and Sex'. *Yale Journal of Law and Feminism* 303, Princeton Law and Public Affairs Working Paper No. 06-009.

PART III
Moralities of Money, Mobility and Intimacy

CHAPTER
7

From *Programas* to Help and Marriage
Transnational Sexual, Economic and Affective Exchanges among Brazilian Women

Adriana Piscitelli

Introduction

On a cold winter morning in 2014, I waited for Veronica, a Brazilian migrant, at the entrance to my hotel in Madrid. I had not seen her for some time. From a lower-middle-class origin, she was the only woman among my interviewees who had not completed college. I had first met her in Barcelona seven years before, when she was a 27-year-old irregular migrant sex worker struggling for 'papers' and hoping to find 'love'. In those days, she offered sexual services in diverse places. Slim, with perfect light skin and dark, curly hair, she was considered highly attractive in the Spanish sex industry. Yet, she was not able to work in the safer venues where only 'legal' migrants worked. Her work as a prostitute had allowed her to make enough money to buy an apartment in Brazil for her mother and sisters, but she had also had a traumatic experience when a client tried to kill her; and that made her decide to abandon sex work – and her income, which ranged between 3,000 and 5,000 euros per month, decreased dramatically. With the mediation of an NGO that supported sex workers' rights, she regularized her migration status and obtained some low paid jobs.

Throughout those years she repeatedly tried to build heterosexual love relationships. Her first boyfriend in Spain was a Catalan. 'It did not work', she said. 'He knew about my work. He had a lot of prejudice regarding Brazil. And in arguments, he brought up that I had been a prostitute.' The second boyfriend was a German with whom she 'fell passionately in love'. The relationship lasted for two years and she suffered a lot. She said that when they argued because he cheated on her, he brought up the issue of prostitution. Since then she had kept her work as a prostitute a secret.

With a Finnish boyfriend, Veronica moved to Madrid and fulfilled her dream of continuing her studies. However, the first months in Madrid became a nightmare. This man turned into a violent person. Leaving him, she found herself with no home, work or money in a city where she knew few people. My meeting with Veronica in Madrid was a couple of months after these events. Over lunch she told me that she was now living with another man, a Spanish professor at her new school. After dating Veronica for a few weeks, this man rented an apartment in order to live with her. This was a relief for Veronica. She said that she liked him, without mentioning love, but highlighting the relevance of his assistance in economic terms and also regarding her studies. When he returned home in the evenings, he helped with her lessons and promised to help her to find what she most wanted: a job as a highly qualified electrician in the construction sector.

Veronica's migratory trajectory synthesizes relevant aspects of the problematic I intend to discuss here: the sexual and economic exchanges in which several Brazilian women with whom I have worked involved themselves. Her story allows us to perceive the coexistence of different modalities of exchanges, not only prostitution but also *ajuda* (help) – a concept broadly disseminated in the lower and lower-middle classes in Brazil. This chapter examines how these exchanges are reconfigured in transnational contexts.

Critical writings about the relationship between global sex markets, tourism and migration (Kempadoo 2004; Cabezas 2009) have revived the anthropological interest in understanding how sociohistoric standards of local organizations of sexuality and emergent norms of sexual and economic exchanges are articulated in encounters between cultures (Sahlins 1990). I extend these frameworks of analysis by addressing the experiences of Brazilian women from the lower and lower-middle classes who entered the transnational sex markets through relationships with foreign tourists in Brazil and in their migratory trajectories in Southern Europe.[1] I consider how economic practices, sex and affection are articulated in the trajectories of these women, exploring the effects of the insertion in the transnational realm in these imbrications. I analyse these effects by considering shifting and interrelated modalities of intimacy and exchange.

In the Brazilian public debate, the insertion of lower-class women in the transnational sexual economies, by means either of sexual and economic exchanges with foreign tourists in Brazil or of Brazilian migrants' sex work abroad, has been frequently perceived as connected to sex trafficking (Senado Federal 2011). Some of the academic studies on these topics share this perception. In line with feminist approaches that consider the practices involved in these economies as new forms of sexual exploitation (Barry 1997), some studies consider that they restate a sexual violence that has affected Brazilian women since the colonial period (Oliveira 2011). However, a growing body of scholarship takes an opposing view that instead highlights how these economies offer fresh possibilities of agency in Brazil, and also in Brazilian migrants' trajectories abroad (Teixeira 2008; Silva, Blanchette and Bento 2013; Piscitelli 2013).

In this chapter, I take a different approach. Considering the dimensions of violence present in the dynamics of transnational sexual economies and the options for agency, I shift the focus from this debate by dialoguing with theories of exchange, affects and materialities. Adopting a sociohistoric perspective, my main argument is that the sexual, economic and affective exchanges in which these Brazilian women involved themselves are reconfigurations of practices and notions that are found in new scenarios. In the movement between social and cultural contexts in Brazil and Europe, these practices, located between 'traditional' and new forms of exchanges, change and acquire new meanings regarding the ways in which they 'improve' the women's lives. Notions of affection are relevant in order to understand these changes.

I begin by describing the ethnography conducted, and outline how different sexual-economic exchanges are formed and perceived in the Brazilian context. Then I analyse the different modalities of sexual-economic exchanges enacted by these women, and discuss how these exchanges are altered in transnational scenarios in Southern Europe. In conclusion, after showing how these different exchanges between Brazilian women and European men are reconfigurations of long-standing incorporated dispositions, I explain how, in spite of risks and occasional violence, the women preferred new modalities to 'traditional' exchanges.

An Ethnography of Brazilian Women within a Transnational Sexual Economy

In Brazil, as in other countries of Latin America and the Caribbean whose histories were marked by colonial relationships and slave regimes (Kempadoo 2004; Padilla 2007), there is a long history of interpenetration between economics and sexuality. Historians and anthropologists who have analysed these interpenetrations in different historical moments and contexts in Brazil, show how sexual and economic exchanges appear to be rooted in inequalities that activate – depending on the context – various distinctions, articulating gender, social class, race and, in certain periods marked by migration, nationality (Fonseca 1997; Schettini 2006).

These interpenetrations began to stir my interest at the turn of this century, when I initiated my fieldwork in the tourist circuits of Fortaleza, the capital city of Ceará State in north-eastern Brazil. At that time, this city, in one of the most impoverished regions of the country, with marked social class divisions, beautiful beaches, busy nightlife and a sudden explosion of international tourism, was considered one of the new centres of 'sex tourism'[2] in Brazil. The intensification of sexual encounters between poor young local women and foreign men, mainly from European countries, raised intense concern. These encounters in beaches, bars and boats by the seaside were read as a manifestation of the increase in prostitution linked to international tourism, and as a risk for women, since they were seen as posing the danger of sex trafficking.

In such tourist settings, there were different modalities of sexual and economic exchanges, marked by diverse modes of commodification. Some of these exchanges related to local concepts of prostitution. These stigmatized practices coexisted with others that involved exchanges of sex for gifts and material benefits, but were not considered prostitution by the women. The latter were, to a certain point, evaluated positively, particularly when they facilitated social mobility. The establishment of new forms of exchanges with foreign visitors changed these practices (Piscitelli 2007). The reconfiguration of these exchanges in transnational realms was delineated with even greater clarity when I turned my focus to Brazilian women in the sexual economies in Southern Europe.

The fieldwork conducted in Fortaleza was the initial phase of a multi-sited ethnography (Marcus 1995), the objective of which was understanding the dynamics and conceptualizations involved in the integration of Brazil into transnational sex markets. During my later fieldwork in Milan, I traced the paths of various women whom I had met in Fortaleza and who had married Italians that they had met in the 'sex tourism' circuits of that city (Piscitelli 2008a). Finally, I researched migrant Brazilians in highly commodified spaces of the sex industry of Spain, mainly in Barcelona. In both settings I ended up exploring the articulation between transnational sex and marriage markets (Piscitelli 2008b).

I followed these women's paths during forty-two months between 2000 and 2017. In this chapter, I use as a basic reference the trajectory of thirty-eight women, several of whom I accompanied during various years.

During the fieldwork periods,[3] I shared part of their everyday lives. I spent time with them in their work spaces, sitting with them in the living rooms and kitchens of in-call flats, helping them to prepare the bedrooms for the next client, or chatting and walking with them on the streets while they waited for clients. I visited some in the headquarters of the sex workers' organizations and accompanied them on political demonstrations, such as the acts of 'Prostitutas Indignadas' in Barcelona. However, I mostly hung out with them in their leisure time, when we went out or else I visited them in their homes.

These women come from various regions of Brazil and they range in age from twenty to fifty. They belong to what are considered the lower and lower-middle classes in this country, taking into account income, years of schooling, and 'colour'. Yet, they are not affected by higher degrees of inequality and are distant from the population that in Brazil is considered to be below the poverty line. In Brazil, the women with whom I worked had had various occupations with low salaries. However, most of them received between one and two minimum wages, with incomes between 270 and 380 euros. They lived in relatively poor neighbourhoods, sometimes in suburbs relatively distant from the city centre, but not in shanty towns. Although some had only completed elementary school, most initiated high school, having at least eight years of schooling, while one also had some higher education. This means that, when I started my research studies, these women had studied for more years than the average of the population. And while in their migratory trajectories they all felt affected by European racial criteria, in Brazil only four women considered themselves to be black or mulatta. The rest perceived themselves as white or *morena* (light brown), categories of 'colour' that are not racialized in derogative terms.

In the circulation between different locations, I perceived how several of these women shifted between one and another modality of sexual and economic exchange, and I also realized how the distinctions between these interchanges altered. These modalities and the distinctions between them tend to be delineated based on the differences associated to two local concepts: *programas* (which roughly translates as 'tricks') and *ajuda* (help, assistance).

Programas and *Ajuda*: Interchanging Modalities of Sexual-Material Exchange

In Brazil, the expression *programa* is a generic term that alludes to prostitution, in the sense of explicit agreements of sexual services for money (Gaspar 1985), involving delimited practices and time periods, which can have different economic values. The *programas* are conducted in different spaces such as apartments, brothels or massage parlours, with different degrees of organization. Some sex work takes place through intermediaries (in some cases called pimps or madams) and some takes place without.

Studies about prostitution in different parts of Brazil show that these modalities of sexual and economic exchanges can involve affection and pleasure, which might promote displacements in the relationships between people who, at the beginning of the encounters, were prostitutes and clients but who may later become lovers or married couples (Olivar 2010; França 2011). However, one of the current ideas dominating the realm of prostitution is that professionalism involves avoiding love and pleasure in the relationships with the clients (Leite 1992).

Ajuda is a broadly used concept in Brazil and also among Brazilian migrants abroad. Among people of the lower and middle classes, this concept refers to economic contributions that, although considered important, do not constitute the main source of resources for subsistence (Gregg 2006). *Ajuda* is frequently exchanged for sex and is often linked to affection. While the concept *programa* evokes a contract for sexual services, *ajuda*, inserted in a tradition of hierarchical exchanges (Fonseca 1996; Rebhun 1999), is related to notions of support, care and affection that are expressed in terms of contributions to economic survival and consumption.

There are different modalities of *ajuda*, which tend to involve men and women in unequal positions, in terms of class or at least of access to economic resources, and often regarding age and 'colour' also. One of these traditional forms is the relationship between a young woman and an older and wealthy man, who provides money and other types of goods. The 'old man who helps' (*ajuda*) is a recognized means of social mobility (Fonseca 1996; Goldstein 2003).

In Fortaleza, the figure of the 'old man who helps' was repeatedly highlighted in the local narratives. In the summer of 2002, I was hanging out with one fifty-seven-year-old Brazilian man who introduced me to a group of married middle-class friends, retired, with monthly incomes around or above 2,000 euros, with whom he met daily at the beach. He commented about the *meninas* (girls), the poor young women who received *ajuda* from these men: 'In this land, age does not count for men. Look at my group, the youngest is fifty, the oldest is seventy-nine. All are married and also have girls, who are twenty, twenty-two. They are good to them, care for them, give them money' (Fortaleza, August 2002).

The monetary value of the presents and the quantities of money that the women receive vary according to the social class and the material resources of the man, as well as the degree of involvement in the relationship. The modalities of sexual and economic exchange encompassed in this category are not stigmatized like prostitution. And a greater degree of respectability is reached when *ajuda* results in a stable relationship, as when 'the old men who help' turn into stable long-term lovers of lower-class women. These men do not come to sustain their lovers' homes, but help to alleviate poverty over long periods, offering diverse material benefits to the women, such as the payment of their rent and medical bills (Paim 1998).

In exchange for *ajuda*, the women offer sex, company and at times domestic care, and this is frequently connected with affection. The presence of what various authors consider to be expressions of romantic love (Illouz 2007) is perceptible in the symbolic universe of the women with whom I worked, challenging the boundary that some researchers draw to separate this form of emotion from the universes of the Brazilian lower classes (Gregg 2006). Notions related to romantic love, such as spontaneity, intensity, passion – in the sense of an uncontrollable not rationally chosen feeling that appears in an encounter with the person of one's dreams – are expressed by the women with whom I worked in terms such as: 'I lost my head, to be in love'. This feeling is sometimes present in the realm of *ajuda*. Nevertheless, the affection linked to this modality of exchange is frequently expressed in other terms, particularly *respeito* (respect) and consideration. Lisette, a light-skinned twenty-eight-year-old hairdresser with long curly hair, was from Fortaleza; she had nine years of schooling and an income of around 350 euros a month. After a divorce, she had managed to open a small beauty salon in one of the rooms of her house in a poor suburb of Fortaleza with the *ajuda* of a fifty-six-year-old married man. She explained to me that she always sought to have affairs with people of means who could support her. Regarding this particular man, she said: 'My business with him is not love. He is a pleasant person, I respect him, he has helped me a lot, and I admire him, but I am not in love with him' (Fortaleza, January 2001).

It is important to observe that *respeito*, present in these sexual and economic exchanges, is also considered an integral part of the constitution of the low-income families by studies conducted in various parts of Brazil. According to scholars in this field, among women of these lower social strata, the term *respeito* alludes to social obligations to sustain families, and it can be given priority in relation to *prazer* (pleasure) (Duarte 1987). In some understandings of these social strata, the interpenetrations between sentiments and economic practices are frequently expressed in notions of affection and consideration, which involve various economic transactions considered as gifts – the provision of food, clothes, access to credit, and employment opportunities (Paim 1998; Rebhun 2006). Yet, in the trajectories of the women with whom I worked, love/passion and respect/consideration, as well as *programas* and *ajuda*, are not necessarily exclusive or static categories.

In recent decades, various studies have questioned the rigid separations and oppositions between gifts and market economies, and the fixed character conceded to goods (Appadurai 1986; Godbout 1999). In an attempt to overcome these oppositions, readings such as those of Appadurai broaden the notion of commodity, considering that many different types of things, including sex, have the potential to become goods in specific moments and situations, in the realm of different modalities of exchanges that vary in the form and intensity of sociality associated to them. The coexistence and the shift between *ajuda* and *programas* found in this universe contribute to dialogue with these readings, problematizing these oppositions in the dominion of sexual and economic exchanges that embrace prostitution as well as other modalities of sexual and economic exchanges.

A number of the women in the study had never conducted a *programa*, but had received *ajuda* from one or more men. Those who considered themselves to work as prostitutes (*garotas de programa*) had established, with a certain frequency, relationships based on one or another mode of exchange. A relationship initiated as a *programa* can, over time, become a relationship of *ajuda*. And a relationship of *ajuda*, initiated within or outside the realm of prostitution, can become long lasting, and even lead to marriage, although it is not common when the partners are Brazilians.

Referring to feelings, relationships that begin with no emotional attachment can lead to respect, or to love. On this point, the considerations of Hunter (2010) related to the interlacing of emotional and material practices and to the places of the birth of love, have echoes in the universe of my interviewees. According to the author, emotional and material practices are always interlinked and, in this sense, sex and love are always material. In contexts of poverty, love can rarely be separated from a world of dependencies. Among my interviewees, the feelings connected with *ajuda* become more understandable, considering that this modality of exchange creates obligations and offers certain support for the women – and frequently, also, for other members of their families. And when *ajuda* is long lasting, and the people become attached, it becomes a 'place' of production of emotional ties.

Asymmetrical Sexual and Economic Exchanges

The fact that the exchanges considered as *ajuda* are distinguished from prostitution in the local conceptualizations is important. The relevance resides not only in that this distinction relates to different styles of commodification among sexual and economic exchanges, but also that it relates to distinctions in the socialities involved, which, in the case of *ajuda*, evokes relationships of reciprocity.

Ajuda calls to mind notions of transactional sex (Kempadoo 2004; Hunter 2010). However, I am hesitant to rely on this notion. The conceptualization of (heterosexual) transactional sex has been criticized for highlighting how women's sexuality is commodified, not taking into account the power of female eroticism or how this power connects to kinship, gender dynamics, and moralities of exchange (Groes-Green 2013). Agreeing with this criticism, I would like to call attention to another problematic dimension of the use of this concept: how it contributes to exoticize 'others'.

Transactional sex is a concept almost exclusively used to allude to sexual and economic exchanges in 'poor'/'non-Western' countries. In a production of knowledge in which only people from some sexualized 'poor' countries are connected with these exchanges, this concept takes part in delineating ethno-sexual frontiers (Nagel 2000) that participate in the construction of global hierarchies between nations. And in the debate about sexual and economic exchanges in Brazil, the notion of transactional sex participates in the production of hierarchies between the upper and middle classes (that supposedly are not involved in such exchanges) and the lower sexualized and racialized classes. Yet, analyses of heterosexual and homosexual sexual, economic and affective exchanges in different parts of the country allow us to perceive that these practices are disseminated in different social classes (Piscitelli 2007; Araújo 2015; Passamani 2015).

Taking into account the problems posed by the notion of transactional sex, Groes-Green (2014) takes an interesting analytical path. Considering how young Mozambican women's migratory trajectories towards Europe are shaped by sexual relationships with older white men and obligations towards female kin, the author understands these relationships through theories of patronage and moralities of exchange.

Categories connected with the concept of patronage (*coronelismo/clientelismo*) are relevant in sociohistorical and anthropological analyses about the political and economic organization in Brazil (de Carvalho 1997). These categories allude to patron–client relationships that, conceived as systems of asymmetrical personal exchange, refer to redistributive processes outside the state and to formal economic institutions, intimately connected with the operation of kinship groups. *Clientelismo* has been considered as a structuring political principle in the country that declined after the first decades of the twentieth century, in the process of expansion of the political arena and of the economy (Kuznesof 1988). In spite of this, some authors consider that in Brazil social status and personal relationships continued having enormous meaning in the ways in which people are perceived and resources are distributed (da Matta 1978).

In the contexts in which I worked in Brazil, the notion of *clientelismo* does not adequately convey my interviewees' lives. Although they did not consider their jobs to be well paid or the government's social programmes to be sufficient for their needs and desires, most of them had access to employment and to public policies without depending on patrons. And a few among them also had strong notions of rights associated to their participation in sex workers' organizations. Simultaneously, in order to 'improve' their lives and fulfil a broader range of desires and needs, involving luxury goods and migratory projects, in the area of intimate relationships they recreated the 'tradition' of hierarchical sexual and economic exchanges that involved loyalties, obligations and reciprocity.

The trajectories of these inteviewees allow us to perceive that the transnationalization of the sex markets has changed the practices and meanings linked to sexual and economic exchanges. In Fortaleza, in the frame of the new possibilities of social mobility and of migration associated with foreign tourists, these relationships acquired new traces. These sexual, economic and affective exchanges were also recreated in these women's migratory trajectories abroad. However, they were differently reconfigured in the South European contexts in which the women's social positions were marked by a more intense precariousness, in spite of the possibility of making more money than in Brazil, particularly when they worked in the sex industry. And, as in the Groes-Green (2014) analysis about the relationships of women from Mozambique with European men, the interchanges between the Brazilian women with whom I worked and their partners were connected with specific moralities of exchange. The emotions associated to these exchanges allude to their alterations in transnational realms.

Reconfigurations in Touristic Scenarios

In the tourist circuits in Fortaleza, relations of *ajuda* involving poor young women and/or those considered to have darker skin and foreign visitors also come to be seen as prostitution and are therefore stigmatized by broader parts of society. Local definitions of prostitution have expanded, encompassing not just sexual practices, but social agents: women with skin that is seen as darker or who embody a sexualized and racialized poverty in the company of foreign male white tourists and who often 'invade' the leisure spaces of the local middle classes, interrupting the territorial segregation of the city. On the contrary, for the foreign visitors, the dissemination of these exchanges and the characteristics assumed by the *programas* make it difficult to see them as prostitution, which wound up being restricted to only a few modalities of *programas*.

The transnational sex markets provide the contact between different sexual and emotional habitus. The foreign men who have intimate relationships with Brazilian women in Fortaleza are marked by heterogeneity in terms of class, age and nationality. These women do not constitute a homogeneous universe either, since women in their twenties, thirties and forties, locally seen as white or *morenas* from the lower but also the middle classes, were interested in the foreign visitors. Nevertheless, without generalizing, it is possible to perceive how these encounters bring together people with differentiated readings and expectations in relation to the codes of interaction, corporality and affection, and also in terms of sexual and economic exchanges.

This point is relevant, considering the readings that allocate different paradigms of prostitution to the 'Third World' and to 'the West' (Bernstein 2007). These approaches trace differences in styles of using the body, and in the spaces and emotions between 'premodern', 'modern' and 'postindustrial' paradigms. Although I do not intend to allocate evolutionist temporalities between 'First' and 'Third' world, it seems to me important to note that in the transnational sex markets, the coexistence of diverse 'sexual cultures', moralities and different modalities of commodified sex that involve distinct interpersonal dynamics and styles of connection between eroticism and emotions, jumble these paradigms.

In the transnational tourism circuits of Fortaleza, paradigms of prostitution are mixed and also confused with modalities of sexual and economic exchanges that are not seen as prostitution by the women involved in them. The foreigners become confused, by reading the corporality of the women and the interactions that they have with them from their own sexual and emotional habitus, and by considering the differences between these interactions and styles of prostitution that they know in their places of origin.

In this realm, the realization of *programas* takes on new connotations. Some 'professionalized' sex workers do not change their practices. But, in the fluidity that marks the tourist circuits in the city, adapting to the foreign visitors, some young women who conduct *programas* opt to not establish time limits or stipulate the cost of the exchange, considering that in this way they can earn more money from the foreigners. Lisette, the hairdresser, who after having several relationships of *ajuda* with local men started to look for foreign tourists, explained that it was necessary to play with those things, to be like a correct, difficult girl. And then she told me about the outcomes of that behaviour, which materialized in the money she got from an Italian man:

> Considering everything he's sent, it's more or less about three thousand euros. But, because I was smart, nearly every time he called me I asked

> for money – two hundred, three hundred euros. Ah, I'm sick. I, I broke a leg. I have a problem in my breast. I used up nearly all the illnesses... So I never charged for a *programa*. He thinks I'm the most correct woman in the world. (Fortaleza, February 2002)

In this scenario, the spatial and corporal limits and the use of invented names found in the traditional forms of *programa* are blurred. The distinctions between the spaces for *programas* and for private life are erased when the young women take the visitors to their homes and to those of their families, as well as, at times, the restriction of feelings. A sweet, slim eighteen-year-old girl, with light complexion and short dark hair, told me about the man with whom she was in love at that moment. She had eight years of schooling and an income of approximately four hundred euros per month, and considered herself to be a *garota de programa*. She had started dating foreigners when she was sixteen, dreaming of marriage:

> This Russian is the love of my life – an old man, but I never liked boys. He is blond, with light eyes. He travels once a month, for work, and spends two or three days in Fortaleza. At the hotel [where we stay], everyone knows me. He says that it's our home. I am very upset when he goes away, and he is concerned about this, and says I shouldn't get like that. (Fortaleza, January 2001)

In these tourist circuits, these blurred arrangements obscure the borders between modalities of exchanges, between the *programas* and the styles of *ajuda* established by young women who substitute the figure of 'the local old man who helps' for 'foreign tourists', who are at times younger, perceived as more attractive than the local potential suppliers of *ajuda* and as offering more care, which is expressed in a broadening of economic support.

The benefits linked to these foreigners are not limited to money. In intimate encounters with them, the exchanges come to simultaneously involve care, sexual pleasure, and possibilities for trips abroad. In some cases they also lead to marriage, which is much more common with foreign men than with the local men from higher classes with whom they also had sexual liaisons. The latter usually engaged in those exchanges with poorer, younger women, in parallel with marriages to women from their own social class.

Circulating with foreigners in their own neighbourhoods exposed the women to stigmatization as prostitutes, including by their families, relatives and acquaintances, since the common view was that foreign visitors were only with them in search of sex. However, the stigma was neutralized if a relationship was long lasting and offered material resources that were redistributed within the family, but mainly supporting the women's children, their mothers and sometimes also young brothers and sisters.

In the accounts about the sexual encounters in these transnational scenarios, scenarios the notions linked to romantic love appear with greater frequency. Karla was a cheerful twenty-four year-old *Morena*. She was a single mother who had given birth when she was fourteen and had started to date foreigners while working as a waitress in the main disco where tourists in search of sex and local women met, providing her with a monthly income of 450 euros. She told me about her relationship with a Dutch tourist whom she believed would allow her to realize her dream of migrating to Europe:

> When I saw him, I [thought] 'This man, I could eat him up!' He's big and strong... just uses white clothes, a white shirt... I fell deeper in love every day, you know? I didn't see anyone, just him! I left everything behind [for him] ... That day he waited for me until [I had left work] in the morning. Then he took me home and told me he loved me... He said 'Do you want to come to my house [in Europe]? I said 'I do!'. He replied: 'So, get a passport – I will send you money for you to get one'. (Fortaleza, February 2002)

The attraction that the foreign men have for these women cannot be separated from the fascination provoked by the contact with the idealized differences attributed to the 'rich' and 'white' worlds that they represent. This attraction is expressed in the aestheticization of these countries and their inhabitants, racialized as white, and in the emphasis and respect for their styles of masculinity, perceived as more egalitarian than those of the local men, with a strong importance given to the care they are seen to have. This idea of care was precisely the key that operated in the foreigners' substitution of the 'local old man who helps'. These relationships could lead to migration and marriage but, with a certain recurrency, they also disappointed the women. Occasionally, sometime after leaving Fortaleza, the foreign tourists would 'abandon' the girls, interrupting their phone calls and remittances of money. And sometimes they changed their minds regarding their invitations to visit them in Europe and/or their marriage proposals.

On some occasions, after spending some time in their own countries, the men considered that what they felt for the women was not sufficient for them to be willing to face the difficulties posed by the differences that are present in these relationships. Karla, the waitress from Fortaleza, visited her Dutch boyfriend in Holland and stayed with him for three months. Fascinated with her experience abroad, she returned to Fortaleza in order to do the necessary paperwork in order to marry him – however, a month later he told her that they were not going to marry anymore. With a broken heart and feeling depressed, Karla explained that he had said that, after she left, he had realized that although she was very good in bed, he wanted to marry a woman from his own country, with a similar education (Fortaleza, January 2002).

In this context, the relationships with foreign tourists, which in the perception of a number of my interviewees offered more material resources, fun, pleasure and 'future' (in the sense of long-term material possibilities) also posed risks. Two of my interviewees from Fortaleza had rough times in the hands of their foreign boyfriends: one was kept in a private prison and the other one was almost strangled. But in the majority of the cases, the risks were mostly emotional. Yet, going beyond the failures and successes of these relationships, the point that I would like to highlight is that in this transnational scenario the alterations and relative blurring in sexual and economic exchanges were accompanied by a more intense presence of 'love', which was mentioned as being connected with both *programas* and *ajuda*. And 'love', a feeling anchored in materialities but also associated with the idea of a certain egalitarianism, evoked the transformations in both modalities of exchange.

Alterations in Migratory Contexts: *Programas* and *Ajuda* in Southern Europe

In the highly organized sectors of commercial sex in Spain, among the women with whom I worked, the notion of *programa* was also reconfigured. But in this context, it brought to mind the idea of a contract for services in a much more restricted manner than in the versions found in Brazil. This was particularly evident in the clubs that had a high concentration of sex workers, where Brazilian migrants competed for clients with women from various nationalities, following norms in relation to hours, the time to occupy a space, the minutes to be used in the realization of the *programas*, the range of sexual services and the payment attributed to each of them.

The difference in the style of work, compared with Brazil, however, was not necessarily perceived as negative. For example, I interviewed a twenty-two-year-old *morena*, with eleven years of schooling, who had migrated to Spain from the 'sex tourism' circuits of Natal, a city in north-eastern Brazil where she had had an income of only around 400 euros a month. She came to work in a club in Bilbao where she obtained around 3,500 euros per month. Also, in Brazil she would spend all night with one man, whereas in Bilbao it was only twenty minutes. She thought that was a good thing because she did not get tired of the men anymore: 'Like, you are with a person who you don't like, an old fat guy. To spend the night with this man would be horrible... but with a few men, no, you find one more handsome, another more pleasant – it changes' (Bilbao, November 2004).

In this style of *programas*, a number of Brazilian sex workers considered the embodiment of an affectionate (*carinhoso*) style of relationship to be important, to affirm and give value to a national specificity, in the competition for clients. And Spanish clients from the middle layers of prostitution appreciated this affectionate style. By performing this loving style of relationship, anchored in 'care' for the men, some women converted their clients, or other frequenters of the spaces in which they provided sexual services, into men who 'helped them'. A few even ended up marrying the men as a result of these intimate interactions.

In such cases, *ajuda* was sometimes provided by a man who had been met outside the realm of prostitution. The Internet, where contacts with clients can be made on specific websites designed for romantic relationships, also allows obtaining *ajuda*. In February 2011, I conducted repeated visits to an in-call apartment in Barcelona where sexual services were being offered. Here I met two Brazilian women who had recently begun prostitution, after having lost their jobs – one as a waitress, the other one as nanny – believed to be a result of Spain's economic crisis. They told me about the possibilities of 'netdating'. One of them had met an Italian through a dating site. She mentioned her debts to the man, told him about the economic difficulties she was facing, and her need to send money to her daughter in Brazil. The Italian man almost immediately began to send her money. The first time he transferred 200 euros. A few weeks later, another 100 euros. Only then did he go to meet her in Spain and, while spending time together, visiting tourist spots in Barcelona, they had sex. When I interviewed the woman, she explained that this arrangement was not a *programa* but only *ajuda*, because in contrast to the tricks she performed in the apartment, she was not offering sexual services. Sex and money were part of a broader relationship.

In the migratory contexts of Southern Europe, *ajuda* often takes on different connotations from those found in Brazil. Sometimes, it involves economic benefits. However, it also relates to obtaining the various resources needed for the incorporation in these contexts. It is worth noting that, in the period before the economic crisis in Southern Europe, some of the women I interviewed who offered sexual services had considerably higher incomes than those of some of the European men who 'helped' them. But being with these men gave them the advantage of knowing a person who was allowed to sign rent and housing contracts – something they could not do, being without papers or citizenship. Also, the men were often able to help those women who wanted to leave prostitution to find work in other sectors. And *ajuda* could involve marriages that allowed the regularization of their migratory status.

Olivia, a fifty-year-old Brazilian migrant in Barcelona, was a plump blonde woman with large buttocks, light skin and lively green eyes. With eleven years of schooling, she was offering sexual services in the streets of the Raval where, before the economic crisis in Spain, she had earned around 4,000 euros per month. She told me about her marriage to a good-humoured waiter from Andalusia during a lunch that both had offered me at their apartment. She told me that when she met him she was working and living in what she considered an expensive hotel, paying nearly 400 euros per month for a very small room. Laughing, she said that when they started dating she went to his house one day and thought: this is where I want to live to share expenses and everything. And then he fell in love and called her to live with him. Since they lived happily together he said: 'To help you, we'll get married and you will get papers'. And one year later they got married (Barcelona, February 2009).

The category *ajuda* also relates to the economic contribution that the partners offer to sustain members of the families of my interviewees in Brazil. Karla, the waitress from Fortaleza who fell in love with a Dutch tourist who then 'abandoned' her, later on married an Italian man whom she had met in the tourist circuits of Fortaleza, and they moved to Milan. She told me that her husband had promised that he would send money to her daughter in Brazil every month, and he never failed to do so. On the 15th of every month he sent her 200 euros (Milan, April 2004).

For several of the women I met in Spain and Italy, *ajuda* also implied affection. Sometimes the emotional ties produced in these relationships related to love (*amor*), but mostly, as in the 'traditional' *ajuda* relationships I found in Fortaleza, to respect (*respeito*). Sometimes romantic love appears in stories about relationships with European men. This can be illustrated with the story of Veronica, the Brazilian migrant in Spain with whose story I started the chapter. Telling me about the end of the relationship with her German boyfriend, she explained that she had suffered so much from love that she felt she had 'nearly died'. She could not eat, it hurt her so much (Barcelona, November 2009).

Judging from my interviews in Barcelona, there seems to be a tendency among some Brazilian sex workers in Southern Europe to expect that relationships based on love will not work, due to specific tensions they have experienced in love affairs that have begun in clubs or with clients met in the sex industry. Among the few who have longer lasting relationships, intimate ties are frequently described through notions of respect, fed by gratefulness for the contributions of support and the recognition of opportunities provided. Explaining her feelings for her husband, the waiter from Andalusia, Olivia told me: 'See how it is? He's good. I am good to him, although I am not in love. But love passes, he is good, he is happy... he likes parties, and is a good partner' (Barcelona, February 2010).

In the story of one of the interviewees who left the ambiguous transnational sex markets in Fortaleza to marry in Italy, respect turned into love. In 2004, Karla told me that initially she had 'respected' her husband. He had supported her in Italy and her daughter in Fortaleza, and she was entirely faithful, took care of him and was grateful for the opportunities he gave her – marrying her, introducing her into his family, and finding her a job (Milan, April 2004). But, later on, when she got pregnant and felt surrounded by an intensified care from her husband and his family, her feelings again started to change. Since her youngest child was born, in 2006, and maternity consolidated her status as a member in her husband's kinship group, she has declared herself to be passionately in love with her husband – something she constantly reiterates in her Facebook posts.

Considering my interviewees' narratives, Karla's experience, with a marriage relationship perceived as successful, leading from 'respect' to 'love', is singular. In the reconfigurations of the sexual, economic and affective exchanges that take place in these migratory contexts, 'love' is far from appearing with the recurrence it had in the tourism circuits of Fortaleza. In that city, this feeling acquired relevance in the frame of the blurring of boundaries between modalities of exchange, associated to the illusion of marrying and migrating.

In the migratory contexts in Southern Europe, in which the frontiers between *programas* and *ajuda* are clearly delineated, the experiences of a number of my interviewees, particularly those engaged in the sex industry in Spain, have led them to disappointments regarding the potential strength of 'love' to neutralize the effects of the stigma associated with prostitution in their intimate relationships. In this frame, for several of them 'respect' – perceived as a feeling with less emotional intensity, associated with help involving diversified benefits and protection – reappears as one of the predominant sentiments.

Final Considerations

The trajectories of my interviewees suggest that with the transnationalization of sex markets, the modalities of sexual and economic exchanges are altered in diverse ways. And the shifting styles of affection are related with these changes. Some women move from *programas* in Brazil, conducted on a cottage scale, to sexual and economic exchanges in the European sex industry that require more intensive work, but that offer much higher incomes than in Brazil. In the tourist circuits of Fortaleza, sometimes the lines between prostitution and other sexual and economic exchanges are blurred. Regarding *ajuda*, in this city, some women shift from sexual and economic exchanges aimed at survival and consumption with local partners to a style of help offered by foreign visitors that enlarges the possibilities to improve life in Brazil, and also contributes to delineating a plan to leave the country and become part of the sexual economy in Southern Europe. And in the migratory processes of several interviewees in Italy and Spain, *ajuda* is reconfigured in a different way, offering resources for a better insertion in those contexts. Finally, the stories of various women with whom I worked point to shifts between the styles of affection linked to *programas* and *ajuda* that are part of these reconfigurations.

In the tourism circuits of Fortaleza, there is a relative intensification of the notions related to 'romantic love' connected both to *programas* and *ajuda*. For several of my interviewees in that city, this style of love is frequently regarded as an ideal feeling, endowed with the capacity of surpassing inequalities. Notwithstanding, in the case of a number my interviewees in Spain and Italy, the predominant feeling regarding *ajuda* is 'respect'. However, in these cases, differently from what happens in exchanges in the sexual economy in Fortaleza, feelings of respect and consideration are valued as positive choices that for some women open the best ways to materialize their broad range of desires and needs.

Some authors who analyse how the imbrication between economic practices and intimate social relations affecting North–South relationships is experienced by those involved in them, consider the relational possibilities of love. In Simoni's (2012) analysis of the relationships between Cubans and foreign visitors, for the participants of transnational encounters, love might open ways for being together in what they perceived as shared social worlds that were not dominated by material concerns and structural inequalities.

The imbrications between material benefits and feelings present in the economic, sexual and affective exchanges analysed in this chapter point to other possibilities. The acknowledgement of inequalities connected to nationality, class, race and gender, combined with the desire to 'improve one's life', are central aspects of several of the relationships my interviewees established in transnational spaces. But this combination frequently operates as a place of production of feelings, of attachments, and sometimes also of (romantic) 'love'.

Adriana Piscitelli is a feminist social anthropologist, professor at the University of Campinas (Brazil), National Science Research Council researcher (CNPq/Brazil), and associate coordinator of the State University of Campinas Centre for Gender Studies – PAGU. She has been a recipient of Ford, MacArthur, Guggenheim and Rockefeller foundations' awards.

She has published diverse articles, including 'Windsurfers, Capoeiristas and Musicians: Brazilian Masculinities in Transnational Scenarios', in *Masculinities under Neoliberalism*, edited by Andrea Cornwall, Frank Karioris and Nancy Lindisfarne (Zed Books, 2016), and 'Erotics, Love and Violence: European Women's Travels in the Northeast of Brazil', in *Gender, Place and Culture: A Journal of Feminist Geography* (2015).

NOTES

1. I focus the analysis on the experiences of Brazilians from the lower classes. This empirical focus is due to the fact that the women of these social classes have been the most affected by suspicions of involvement in 'sex tourism' and with the sex industry abroad, and thus compose the most important target group of the industry of recovery, and who are marked by victimization, according to discourses by Brazilian and international media and NGOs (Agustín 2005).
2. I use this expression between quotes, considering that, in Brazil, it has become an 'emic' category, linked to prostitution, and above all to the commercial sexual exploitation of children and adolescents.
3. I conducted a total of twenty months of fieldwork in 2000–2008 and 2016–2017 in Fortaleza. The initial fieldwork involved intense ethnographic work, combining observation, non-structured conversations, and in-depth interviews wth ninety-six men and women, both foreign and local, involved in transnational relationships, and agents linked by their work to tourism, sex work and human trafficking in Ceará State. I conducted research in Italy from May to July 2004, and I re-encountered some of the couples that I had interviewed while in Italy on holiday in Fortaleza in 2005 and 2006, and in Milan in 2016. The ethnographic work in Italy encompassed in-depth interviews with twenty-five people, including Brazilian women who had migrated through tourist circuits in Fortaleza, their Italian husbands, and key people linked to non-governmental organizations dedicated to working against prostitution and trafficking, and agents of the Brazilian Consulate in Milan. The research phase in Spain took place between 2004 and 2015 in Madrid, Bilbao, Granada and (mainly) Barcelona, and included interviews with fifty-seven people: Brazilian women and transvestites who offer sexual services, clients, owners of prostitution establishments, and agents linked to various support entities for migrants and/or sex workers.

REFERENCES

Agustín, L. 2005. *Trabajar en la industria del sexo, y otros tópicos migratorios*. Donosti: Tercera Prensai.

Appadurai, A. (ed.). 1986 *The Social Life of Things: Commodities in Cultural Perspective*. Cambridge: Cambridge University Press.

Araújo, A.P. Moreira de. 2015. 'O trabalho de promotora de eventos'. Paper presented at the XIth Reuniao de antropologia do Mercosul, Montevideo.

Barry, K. 1997. 'Prostitution of Sexuality: A Cause for New International Human Rights'. *Journal of Loss and Trauma* 2(1): 27-48.

Bernstein, E. 2007. *Temporarily Yours: Intimacy, Authenticity and the Commerce of Sex*. Chicago, IL: The University of Chicago Press.

Cabezas, A. 2009. *Economies of Desire: Sex and Tourism in Cuba and the Dominican Republic*. Philadelphia, PA: Temple University Press.

Carvalho, J.M. de. 1997. 'Mandonismo, Coronelismo, Clientelismo: Uma Discussão Conceitual'. *Dados* [online] 40(2) [cited 12 January 2016]. Available at http://www.scielo.br/scielo.php?script=sci_arttext&pid=S0011-52581997000200003&lng=en&nrm=iso. ISSN 1678-4588.

Duarte, L. Fernando Dias. 1987. 'Pouca vergonha, muita vergonha: sexo e moralidade entre as classes trabalhadoras urbanas', in José Sérgio Leite Lopes (ed.), *Cultura e Identidade Operária: aspectos da cultura das classes trabalhadoras*. Rio de Janeiro: UFRJ/Marco Zero, pp. 203-26.

Fonseca, C. 1996. 'A dupla carreira da mulher prostituta'. *Revista Estudos Feministas* 1: pp. 7-33.

_____. 1997. 'Ser mulher, mãe e pobre', in Mary Del Priore (ed.), *História das Mulheres no Brasil*. São Paulo: Editora Unesp, Editora contexto, pp. 510-53.

França, Marina Veiga. Dentro de fora do programa: interações afetivo-sexuais de prostitutas da zona boêmia de Belo Horizonte. Paper presented at the *35º Encontro Anual da ANPOCS*, Caxambu-MG, October, 2011.

Gaspar, M.D. 1985. *Garotas de programa: Prostituição em Copacabana e Identidade Social*. Rio de Janeiro: Jorge Zahar Editor.

Godbout, J. 1999. *O espírito da dádiva*. Rio de Janeiro: Fundação Getúlio Vargas Editora.

Goldstein, D. 2003. *Laughter out of Place: Race, Class, Violence and Sexuality in a Rio Shantytown*. Berkeley, CA: University of California Press.

Gregg, J. 2006. 'He can be sad like that: Liberdade and the Absence of Romantic Love in a Brazilian Shantytown', in Jennifer Hirsch and Holly Warlow, *Modern Loves: The Anthropology of Romantic Courtship and Companionate Marriage*. Ann Arbor, MI: University of Michigan Press, pp. 157-173.

Groes-Green, C. 2013. '"To Put Men in a Bottle": Eroticism, Kinship, Female Power, and Transactional Sex in Maputo, Mozambique', *American Ethnologist* 40(1): 102-17.

_____. 2014. 'Journeys of Patronage: Moral Economies of Transactional Sex, Kinship, and Female Migration from Mozambique to Europe'. *Journal of the Royal Anthropological Institute* (N.S.) 20: 237-55.

Hunter, M. 2010. *Love in the Time of Aids: Inequality, Gender and Rights in South Africa*. Bloomington, IN: Indiana University Press.

Illouz, E. 2007. *Consuming the Romantic Utopia: Love and the Cultural Contradictions of Capitalism*. Berkeley, CA: University of California Press.

Kempadoo, K. 2004. *Sexing the Caribbean: Gender, Race and Sexual Labour*. Abingdon: Routledge.

Kuznesof, E.A. 1988. 'A família na sociedade brasileira: parentesco, clientelismo e estrutura social (São Paulo, 1700-1980)', in Eni de Mesquita Samara, *Família e Grupos de Convívio*. Revista Brasileira de História. São Paulo: ANPUH/Marco Zero 9, pp. 37-64.
Leite, G. 1992. *Eu, mulher da vida*. Rio de Janeiro: Editora Rosa dos Tempos.
Marcus, G. 1995. 'Ethnography in/of the World System: The Emergence of Multi-sited Ethnography'. *Annual Review of Anthropology* 24: 95-117.
Matta, R. da. 1978. *Carnavais, Malandros e Heróis: Para uma Sociologia do Dilema Brasileiro*. Rio de Janeiro: Editora Rocco.
Nagel, J. 2000. 'Ethnicity and Sexuality'. *Annual Review of Sociology* 26: 107-33.
Olivar, J.M.N. 2010. *Guerras, trânsitos e apropriações: políticas da prostituição feminina a partir das experiências de quatro mulheres militantes em Porto Alegre*. Tese de doutoramento, PPGas Antropologia Social, UFRGS.
Oliveira, M. 2011. *Las paradojas de la trata y el tráfico de mujeres de la amazonía brasileña en España*. Dissertação de mestrado Máster Oficial en Género, Identidad y Ciudadanía. Universidad de Huelva.
Padilla, M. 2007. *Caribbean Pleasure Industry, Tourism, Sexuality and AIDS in the Dominican Republic*. Chicago, IL: University of Chicago Press.
Paim, H.H.S. 1998. 'Vivendo como amante de um homem casado: entre a legitimidade e a ilegitimade das uniões extraconjugais'. Masters dissertation. Universidade Federal do Rio Grande do Sul.
Passamani, G.R. 2015. 'Batalha de Confete no Mar dos Araxás'. PhD dissertation. São Paulo: State University of Campinas.
Piscitelli, A. 2007. 'Shifting Boundaries: Sex and Money in the Northeast of Brazil'. *Sexualities* 10(4): 489-500.
_____. 2008a. 'Tropical Sex in a European Country: Brazilian Women's Migration to Italy in the Frame of International Sex Tourism' (translated by Miriam Adelman). *Estudos Feministas* 4, special edition Available at http://socialsciences.scielo.org/scielo.php?pid=S0104-026X2008000100003&script=sci_arttext.
_____. 2008b. 'Transits: Brazilian women migration in the context of the transnationalization of the sex and marriage markets', (translated by Daniel Etcheverry Burgueo). *Horizontes Antropológicos* 4, special edition. Available at http://socialsciences.scielo.org/scielo.php?script=sci_arttext&pid=S0104-71832008000100011&lng=pt&nrm=iso. ISSN 0104-7183.
_____. 2013. *Trânsitos: Brasileiras nos mercados transnacionais do sexo*. Rio de Janeiro: Editora Garamond.
Rebhun, L.A. 1999. *The Heart is Unknown Country. Love in the Changing Economy of Northeast Brazil*. Stanford, CA: Stanford University Press.
Sahlins, M. 1990. *Ilhas da História*. Rio de Janeiro: Editora Jorge Zahar.
Schettini, C. 2006. *Que tenhas teu corpo: Uma história social da prostituição no Rio de Janeiro das primeiras décadas republicanas*. Rio de Janeiro: Arquivo Nacional.
Senado Federal. Comissão Parlamentar de Inquérito, 2011. [Parliamentary investigation] Senado Federal, Brazil, December 2011.

Silva, A.P., T.G. Blanchette and A.R. Bento. 2013. 'Cinderella Deceived: Analyzing a Brazilian Myth Regarding Trafficking in Persons'. *Vibrant – Virtual Brazilian Anthropology* 10(2): 378-419. Available at http://www.vibrant.org.br/issues/v10n2/ana-paula-da-silva-thaddeus-gregory-blanchette-andressa-raylane-bento-cinderella-deceived/.

Simoni, V. 2012. 'Love, Interest and Morality in Touristic Cuba'. Paper presented at the International Congress of Americanists, Vienna, on 15-20 July 2012.

Teixeira, F. do B. 2008. 'L'Italia dei Divieti: entre o sonho de ser européia e o babado da prostituição'. *Cadernos Pagu* (31), Campinas- cadernos pagu (42) SP, Núcleo de Estudos de Gênero-Pagu/Unicamp. Available at http://dx.doi.org/10.1590/S0104-83332008000200013.

CHAPTER
8

True Love and Cunning Love
Negotiating Intimacy, Deception and Belonging in Touristic Cuba

Valerio Simoni

Introduction: 'The Error of the Spy'

It was late into the night, as we were walking along the Malecón (Havana's seaside promenade), when my friend Ernesto[1] and I came across Carlos, a fellow Afro-Cuban man. Like Ernesto, Carlos was also part of the loose 'Rasta'[2] circle that used to hang around tourist places in Havana. I had first met Carlos a few years earlier, and this familiarity between us helped to create a convivial atmosphere as we began chatting about each other's lives and what had happened since our last encounter. Carlos had just been released from prison, where he had spent a year for a minor offence, and was now preoccupied by the deterioration of his relationship with Ursula, the Swiss woman with whom he had been together, on and off, for about twelve years. While complaining about her intractable, bossy behaviour and all the other things he disliked in Ursula, Carlos' engrossed talk also revealed that he was still somehow taken by this relationship. 'You're in love with her, aren't you?' provoked Ernesto, sensing where the key problem was. Leaving Carlos with an embarrassed smile, Ernesto started laughing at his own perspicacity. 'You see, there it is – the error of the spy (*el error del espía*)!'[3] That was Ernesto's way of accounting for Carlos' absorption in this story and his current predicament: by falling in love with the tourist, he had lost control of the situation, of the objective he was after, which, the reasoning implied, was to get married and join Ursula in Switzerland. The error of the spy had been to get so emotionally involved in the relationship as to lose track of its ultimately instrumental goal. The logic at play here was that such relationships were to be informed by cunningness, by skilful and detached playing with emotions and love. In spite of his decade-old experience in dealing with tourists, Carlos had obviously failed to maintain such detachment, going a step too far, and therefore revealing a certain naïveté.

For Ernesto, however, this was just one way of seeing things, and it was with light-hearted amusement that he had hinted at Carlos' failure to play with love. Indeed, as he then elaborated, what was more reproachable for Ernesto was that Carlos was now letting go of his lover without doing anything to win her back, failing therefore not so much in cunningness, but in heeding the call of his feelings. Carlos told us how Ursula used to get mad at him for always hanging around with his Cuban friends, neglecting her, and using her money to party with other Cubans. For Ernesto, this showed that Carlos had been unable to compromise with his 'pride' (*orgullo*) and forgot to put love first. Such pride was typical of most Cuban men, said Ernesto. Led by peer pressure, people tended to show off girlfriends from abroad while taking advantage of them economically for the benefit of their friends. According to Ernesto, this sort of attitude was vain and ruinous, especially since it led to forgetting, as in Carlos' case, that love was more valuable than friendship, and that friends were coming and going, whereas a woman that had 'touched your heart' was there to stay. Ernesto presented us with an abstract reflection about love, encouraging Carlos to realize its essential value, and to forget how his friends might judge him if he did not follow the typical script of taking economic advantage of the rich tourist. '*Está en talla*' ('he has stature/wit'), was Carlos' way of acknowledging Ernesto's lesson, and of giving credit to his advice.

This insightful conversation, which left Carlos wondering about what to do next with Ursula, acts as an illustration of the competing moral worlds, subjectivities, and spheres of belonging that my research participants navigated and inhabited while enacting and making sense of relationships with tourists. Two opposing narratives tended to frame the way intimacy with foreigners was perceived and evaluated: narratives of love relationships (or true love) on the one hand, and narratives of instrumental relationships (or cunning love, based on interest) on the other. It is by understanding the moral, emotional and pragmatic demands to which these two interpretative frames responded, and by realizing their global circulation and diffusion, that I believe we can ultimately grasp their affordances and consequences, as well as the challenge of overcoming them.[4]

Cunning Love

We were driving together towards a popular disco in Havana, when Jan, a young Norwegian man in his thirties who had been visiting Cuba regularly for three consecutive years, started explaining to me about the 'girls' on the island, of which, according to him, there were three kinds:

> The ones that you meet and ask you straightforward for money, say 40 dollars [US]. The ones with whom you make love, and only afterwards ask you for some money, for a taxi to get home. And the ones who don't ask you anything, generally the most beautiful ones, and that when you come back to your country you can't stop thinking about them, about their needs and poverty, and you keep writing to them, sending them money, 100, 200 dollars, while in the meanwhile they are here in Cuba enjoying their [Cuban] boyfriends, and fucking other tourists.

Jan's cynical view, as he went on to explain, was informed by the negative experiences he had had with two Cuban girlfriends, one of whom was now carrying his child. According to his typology, both women had proven to be of the third and most deceptive kind. His relationships with them had led him to confront the challenges and complications of 'falling in love', as a foreigner, with Cubans. These 'failed relationships' had brought Jan 'back to earth', and made him realize the predominance of *jineterismo* as far as relationships between tourists and Cubans were concerned. From the Spanish word for 'rider' (*jinete*), in present-day Cuba *jineterismo* has become a contentious term that can potentially encompass 'any dollar-generating activity or connections with foreigners' (Fernandez 1999: 85). In the realm of tourism, *jineterismo* indicates the 'riding of tourists' for instrumental purposes, and tends to evoke notions of 'tourist hustling' and 'prostitution'. Scholars have shown how ascriptions of *jineterismo* are often ambiguous, and bring issues of morality, nation, race, class and gender into play (e.g. Fernandez 1999; Berg 2004; Cabezas 2009; Daigle 2015; Simoni 2016a). Given also that an accusation of *jineterismo* could carry legal sanctions, any such categorizing could be fraught with controversy, making it extremely important to consider who was using this notion, in which context, and to what end (Simoni 2008).

From advice in guidebooks, to the tips exchanged by tourists in Cuba, narratives of deceitful relationships with Cubans and *jineterismo* have spread widely since the booming of tourism in the early 1990s (Simoni 2016a), warning tourists of the eminently instrumental character of these encounters from the locals' point of view. One of the places where *jineterismo* and 'cunning love' were much talked about was Santa Maria beach, a place frequented by many heterosexual white men who came to Cuba year after year with a desire for sexual adventures with Cuban women. 'You must be crazy to fall in love with a Cuban girl', was the frequent comment that circulated among these tourism 'veterans'. Accordingly, newly arrived visitors who 'fell in love' with a Cuban partner could easily be scorned for their naïveté, and be derided as the 'suckers' who still fail to understand how such things work in Cuba. What was highly valued instead in this milieu, were the tales of deceptive countermoves at the expenses of *jineteros* and *jineteras* – narratives that highlighted the tourists' own cunningness in coping with the 'typical Cuban trickery' (see Simoni 2014b). Such were the stories of tourists who had outwitted Cuban women and managed to have sex with them for as little economic investment as possible, or even 'for free', as some boasted. A well-known script advised tourists to feign love, to pretend one was totally taken by the relationship, and thus play with the mirage of a possible long-term engagement filled with potential economic advantage for the Cuban partner, perhaps even the promise of marriage and migration to the tourist's country of residence. This, it was argued, could easily grant sexual access to a Cuban woman without giving money in return. Nor did this trick imply any sort of commitment, as the tourist could always withdraw or disappear whenever he liked.

Manuele, an Italian man who had been coming to Cuba since he was a teenager in the early 1990s, explicitly outlined such a scenario. Every time we met at Santa Maria beach, Manuele liked to gossip about his ongoing intimate adventures with Cuban women. That day, which was the last one of his 'Cuban winter holidays' (within a few hours he was due to take the plane back to Italy), he started telling me and some fellow Italian tourists that he had promised his current 'girlfriend' – a Cuban woman he had met a couple of weeks earlier – to bring her a TV and DVD player as presents the following evening. 'But weren't you leaving tonight?' was my reaction. Manuele burst out in a laugh, before explaining that this was precisely why he had told the woman he would give her the gifts 'tomorrow'. He was never going to do it, and would never see that woman again. She would never be able to track him down in Italy, anyway. He had spent a nice two weeks in her company, had had lots of sex, but that was it. He was not a 'sucker' who would fall in love or commit to a long-term relationship with a Cuban woman.[5]

As Manuele put it on other occasions, deploying a very cynical view of tourist–Cuban relationships in general, one had to rely on the 'same weapons' (*le stesse armi*) that Cubans used, and play according to their rules, which were, allegedly, the rules of trickery and deception. According to such reasoning, the two teams involved in the game remained forever anchored in their very own worlds and agendas, and it seemed ludicrous to think that they would one day share more than short-lived moments of sex and intimacy. 'Their family is one and one only!' (*'La loro famiglia é una sola!'*, with the Italian *famiglia* metonymically evoking here the Cuban nation more at large); 'You'll never be able to (fully) trust them!' Such were the kind of recipes that emerged in these moments of male tourist sociability and gossip in Santa Maria. No matter how long you stayed with a Cuban partner, you would always remain a foreigner to them, and they would never come to treat you as they did their fellow nationals. While the views of these experienced tourists were rather extreme and may be located at one end of a continuum of tourists' assessments of intimate relationships with Cuban people, my ethnography suggests that most tourists in Cuba, both women and men, were highly sceptical about the wisdom of getting entangled in any long-term relationship with a local. The spectre of possible deception, contrived emotions, interested love and marriage,[6] and other instrumental machinations at their expense, was often lurking at the back of their minds.

These lines of reasoning were reifying a divide between Cubans' self-presentations to outsiders and their actual motivations and agendas, which were deemed ineluctably strategic. As I have argued elsewhere (Simoni 2013, 2014a, 2016a), this interpretive logic is extremely widespread in an increasingly globalizing field of tourism discourse and critique, and needs to be understood in relation with tourism's drive to reach into the most intimate realms of the places and lives that come onto its path, and with the tourists' preoccupation of being deceived by 'fake' touristic displays.[7] Most tourists I met during fieldwork despised the idea of being cheated, and were constantly puzzled about the 'real' intentions and motivations of the Cubans interacting with them. Here is where narratives of *jineterismo* could act as a key interpretative resource to 'unmask' the locals' 'secret' motivations. In terms of social scientists' approaches, similar frames of legibility still retain much analytical purchase when assessing touristic encounters from a critical (-cum-cynical) perspective (Simoni 2014a). Such interpretive grids may appear all the more compelling, operative, and theoretically limitless when combined with a strong focus on structural inequalities, an emphasis on local resistances to global forces, and a conceptualization of the (liberal) individual that foregrounds economic agency. The risk here lies in adopting such a framework a priori (Fassin 2008), by 'romanticizing resistance' (Abu-Lughod 1990; Piot 2010) and overemphasizing the image of the cunning locals who, in spite of their subaltern position, are able to trick and deceive the structurally advantaged tourists – a category of people for whom academics have traditionally displayed little sympathy (see Crick 1995). Going a step further, I argue that we may be easily tempted by the notion that the disadvantaged inhabitants of tourism destinations in the South are not only able to take advantage of tourists, but that they should legitimately do so; and we – as critical researchers sensitive to domination and ways of resisting it, and eager to highlight their economic agencies and rationalities – expect them to act this way.

This is a line of interpretation that I think we should refrain from deploying too swiftly, and one that may become even more tempting and self-evident – and its moral underpinnings therefore less likely to be reflexively acknowledged – in a Caribbean context where cunning responses to colonial domination have captured much anthropological attention (Browne 2004; Freeman 2007). The notion of disadvantaged people deploying subtle tactics and 'economic guile' to get by in unfavourable contexts of existence is indeed a long-standing one in anthropologies of the Caribbean region, where such features have been considered 'to embody the most authentic in Caribbean culture' (Wilson 1964, cited in Freeman 2007: 5). An interesting parallel may be drawn here with Cole's assessment of recent scholarship on African intimacies, which tends to foreground 'the instrumental, as opposed to the emotional, nature of intimate male–female relations ... either to highlight African agency despite difficult social and economic conditions or to illuminate the underlying logic behind seemingly promiscuous behaviour' (Cole 2009: 111). The risk of putting too much emphasis on 'the strategic nature of relationships', argues Cole, lies in reproducing stereotypes that see Africans – and particularly African women – as 'purely instrumental' (ibid.), a risk that I see very much present in the Cuban case discussed here.

Thinking about the 'romance of resistance', it is also important to consider that in Cuba, the socialist government itself rests on a long tradition of nationalist rhetoric of resistance to colonial and imperialist powers. In this context, it becomes interesting to follow how the notion of *la lucha* ('the struggle') – one of the key terms of revolutionary symbolism – progressively turned in the 1990s into a common expression to indicate Cubans' day-to-day struggle to get by (Palmié 2004: 241), to look for dollars 'in the street' (*en la calle*) (Berg 2004: 84; see also Stout 2007 and Bisogno 2010). In the generalized climate of crisis that characterized Cuba after the demise of its Soviet ally, Cuban people engaging informally with foreign tourists were able to inscribe their actions within the moral framework of *la lucha* (Bisogno 2010; Garcia 2010; Roland 2011). This is when *jineterismo*'s justificatory logic and moral footing could be brought to the fore. Grounded on the reification of a radical asymmetry of resources, *jineterismo* could embody among my research participants a just struggle, and be seen as a sort of redistributive tactic in an unequal world in which wealthy tourists visited poorer countries like Cuba. Indeed, and in line with what many believed the government was itself doing – 'squeezing' foreign visitors to bring in as much hard currency as possible – *jineterismo* could be portrayed as a rightful way to get a slice of the tourism cake, part of a nation's cunning tactics to siphon capitalist wealth. If some deception at the tourists' expense was involved, this could easily be justified by the Cubans I engaged with in the frame of an 'Us' (poor) Cubans vs. 'Them' (rich) tourists approach.

It is in relation to this moral frame of justification that Ernesto's reference to the 'error of the spy' should be understood. Indeed, in such moments of peer sociability, the instrumental idiom of *jineterismo* could easily take centre stage, encouraging people to assert their cold-heartedness in dealing with the rich foreigners. The remarks of Brennan (2004) on the normative expectations that exist among female sex workers in Sosúa, Dominican Republic, regarding ways of talking about love with foreign partners, provide an interesting point of comparison here: 'Positing love could make Sosúan sex workers appear foolish. No matter what they feel for their foreign boyfriends, these women have an incentive to portray themselves as not naïve enough to actually fall in love' (Brennan 2004: 96). In his article on transactional sex in Maputo (Mozambique), Groes-Green (2013) similarly shows the risks inherent in local women getting too emotionally involved and giving in to love with their white partners. According to this author, '[t]he most feared consequence of doing so would be to suddenly "forget themselves or their families"' (Groes-Green 2013: 113), a reasoning that draws attention to the wider importance that intimacies can acquire as key indicators of one's allegiance and belonging, in delineating and signalling the community one identifies with, feels part of and commits to.

The expectation of instrumentalizing tourists, and its 'taken for granted-ness', had also become a target of Ernesto's criticism, as he warned Carlos of his vanity, and urged him not to be guided solely by concerns for his reputation and 'what friends might say'. Ernesto certainly had a point there, given that what tended to prevail when Cubans gossiped about their relationships with tourists were boastful stances and displays of one's cunning exploitation and instrumentalization of naive tourists. In a sense, the image taking shape in moments of peer sociability was that of a unified Cuban community taking rightful advantage of the privileged Other, embodied by the foreign tourist. Accordingly, tourists could be objectified and literally treated like *piezas* ('pieces') in a game geared at satisfying the interests and desires of the Cuban person involved, of their family and friends, and of the Cuban population at large.

Economic guile and cunning resourcefulness, which Wilson (1969) ascribed to the Caribbean prestige system of 'reputation', may be seen here as values embraced by my Cuban research participants. Following this author's insights, such values can be traced back to 'Caribbean work histories in which moral rights to self-reliance and autonomy, even if exercised in illicit ways, are widely accepted and highly prized achievements' (Browne 2009; see also Browne 2004 and Prentice 2009). The Cuban version of

Browne's 'creole economics' may thus be interpreted also as a way for my interlocutors 'to signal their valued membership' (Browne 2004: 196) to the world of Cuban *luchadores*, and to assert 'personal autonomy and cultural difference' from tourists – with the tourists, and perhaps to some extent also Cuba's formal officialdom, replacing in this case the French control in Browne's Martinique. Seen in this light, the instrumental narratives of *jineterismo* worked towards the maintenance of a clear dividing line between Cubans and tourists. They also drew on the assumption that the cunning intimacies Cubans were developing with tourists were ultimately economic in nature and geared at benefitting one's 'insider' community (that is, other Cuban people), and that such community was the realm where true intimacy was to be deployed.

By contextualizing the instrumentality of their relationships with tourists within an 'Us–Them' divide, Cubans could avoid restricting the measure of their worth to economic agency and morality alone, and could cultivate in parallel the image of virtuous Cuban subjects generously sharing with their community what had been gained from the touristic *lucha*. Often implicit, such assumptions about redistributing gains among fellow Cubans became visible when people talked about all the good things they had been (or would be) able to do with the tourists' resources, such as helping poor relatives living out in the countryside, buying new furniture and home appliances for their parents, and providing good food and clothing for their children.

The positing of the Cuban 'we' as one's primary sphere of allegiance and belonging was mirrored by the assertion, made by several of my tourist research participants, that the Cubans' family was and would always be one and only one: the Cuban nation (see above). For the tourist, this stance and the equally cunning responses it justified from their part could also help to delineate and safeguard their 'back home', the communities in which they spent their everyday life, as the ultimate place in which their ability to relate intimately with other people had to be judged. This way, their tricks to obtain 'cheap sex' with Cuban women could be presented as departing from their 'normal' moral ways of being, as exceptional modes of action that responded to an 'imperfect world' (Povinelli 2006: 198) of insurmountable North–South inequalities and *jineterismo* – a context in which any attempt to integrate the Cuban community was cast as a naive illusion at best (see Simoni 2014b).

The tourists' equation, when discussing issues of intimacy, of the Cuban family with the Cuban nation, and the related assumption that as far as Cubans' professions of love to a foreigner were concerned, none should be trusted, contributed to reify the Cuban 'we' frame of reference and the cleavage between 'Us' and 'Them' – the same divide that the narratives of *jineterismo* examined above also helped to sustain. As some tourists put it, even in the event of marrying a Cuban, you could be sure on which side of the tourist–Cuban frontier your partner's allegiance would remain: on the Cuban one. Hence the refrain I heard from an Italian man in Santa Maria, *'Moglie e buoi dei paesi tuoi!'* ('Wife and ox [should be] from your own land!'). Accordingly, as far as serious decisions like marriage were concerned, one had better choose someone from one's own country. These considerations seem to support Fernandez's argument, building on Povinelli (2002), that for modern states '[i]ntimate love is ... the foundation not merely of true families but also of true nations' (Fernandez 2013: 4). We may also recall Stoler's (1989) groundbreaking analysis of how intimacy in colonial cultures became a moral locus for defining the very notions of colonizer and colonized, which is a further reminder of the importance of moral investments of intimacy in establishing boundaries of belonging and exclusion, and in fixing cleavages between 'Us' and 'Them'.

We are thus confronted here with a kind of split and hierarchy between two realms – the 'touristic contact zone' and the 'local/home environment' – with precedence being implicitly given to the latter, made to act as the 'normal' realm of life, the context into which one belonged, in the sense of being and feeling part of a community and having a valued place in it. By way of contrast, the touristic contact zone became the exceptional realm of instrumental endeavours, of playful love and *la lucha*, in which cunning deployments of intimacy where justified as expressions of economic rationality. Contextualized in tourism, love's instrumentality did not necessarily threaten one's overall capacity for true love, and could help counter judgement as someone exclusively guided by self-interest, economic imperatives, and a desire for material wealth.[8]

True Love

In spite of the prevailing narratives of *jineterismo*, of reciprocal trickery and deception as 'fair game' in tourist–Cuban intimate relationships, and of the scornful attitudes of experienced visitors towards foreigners who 'fell into the traps' of Cubans' cunning love, competing narratives also existed among the tourists I met in Cuba. After all, there were foreigners who engaged in long-term relationships and ended up marrying a Cuban partner. Even in the context of Santa Maria beach, which tended to be averse to any sort of romanticism, I heard foreign men 'admitting' to falling in love with a Cuban, and cherishing the notion that true love could be found on the island. In most such cases, the Cuban partner was presented as someone who had been met outside of the main tourism circuits, thanks to fortuitous and uncalculated encounters, and this was contrasted with the more common scenario of encounters in highly tourist areas, bars and clubs, where *jineterismo*, hustling and prostitution were said to predominate.[9]

In the love story between Gianluca and Yara, however, their first encounter had not followed the more virtuous script. Gianluca was an Italian man in his mid-thirties on his first trip to Cuba; Yara, a Cuban woman in her early twenties, was from very humble origins and had recently migrated from Ciego de Ávila (one of Cuba's eastern provinces) to Havana in search of better livelihood opportunities. The two had only been together for a couple of weeks when I first met them. Their first encounter had been in one of the popular discos of Havana, which was widely known among tourists as the typical 'den' of *jineteras*. Gianluca was well aware of the warnings that circulated in Santa Maria about the dangers of getting too seriously involved with Cuban women. In a rather apologetic and self-mocking tone, and feeling he had to justify such a 'crazy' endeavour, he said he knew that this was 'the worst mistake one could make on a first visit to Cuba'. However, he also added that he did not care, as his feelings for Yara were so strong that he simply had to go with it. He sensed that their relationship could probably work out, and the two of them were already planning for his next visit to Cuba in a few months' time. Meanwhile, Gianluca would provide Yara with a mobile phone to communicate with him while he was in Italy, and would help her with the money she required to satisfy her everyday needs, so that she would not have to continue hustling in Havana to get by and to help her family back in Ciego de Ávila. In telling me this, Gianluca was aware that most other foreign men on the beach would frown upon such a naive and risky endeavour. As Giulio, one of the Italian veterans, said, 'It's like getting a brick on your head'. By this he meant Gianluca would certainly be left 'bleeding' and losing most of his economic resources to Yara, who was sure to capitalize on such reckless love. While I do not know how their story continued, what matters here is that Gianluca treasured his deep feelings for Yara, felt that such feelings were reciprocated, and strived to build a path that could help them to reach beyond the scenarios of a cunning and deceptive love.

Getting back to Cubans' claims and enactments of love, I would like to return to the example that opened this chapter. In his advice to Carlos, Ernesto had ultimately urged him to follow his heart and let love prevail over his reputational concerns about what his Cuban friends might say. The love to which he referred was not of the calculative cunning kind, but one that called for emotional involvement and abandonment. Seen from a *jineterismo*'s perspective, such loss of control would have been a mistake, *el error del espía*, but for Ernesto, the hierarchy of values that ought to guide one's life seemed rather clear: sentiment and love had to be prioritized. But what then about the notion, discussed above, that 'true sentiments' ought to be reserved for the Cuban 'we', namely for one's Cuban family, friends and lovers? The problems with this scenario, for people like Ernesto, became apparent upon assessing the state of intimate relationships among Cubans, and the way these were being tainted by people's economic needs. 'Everyone is in need (*tiene necesidades*)', and needs 'deform everything', Ernesto told me. '*El amor ya no existe*' ('love does not exist anymore'), echoed Ernesto's friend Aurelio in the course of the same conversation. He was referring to the fact that Cuban women were nowadays *interesadas*, interested in what you had, in your money. As a result of this, it was impossible to have a 'normal' relationship with them. That was why Aurelio was more inclined to start a relationship with foreign women. 'European women are good; they only want love and sentiment. Cuban women have much wickedness (*maldad*)', he maintained.[10] The two young Cubans were articulating here a very widespread critique, in contemporary Cuba, of the generalization and increasing predominance of *relaciones de interés* ('relations for interest', i.e. instrumentally motivated), as opposed to normal, 'real' relationships (Fosado 2005) and 'true love' (Stout 2014; Lundgren 2011).

But while actualizing the typical narrative of 'moral decline, evidenced by materialist interests in romantic relationships' (Fernandez 2013: 12), Ernesto and Aurelio were also quick to justify it, arguing that in the present climate of crisis it was normal for Cuban women to put economic considerations above love (Simoni 2015a). Rather than being simply seen as a sign of immorality, these women's behaviours were thus assessed as responding to another horizon of moral demands: the imperative of providing for oneself and for one's elder and younger kin, in line with the morality of economic responsibility and *la lucha* considered in the previous section. Discussing the issue further, Aurelio also clarified that it was the fault of the system (*es el sistema*) in Cuba that everything now was *por interés*. In so far as the Cuban context was judged responsible for 'deforming' how things should have 'normally' been, we are confronted here with a discourse of exception, a 'normative politics' (Povinelli 2006: 208) that did not tarnish the ideal of pure love, but simply displaced it elsewhere, in other places or other times. For Aurelio and Ernesto, such 'regulatory ideal' (ibid.) ought to inform people's practices under normal conditions, but since these conditions were now lacking in the Cuban milieu, the two of them were looking towards relationships with foreigners as a possible ground for its realization. Indeed, Ernesto and Aurelio aspired to something more than a life dominated by economic needs and responsibilities, and were hoping for emotional fulfilment in true love and intimacy – ideals that they valued highly. In contrast to the bleak prospects they projected on relationships with Cuban women, intimacy with foreign women appeared in this sense as the realm in which true love was still possible.

These reflections offer us a good vantage point from which to re-examine the issues of belonging that I addressed above when discussing the moral framework of *jineterismo* and tourists' cynical responses to it. Seen as a legitimate economic endeavour to access tourists' wealth for the benefit of a collective Cuban 'we' (often embodied in family and peers), *jineterismo* indicated an allegiance to Cuba as the place of belonging, the context where one's emotional and moral self could find their true expression, be actualized, and ultimately be recognized as worthy by fellow Cubans. In the interpretative frame deployed here by Ernesto and Aurelio, by way of contrast, people's fulfilment of their moral aspirations for love, and for emotionally gratifying relationships more generally, was outward-looking, oriented towards an outside world represented by tourism and tourists. Accordingly, encounters with tourists could help them materialize and inhabit a world that was in no state of exception – a world beyond economic hardship and its ensuing 'deformities', a world of 'normality'.

Criticizing Cuba as a dysfunctional place where 'normal' relationships could hardly be found, this cosmopolitan approach shifted the ideal grounds of belonging, and the related standards for assessing one's moral worth, from Cuba to the wider world, be it only on an aspirational and virtual level. Many among my Cuban interlocutors spent most of their days trying to interact with tourists, and it was also in relation to this foreign world that they would constantly measure each other – judging, comparing and deliberating on one's ability to understand and engage with foreigners on the same moral grounds, according to the same ideals of relationships. In some cases, the dissatisfaction expressed with everything Cuban, and the obsession with 'the abroad' and with moving abroad, prompted comments that a person was already – in terms of mind-set at least –more 'there' than 'here'.

A case in point was Raydel, an Afro-Cuban Rasta in his forties, who was often teased by his peers for his extravagant behaviour and his 'tourist-like' attitude. Raydel was in a long-term relationship with Rebecca, an Austrian woman with whom he had a child. He had spent the last few years trying to get all 'the papers' done so he could join the two in Austria, but the Cuban authorities had kept denying him the 'exit permit' (*permiso de salida*) needed to leave the county, so that when I last saw him in April 2013, to his disbelief he remained stuck in Cuba.[11] Among other things, Raydel liked to hang around the touristic areas of Havana with a camera, dressed like a *yuma* (as he put it, employing a popular term for 'foreigner'), and acting as such. Going around with him, his Cuban friends and I could not help noting, sometimes with a certain embarrassment, his conspicuous endeavours in taking pictures in a tourist fashion, filming other Cubans singing and dancing on the Malecón, or the occasional English sentences he addressed to fellow countrymen, who were sometimes left puzzling about his actual origins. Raydel also liked to report on his open arguments and confrontations with the Cuban police, who regularly questioned him for being in the company of tourists, as well as with the owners and staff of bars and restaurants, who could discourage him from entering their premises. Being present on some of these occasions, I saw him argue for the recognition of his 'human rights' to be wherever he liked, and in the company of whomever he liked, and he supported his claims with reference to his Austrian visa and the fact that he was just about to leave Cuba for good. Raydel used to go around with his passport, a document associated with imminent travel, which few Cubans possessed, and which could create further frictions with police officers who asked for the usual ID card that every Cuban was expected to carry. 'They lost me already', he once told me referring to his breaking away from the Cuban 'system', suggesting that all his hopes, desires and aspirations were nowadays located somewhere else, out of Cuba. An imagined Europe was the place where Raydel – self-proclaimed 'citizen of the world' (*ciudadano del mundo*) – felt he belonged, and deserved to be.

Spending much of his everyday life in the company of foreign tourists, Raydel's talk was all about pure, sincere friendship and love, and about the value of sentiments. Explaining this to me, he insisted that he had never asked anyone for anything: all he had received from foreigners had always resulted from the free will of people who cared for and loved him. Such emphasis on sentiment as the key driver of relationships, and the ensuing (re)qualification of any material benefits as by-product, was grounded on the notion that it was simply normal for true lovers and friends to share everything without calculation, and seemed essential for people like Raydel, marking a clear difference with intimacies that were motivated by material interests, or even by a 'mix' of interest and sentiment.[12] In spite of never having been asked for anything, Rebecca had always been very generous with him. Thanks to that, Raydel had been able to improve the lives of his relatives living in the remote countryside from where he originally came, in one of Cuba's eastern provinces. As a result, he felt he had finally achieved what he had always dreamt of doing for his Cuban family. Praised as a generous benefactor in his home town, what he now wanted for himself was to move on with a life abroad, an abroad for which he felt he was perfectly prepared already, able to behave like other citizens of the world did. His way of relating with tourists and fellow Cubans, as described above, exemplified the cosmopolitan subjectivity he wished to assert.

Albeit rather extreme in this case, Raydel's outward-looking stance was far from exceptional among my Cuban research participants, and many were those who expressed similar desires and aspirations for a 'normal life' abroad, for setting up family and raising children with a foreign partner in

Europe. Such longing for 'normalcy'[13] was also signalled by the idioms of love and friendship people assumed would hold sway in normal conditions of existence (Simoni 2014c). Affirmations of true love and friendship indicated in this sense one's ability to live in accordance with the same moral standards ascribed to tourists, and reclaimed the same kind of 'emotional interiority' (Faier 2007: 149).[14] Following Povinelli (2002, 2006), we may argue that what was brought to life here was the ideal of an 'autological subject' freed from societal constraints, as opposed to its 'mirror image' (Povinelli 2006: 208) and 'contrasting evil' (ibid.: 199), a 'genealogical society' made of socially determined subjects.[15] Subscribing to these ideals of a 'normal', true love, untarnished by material considerations, could thus be seen as a way for Cubans like Raydel to assert the aspiration to overcome the context of exceptionalism, of enduring crisis, scarcity and isolation associated with Cuba, and to claim 'membership' of a 'global society' (Ferguson 2006) from which many of my Cuban research participants felt excluded.[16]

When accounting for these assertions of true love or friendship to tourists, we may still argue that what we are dealing with are essentially discourses, ideals and aspirations that have little to do with how things actually take place in practice, and which can hardly be grounded in any contextualized ethnographic description of people's everyday lives and actions.[17] In deploying this kind of criticism, however, we should not forget 'the enabling and animating aspects' of people's hopes and desires (Moore 2011: 25). According to Moore, it is this 'ethical imagination' – '[t]he forms and means … through which individuals imagine relationships to themselves and to others' (ibid.: 16) – that ultimately 'links human agency to the forms of the possible' (ibid.: 18). Recognizing the importance of 'the aspirational character of our relations to others' (ibid.: 10), and paying attention to our research participants' interest 'in creating new connections, new meanings, novel forms of relation' (ibid.: 9), is a productive way to shift the focus of our analyses towards the future and its potentialities. Such a move seems all the more sensible, and analytically sound, when we find that our research participants are themselves clearly pushing in that direction, as was the case for Raydel, whose everyday life and behaviour was frequently informed by anticipations of his future abroad and by concrete examples of his proficiency in relating with such 'Euro-otherness' (Piot 2010: 169).[18]

Another element that is also important to consider at this point is that for many of my Cuban research participants, tourist girlfriends kept coming and going, their promises of return often left unfulfilled, so that fantasies of true love were frequently frustrated. Such ruptures and (heart)breaks could lead to further recalibrations of one's sense of self and its relations to the tourist Other. In April 2013, spending more time with Ernesto one year after our first encounters and conversations (including those referenced above), he told me that he was getting more and more *negativo* (negative) in his dealings with tourists. In the last year or so, he had received many blows, and had been very disappointed by how relationships in which he had invested a lot, emotionally, did not match up to their promises. A year earlier, Ernesto had insisted that his way of relating with tourists was grounded on 'truth' (*la verdad*) and 'sentiments' (*los sentimientos*), but now, even if he himself did not like it, he was getting more and more cynical and full of *maldad* ('wickedness'). However, true love could still be on its way, he maintained, and so he kept a certain disposition to work positively on his feelings and give it all when a promising relationship was in sight.[19]

Such openness, we may argue, could in itself be a very demanding moral disposition to retain. It implied devoting a lot of energies and emotional commitments in what were often very transient intimate encounters with women one was never sure to ever see again. To evaluate whether a given relationship deserved such intense engagement, Ernesto strived to get a sense of how truthfully the tourist in question was ready to 'surrender' (*entregarse*) to love. He himself was always ready to do so – 'when someone gives you love, you have to give love back' he argued – but tended to back away if he felt there was no corresponding predisposition or response from his partner. The suffering one had to endure when love was not reciprocated, Ernesto told me, was hard to bear.[20] He was particularly disappointed by tourists who, having given in to incredibly intense relationships, upon leaving Cuba started to have doubts about the genuineness of his commitment. According to Ernesto, the tourists' friends and peers, back home, with their warnings about Cubans' wickedness, deceptiveness, and cunning professions of love, were responsible for cultivating these uncertainties, but so were his partners, for letting themselves be influenced by such insinuations, and for believing these people more than him. Those were tough situations to cope with for Ernesto, and a cause of much anger and frustration. He complained that when these women had been with him, they had unpacked together the phenomenon of *jineterismo*, and that he had been able to prove to them that he was not a *jinetero*, someone guided by *interés*. In a way – and reversing the more common assumptions on the matter – it was Ernesto here that was urging tourists to embody Povinelli's autological subject: the autonomous self-determining protagonist of 'intimate events', immune to external societal constraints and determinations. His love acted as a moral demand to be loved in similarly unconditional ways, but tourists were failing him on this, showing their own weakness and lack of autonomy. What these last considerations suggest is also the importance of looking at people's personal trajectories in order to understand the vicissitudes of their engagements with true love and its cunning Other.[21]

Conclusion

In spite of their different life trajectories, successes and failures in intimate engagements with tourists, Ernesto, Carlos and Raydel all seemed to share similar aspirations for true love with foreign women, a love that could eventually enable them to join their partners abroad. For them, love had progressively come to be associated with the outside world, a world to which they in many ways also strived to belong. For the moment, however, and notwithstanding the ascendancy of this virtual scenario on their everyday lives, they were still physically anchored in Cuba, with no immediate solution to actualize their prophetic visions. Socializing with their Cuban friends and peers, they were all equally well versed in the idiom of cunning love, and familiar with the world of *jineterismo* and *la lucha*, 'the struggle' on which they often also relied to get by and make a living. Their engagements along the terms of *la lucha*, and the deployment of its semantics and moral ways of being, also signalled their belonging to a shared Cuban 'we', and enabled them to embody the ideal of a competent Cuban subject skilfully coping with economic adversity, cunningly resisting unequal structural forces, and gaining its rightful - if too meagre - share of global wealth. Within this frame of legibility, and from this Cuban 'we' perspective, even when they explicitly behaved as *jineteros*, they could be seen as acting morally - a morality assessed in terms of worthiness as economic agents, and also grounded on the assumption that what was gained by deceiving the foreign Other would be put to the benefit of a community of Cuban friends and relatives.

If on the one hand this perspective justified Cubans' cunning deployments of love, on the other it made true love with a tourist potentially problematic - the 'error of the spy' - shedding doubts on one's ultimate allegiance (the tourist Other or the Cuban 'we'?). One may indeed argue that it was precisely the perceived transgressions of such cleavage, threatened by love relationships between tourists and Cubans, that prompted moral anxiety among the tourist and the Cuban populations.[22] In other words, while it could be seen as acceptable to engage in hedonistic sexual pursuits in the exceptional spatio-temporal frame of a holiday for tourists, or to make money out of sexual interludes with foreigners for Cubans - what, in both cases, could amount to the cunning deployment of love - affirmations of true love and intimacy crossing the tourist-Cuban divide could be eyed with scepticism and suspicion by cynical peers, as well as by the tourist and Cuban communities at large, generating feelings of awkwardness and inadequacy among the protagonists involved. In such a view, predicated on the typically normative isomorphism between community, nation and belonging (see Gupta and Ferguson 1992), the proper place for love was 'at home', and not in messy contact zones. Bringing this reflection to bear on yet another ramification of these cross-border intimacies, we may also consider that similar frames of legibility find forceful expressions in European public discourses and legal apparatuses patrolling the boundaries of 'proper' marriages – the so-called 'arranged', 'strategic', or 'sham' marriages controversy (see Fernandez 2013). We thus find a convergence of representations and moral assumptions operating at various levels and spheres ranging from Cuba to Europe, from tourism to migration, from institutional to public discourse – a convergence that needs to be critically unpacked and reflexively accounted for in our investigations.

But even if we were to follow, to their logical end result, these protectionists and often nation-bound readings of intimacy and belonging, we might still wonder about the hopes of fulfilling love 'at home' for the people with whom I had worked. To conclude with Ernesto, Carlos and Raydel, the three main protagonists of this chapter, it seemed clear for them that present-day Cuba was hardly the place where they felt they could realize the kind of 'intimate recognition' (Povinelli 2002: 234) to which they aspired. Instead, a good deal of their engaging in intimacy and delving into love was outward and future oriented, and had an abstract global community as its ultimate moral benchmark and site of belonging.

Acknowledgements

The research for this article benefitted from the support of the Portuguese Foundation for Science and Technology (Post-Doctoral Grant SFRH/BPD/66483/2009) and the Swiss National Science Foundation (*Ambizione* Fellowship, PZ00P1_147946).). I am particularly indebted to Nadine Fernandez and Christian Groes-Green for their useful remarks and suggestions on earlier versions of the chapter. Last but not least, my gratitude goes to the foreign tourist and Cuban men and women whom I encountered during my ethnographic fieldwork in Cuba, which made my research possible.

Parts of this chapter have previously appeared in *The Cambridge Journal of Anthropology* and the *Journal of the Anthropological Society of Oxford* (see Simoni 2015b, 2016b).

Valerio Simoni is Senior Research Fellow in the Anthropology and Sociology Department at the Graduate Institute in Geneva, Switzerland, and has held research positions in the UK and Portugal. He has published in edited books and journals in the fields of anthropology and tourism studies, including *Anthropological Theory, The Cambridge Journal of Anthropology*, and the *Journal of Tourism and Cultural Change*, as well as the monograph *Tourism and Informal Encounters in Cuba* (Berghahn Books 2016). With ethnographic field research in Cuba and Spain, his work contributes to social science scholarship on intimacy, economic practice, morality, tourism, migration, transnationalism and globalization.

NOTES

1. All personal names and some details in the examples presented in this chapter have been changed to protect the anonymity of research participants.
2. The people I got to know as Rasta in tourism milieus in Havana were mainly Afro-Cuban men adopting a subculture style that may summarily be characterized as valorizing blackness and Afro-related cultural expressions, sporting dreadlocks and Rastafari-inspired accessories and clothing, and privileging a laid-back approach to tourists. These people generally self-identified, and were seen by others, as Rasta. For a more comprehensive overview of the Rastafari movement in Cuba, see Hansing (2006).
3. The author has translated all direct quotes from research participants, when not already in English.
4. This chapter is based on fifteen months of ethnographic fieldwork (mainly participant observation) carried out in Cuba between 2005 and 2016 in the tourist locations of Havana, the rural town of Viñales (about 200 km west of the capital), and the beach resort of Santa Maria (in Playas del Este, a thirty-minute drive east of Havana). The findings are not representative of the wide variety of tourist–Cuban interactions taking place in this country, and are mostly biased towards the experiences of disadvantaged Afro-Cuban men from humble origins engaging in intimate relationships with wealthier foreign women.
5. Elsewhere (Simoni 2016a), I examine ethnographic material showing how Cuban women themselves could well be aware of the risks and opportunities inherent in engaging in ambiguous sexual encounters in which the role of money and economic compensation remained unclear and non-explicit, as opposed to the more commoditized 'sex for money' transactions.
6. Recent work by García Moreno (2010), García Moreno and Pujadas Muñoz (2011), Berg (2011), and Roca (2013) on Cuban migration to Spain shows the widespread diffusion, in this country, of tourism-related stereotypes regarding Cuba and its people, and of the suspects of 'arranged' and 'economically motivated' marriages between Cubans and Spanish citizens. My own fieldwork in Cuba suggests that similar suspicions thrive in most tourist-sending countries, particularly in Italy.
7. Dean MacCannell (1973, 1976), one of the first theorists of modern tourism, made of such quest for the 'real' and 'authentic' Other the key tenet of his theorization. Drawing on Goffman's front versus back distinction (1959), MacCannell maintained that modern tourists were longing to 'enter the back regions of the places they visited', regions 'associated with intimacy of relations and authenticity of

experiences' (MacCannell 1973: 589). For him, this quest was ultimately doomed to failure, given that 'tourist settings are arranged to produce the impression that a back region has been entered even when this is not the case' (ibid.). As shown by my ethnographic material, the basic tenets of MacCannell's conceptualization seem to have gained much popular recognition and, at least in destinations like Cuba, to have trickled down to inform the practices and interpretive frameworks of tourists.

8. In spite of the widespread acceptance of these lines of reasoning among my research participants, it is significant to note that the Cuban authorities' condemnations of *jineterismo* did not follow the same interpretation, and misrecognized any such moral underpinnings. As the studies of Berg (2004), Stout (2007), Garcia (2010) and Daigle (2015) have shown, official views of *jineterismo* do not see it as a justifiable economic endeavour, or a legitimate realm of *la lucha*, but rather as a sign of psychological weakness and moral degradation – a marker of self-harming and decadent selves (mis)guided by a lust for luxuries and capitalist consumption. To speculate further on such antagonistic moral judgments of *jineterismo*, we may draw on Povinelli's (2002, 2006) reflections on the 'intimate event', and the way it shapes modern selves and nations. Accordingly, we may argue that from the perspective of the Cuban authorities, *jineteros'/-as'* alleged inability to appropriately deploy intimacy posed a threat to the 'humanity' of the nation. In the light of her argument that 'to be human is to engage in practices of intimate recognition', Povinelli considers indeed how in the post-colony 'some people are foreclosed from entering the human realm in order that a nation can be made more human(e)' (Povinelli 2002: 234; see also Fernandez 2013).

9. See Simoni 2016a for more on the different narratives of how encounters originated, and their relevance in the qualification of people and relationships as more or less strategic, instrumental and 'professionalized'. In narratives of Danish women and Cuban men who had married, Fernandez (2013) also draws attention to the importance of the unintentional nature of their first connection; this being a key element used to distinguish these relationships from the allegedly more widespread instrumental ones.

10. The clearly gendered dimensions of these discourses would deserve more attention here. Drawing on recent ethnographic research in African contexts of economic decline on the gendered struggles 'over the balance between love, sex and money', Mains considers for instance how, '[a]t least in theory, an ideal of pure love supports young men's ability to engage in romantic relationships, despite their inability to offer economic support to their partners' (Mains 2013: 342). See Simoni (2015a) for a more thorough consideration of the entanglements between discourses of romantic love and masculinities in touristic Cuba.

11. Cuba's new Migratory Law, which came to effect on 14 January 2013, abolished the requirement of this permit for Cubans to exit the country. When I saw Raydel in 2013, his friends had began wondering what was he still doing in Cuba, now that this limitation was no longer in place: after years of complaining of being denied (*me denegaron*), people started speculating that there could be other reasons why Raydel was not leaving. On my visit to Havana in July 2014, I was happy to learn

12. that after a long bureaucratic struggle with the authorities, which according to his friends had brought him to the brink of madness, he had finally made it, and was living in Austria with his family.
12. Elsewhere (Simoni 2016a, 2016b) I address and explain the reasons for Cubans' potential resistance to what I call the 'hybridity move', referring to those interpretations that characterize their relationships with tourists as driven by a 'mix' of interest and sentiment.
13. A fruitful parallel may be drawn here with Patico's (2009) reflections on 'normalcy' when discussing how international matchmaking provides Russian women and American men with a way to seek normalcy in their personal lives. In relation to the Cuban context, in her research on *jineteras* and their discourses of love for foreign tourists, de Sousa e Santos similarly quotes one of her informants arguing that '[p]eople here want to have what is normal to have, simply what any person in the world can have [the 'world' here representing Western countries]' (de Sousa e Santos 2009: 422).
14. The recent anthropological literature on love and companionate marriage provides useful insights here, as it shows, for instance, how the ability to engage in 'romantic', 'selfless', 'pure' love becomes a marker of modernization, and of being an autonomous and self-determined subject (see, for instance, the chapters in Hirsch and Wardlow 2006, Padilla et al. 2007, and Cole and Thomas 2009, as well as the writings of Povinelli 2006, Faier 2007, Patico 2009, Hunter 2010 and Fernandez 2013, among others).
15. For Povinelli, 'autology' and 'genealogy' 'are two coexisting and intersecting forms of discipline that are constitutive of postcolonial governance' (Venkatesan et al. 2011: 225):

> 'Autology' refers to multiple discourses and practices which invoke the autonomous and self-determining subject, and which are therefore linked to, but not exhausted in, liberalism's emphasis on 'freedom' more narrowly conceived as a political philosophy. 'Genealogy', on the other hand, is taken to refer to discourses that stress social constraint and determination in processes of subject constitution, and construe the subject as bound by 'various kinds of inheritances'. (ibid.)

16. Drawing on Piot's (2010) theoretical insights on new cultural imaginaries taking shape in contemporary West Africa, such professions of true love and friendship may also be read as a way for Cubans to 'embrace the future, through acts of mimetic engagement with that which they desire' (Piot 2010: 10). In order to account, without condescension, for these mimetic endeavours, Piot urges us 'to fight the impulse to make theory adequate to political desire' (ibid.: 169), to resist 'the romance of resistance' (ibid.), and to be ready to 'measure "agency" through engagement with rather than rejection of Euro-otherness' (ibid.: 10), an engagement that people like Raydel were also keen on foregrounding.

17. See Simoni and Throop (2014) for a response to such critique in relation to recent literature in the anthropology of friendship and its calls to 'making friendship impure' (Coleman 2010).
18. A similarly productive path to rethink the relation between practices and ideals, the 'actual' and the 'virtual', has been recently proposed by Willerslev (Venkatesan et al. 2011) based on his research on love and the significance of ideals of love among Siberian Yukaghir hunters. Drawing on this author's work are also Zigon's remarks on love and the remaking of moral subjectivity, when he argues that '[a]s a motivating ethical demand … love guides moral experience in ways that may not always be contained by the local' (Zigon 2013: 203).
19. Confronted with similar disillusionments, my friend Manuel, a young Cuban man from Viñales, reached the conclusion that the game was too unsettling for him, and that continuous investment in intimate relationships with tourists made for a 'crazy life' (*una vida loca*), offering no guarantee whatsoever that one would ultimately be able to find a true lover, settle down, and fulfil 'normal' family life aspirations.
20. An interesting parallel may be drawn again here with the work of Groes-Green (2013) on relations between local women and their white partners in Maputo (Mozambique), and these women's struggles to keep their emotions in check, so as to avoid becoming 'too emotionally dependent on the man', given the risk that 'the man might back out of the relationship' (ibid.: 113).
21. An interesting scenario to explore, in order to track people's love trails in the longer term and in relation to changing conditions of existence, is to follow relationships that originated in Cuba as they develop into marriages and migration to the tourists' country of residence, a path that I started to explore in relation to the case of Spain (Simoni 2015b). As Fernandez (2013) research on Cubans' marriage migration to Denmark seems to suggest, these may be contexts where the key drivers – both moral and pragmatic – for cunning love to exist are no longer there, and where more stable and unified subject formations may take shape.
22. Such anxiety seems to characterize the prevailing reaction of Cuban authorities to the phenomenon of *jineterismo* in Cuba, as suggested by Daigle's (2015) work. A high-level Cuban official interviewed by Daigle (2015, 166-174) goes as far as to maintain that 'no healthy relationship can exist between a Cuban woman and a foreign man' (Daigle 2015: 168) given the economic differences that exist between them. Interpreting such stances, Daigle detects 'nationalist fears of invasion and defilement by foreign influence' (2015: 173).

REFERENCES

Abu-Lughod, L. 1990. 'The Romance of Resistance: Tracing Transformations of Power through Beduin Women'. *American Ethnologist* 17: 41–55.

Berg, M.L. 2004. 'Tourism and the Revolutionary New Man: The Specter of Jineterismo in Late "Special Period" Cuba'. *Focaal – European Journal of Anthropology* 43: 46–56.

———. 2011. *Diasporic Generations: Memory, Politics and Nation among Cubans in Spain*. New York: Berghahn Books.
Bisogno, F. 2010. 'Vivere nell'informalità: *Luchar* nella Cuba post-sovietica'. PhD dissertation. Milan: Università degli Studi di Milano Bicocca.
Brennan, D. 2004. *What's Love Got to Do with It? Transnational Desires and Sex Tourism in the Dominican Republic*. Durham, NC: Duke University Press.
Browne, K.E. 2004. *Creole Economics: Caribbean Cunning under the French Flag*. Austin, TX: University of Texas Press.
———. 2009. 'Economics and Morality: Introduction', in K.E. Browne and B.L. Milgram (eds), *Economics and Morality: Anthropological Approaches*. Lanham, MD: Rowman & Littlefield, pp. 1–40.
Cabezas, A.L. 2009. *Economies of Desire: Sex and Tourism in Cuba and the Dominican Republic*. Philadelphia, PA: Temple University Press.
Cole, J. 2009. 'Love, Money, and Economies of Intimacy in Tamatave, Madagascar', in J. Cole and L. Thomas (eds), *Love in Africa*. Chicago, IL and London: University of Chicago Press, pp. 109–34.
Cole, J., and L. Thomas (eds). 2009. *Love in Africa*. Chicago, IL and London: Chicago University Press.
Coleman, S. 2010. 'Afterword. Making Friendship Impure: Some Reflections on a (Still) Neglected Topic', in A. Desai and E. Killick (eds), *The Ways of Friendship: Anthropological Perspectives*. New York: Berghahn Books, pp. 197–206.
Crick, M. 1995. 'The Anthropologist as Tourist: An Identity in Question', in M.-F. Lanfant, J.B. Allcock and E.M. Bruner (eds), *International Tourism: Identity and Change*. London: Sage, pp. 205–23.
Daigle, M. 2015. *From Cuba with Love: Sex and Money in the Twenty-First Century*. Oakland, CA: University of California Press.
de Sousa e Santos, D. 2009. 'Reading Beyond the Love Lines: Examining Cuban *Jineteras*' Discourses of Love for Europeans'. *Mobilities* 4(3): 407–26.
Faier, L. 2007. 'Filipina Migrants in Rural Japan and their Professions of Love'. *American Ethnologist* 34(1): 148–62.
Fassin, D. 2008. 'Beyond Good and Evil?: Questioning the Anthropological Discomfort with Morals'. *Anthropological Theory* 8(4): 333–44.
Ferguson, J. 2006. *Global Shadows: Africa in the Neoliberal World Order*. Durham, NC and London: Duke University Press.
Fernandez, N.T. 1999. 'Back to the Future? Women, Race, and Tourism in Cuba', in K. Kempadoo (ed.), *Sun, Sex, and Gold: Tourism and Sex Work in the Caribbean*. Lanham, MD: Rowman & Littlefield, pp. 81–89.
———. 2013. 'Moral Boundaries and National Borders: Cuban Marriage Migration to Denmark'. *Identities: Global Studies in Culture and Power* 20(3): 270–87.
Fosado, G. 2005. 'Gay Sex Tourism, Ambiguity and Transnational Love in Havana', in D.J. Fernández (ed.), *Cuba Transnational*. Gainesville, FL: University Press of Florida, pp. 61–78.
Freeman, C. 2007. 'Neoliberalism and the Marriage of Reputation and Respectability: Entrepreneurship and the Barbadian Middle Class', in M. Padilla et al. (eds), *Love*

and Globalization: Transformations of Intimacy in the Contemporary World. Nashville, TN: Vanderbilt University Press, pp. 3–37.

Garcia, A. 2010. 'Continuous Moral Economies: The State Regulation of Bodies and Sex Work in Cuba'. *Sexualities* 13(2): 171–96.

García Moreno, C. 2010. 'Mujeres migrantes cubanas: "resolviendo" e "inventando" también en España'. PhD dissertation. Tarragona: Universitat Rovira y Virgili.

García Moreno, C., and J.J. Pujadas Muñoz. 2011. '"No es fácil..., y aquí tampoco": Trayectorias migratorias de mujeres cubanas en España'. *Revista de Dialectología y Tradiciones Populares* LXVI(2): 455–86.

Goffman, E. 1959. *The Presentation of Self in Everyday Life*. Garden City, New York: Doubleday.

Groes-Green, C. 2013. '"To Put Men in a Bottle": Eroticism, Kinship, Female Power, and Transactional Sex in Maputo, Mozambique'. *American Ethnologist* 40(1): 102–17.

Gupta, A. and Ferguson, J. 1992. 'Beyond "Culture": Space, Identity, and the Politics of Difference'. *Cultural Anthropology* 7(1): 6–23.

Hansing, K. 2006. *Rasta, Race and Revolution: The Emergence and Development of the Rastafari Movement in Socialist Cuba*. Berlin: LIT Verlag.

Hirsch, J.S., and H. Wardlow (eds). 2006. *Modern Loves: The Anthropology of Romantic Love and Companionate Marriage*. Ann Arbor, MI: University of Michigan Press.

Hunter, M. 2010. *Love in the Time of AIDS: Inequality, Gender and Rights in South Africa*. Indianapolis, IN: University of Indiana Press.

Lundgren, S. 2011. 'Heterosexual Havana: Ideals and Hierarchies of Gender and Sexuality in Contemporary Cuba'. PhD dissertation. Uppsala, Sweden: Uppsala University.

MacCannell, D. 1973. 'Staged Authenticity: On Arrangements of Social Space in Tourist Settings'. *The American Journal of Sociology* 79(3): 589–603.

———. 1976. *The Tourist: A New Theory of the Leisure Class*. London: Macmillan.

Mains, D. 2013. 'Friends and Money: Balancing Affection and Reciprocity among Young Men in Urban Ethiopia'. *American Ethnologist* 40(2): 335–46.

Moore, H.L. 2011. *Still Life: Hopes, Desires and Satisfactions*. Cambridge: Polity.

Padilla, M., et al. (eds). 2007. *Love and Globalization: Transformations of Intimacy in the Contemporary World*. Nashville, TN: Vanderbilt University Press.

Palmié, S. 2004. '*Fascinans* or *Tremendum*? Permutations of the State, the Body, and the Divine in Late Twentieth-Century Havana'. *New West Indian Guide* 78(3/4): 229–68.

Patico, J. 2009. 'For Love, Money, or Normalcy: Meanings of Strategy and Sentiment in the Russian–American Matchmaking Industry'. *Ethnos* 74(3): 307–30.

Piot, Ch. 2010. *Nostalgia for the Future: West Africa after the Cold War*. Chicago, IL: University of Chicago Press.

Povinelli, E.A. 2002. 'Notes on Gridlock: Genealogy, Intimacy, Sexuality'. *Public Culture* 14(1): 215–38.

———. 2006. *The Empire of Love: Toward a Theory of Intimacy, Genealogy, and Carnality*. Durham, NC and London: Duke University Press.

Prentice, R. 2009. '"Thieving a Chance": Moral Meaning of Theft in a Trinidadian Garment Factory', in K.E. Browne and B.L. Milgram (eds), *Economics and Morality: Anthropological Approaches*. Lanham, MD: Rowman & Littlefield, pp. 123–241.

Roca, J. (ed.). 2013. *Migrantes por amor: La búsqueda de pareja en el escenario transnacional*. Valencia: Editorial Germania.

Simoni, V. 2008. 'Shifting Power: The (De)Stabilization of Asymmetries in the Realm of Tourism in Cuba'. *Tsantsa: Journal of the Swiss Anthropological Association* 13: 89–97.

———. 2013. 'Intimate Stereotypes: The Vicissitudes of Being *Caliente* in Touristic Cuba'. *Civilisations: Revue internationale d'anthropologie et de sciences humaines* 62(1–2): 181–97.

———. 2014a. 'Revisiting Hosts and Guests: Ethnographic Insights on Touristic Encounters from Cuba'. *Journal of Tourism Challenges and Trends* 6(2): 39–62.

———. 2014b. 'Coping with Ambiguous Relationships: Sex, Tourism, and Transformation in Cuba'. *Journal of Tourism and Cultural Change* 12(2): 166–83.

———. 2014c. 'The Morality of Friendship in Touristic Cuba'. *Suomen Antropologi: Journal of the Finnish Anthropological Society* 39(1): 19–36.

———. 2015a. 'Breadwinners, Sex Machines and Romantic Lovers: Entangling Masculinities, Moralities, and Pragmatic Concerns in Touristic Cuba'. *Etnográfica* 19(2): 389–411.

———. 2015b. 'Intimacy and Belonging in Cuban Tourism and Migration'. *The Cambridge Journal of Anthropology* 33(2): 26–41.

———. 2016a. *Tourism and Informal Encounters in Cuba*. New York: Berghahn Books.

———. 2016b. 'Ethnography, Mutuality, and the Utopia of Love and Friendship in Touristic Cuba'. *Journal of the Anthropological Society of Oxford* 8(1): 143–67.

Simoni, V., and J. Throop. 2014. 'Introduction: Friendship, Morality, and Experience'. *Suomen Antropologi: Journal of the Finnish Anthropological Society* 39(1): 4–18.

Stoler, A.L. 1989. 'Making Empire Respectable: The Politics of Race and Sexual Morality in 20th-Century Colonial Cultures'. *American Ethnologist* 16(4): 634–60.

Stout, N. 2007. 'Feminists, Queers and Critics: Debating the Cuban Sex Trade'. *Journal of Latin American Studies* 40: 721–42.

———. 2014. *After Love: Queer Intimacy and Erotic Economies in Post-Soviet Cuba*. Durham, NC, and London: Duke University Press.

Venkatesan, S., et al. 2011. 'The Anthropological Fixation with Reciprocity Leaves No Room for Love: 2009 Meeting of the Group for Debates in Anthropological Theory'. *Critique of Anthropology* 31(3): 210–50.

Wilson, P.J. 1969. 'Reputation and Respectability: A Suggestion for Caribbean Ethnology'. *Man* 4(1): 70–84.

Zigon, J. 2013. 'On Love: Remaking Moral Subjectivity in Postrehabilitation Russia'. *American Ethnologist* 40(1): 201–15.

CHAPTER
9

The Masculine and Moral Self
Migration Narratives of Cuban Husbands in Scandinavia

Nadine T. Fernandez

The Cuban and international media has lamented that Cubans' morals have been eroded by the severe economic hardship that followed the collapse of the Soviet Union, when people resorted to nefarious scams and pilfering to get by. In a 2013 speech, even President Raul Castro rebuked Cubans for losing their honesty, decorum and decency. He commented, 'I have a bitter sensation that we are a society that is ever better educated, but not necessarily more enlightened' (Burnett 2013). This general shadow of immorality that clouds Cuban society is especially intense around relationships between Cubans and tourists. Even the motives of these romances are doubted as they form in the morally suspect context of the tourist economy where everything is for sale, and at a time when the whole country's moral integrity is in question.

Instrumentality, in many ways, forms the foundation of the migration literature. Perhaps for too long, researchers have employed an economic lens to analyse the cost–benefit factors and working lives of migrants and their families, overlooking emotional and affective elements of people's motivations and experiences of migration (Mai and King 2009). Likewise, within marriage migration research, scholars have appealed to move beyond the focus on strictly economic or kin motivations for cross-border marriage and the paradigms of exploitation and instrumentality rooted in the idea of a universalized category of women's subordination (Ebron 2002; Williams

2010; Charsley 2012). In fact, women are not the only marriage migrants, though most scholars analysing these marriages have explicitly examined gender and power in couples formed by migrant brides from the global South with Western men. The experiences and perspectives of male marriage migrants are seldom the focus of cross-border[1] marriage studies (Charsley 2005; Gallo 2006). Williams notes that gender sensitive studies examining the male perspective are still rare, and urges that 'gender in its broadest sense should clearly be factored into the analysis of all migration' (Williams 2010: 21).

In this chapter I attempt to heed these calls away from instrumentality and towards an 'emotional and sexual turn in migration studies', and at the same time to broaden our gendered view of migration by examining the stories of men as gendered individuals (Mai and King 2009). Their narratives of marriage migration reveal a moral discourse tied to self-making which emerges in these heterosexual, and mostly interracial, unions. I frame these narratives using Oxfeld's idea of 'dialogic morality', where morality forms in response to the current situation (Oxfeld 2010). The flux and transformation of post-Soviet Cuba has resulted not in a moral decline, as Raul Castro and the press lament, but rather a dialogic reworking of ideas about people's obligations (to themselves and others) as they respond to changing economic conditions, social structures and social mores. This 'dialogic morality' connects to notions of subjectivity and self-making as Biehl, Good and Kleinman suggest, in that subjectivity becomes 'the ground on which a long series of historical changes and moral apparatuses coalesce' (Biehl, Good and Kleinman 2007). Put more simply, both they and Oxfeld are talking about how people 'do the right thing' while giving meaning to their lives and envisioning new possibilities for themselves and their relationships. It is an approach that finds parallel in what Sykes calls 'the ethnography of moral reason' (Sykes 2009: 15, as quoted in Simoni 2015). In the Cuban men's narratives, we see a moral discourse of their migration experiences that shows an unfolding and interconnecting of self and different aspects of masculinity (the manly lover, the autonomous modern subject, the family breadwinner). Empirically shifting the gendered focus from mobile brides from the Global South, to mobile grooms from the Global South, I explore how the Cuban men themselves understand these relationships in terms of morality and masculinity.

Methodology

This research is based on ethnographic fieldwork and over fifty open-ended interviews I conducted in 2011–12 with Cubans and their Danish or Swedish spouses. About 550 Cubans (nearly equal numbers of men and women) live in Denmark. While determining exact numbers entering through marriage is difficult, over 300 family reunification permits[2] were issued to Cubans between 2000 and 2010 (Statistics Denmark 2018). In Sweden where over 2,800 Cubans reside (Statistics Sweden 2018), I contacted a smaller number of couples in the cities of Malmö and Stockholm. There are slightly more Cuban men than women living in Sweden, and roughly 40 per cent of all the Cubans in Sweden arrived there after 2000.

Like Cubans in Spain (Berg 2011), Cubans in Scandinavia do not form an ethnic community in any meaningful or visible way, so finding interlocutors required relying on personal contacts. Locating Cubans through diverse networks, I then used snowball sampling to identify additional participants. The interviews were supplemented with participant observation at venues frequented by some of the Cuban–Scandinavian couples. About 60 per cent of the couples I interviewed were Cuban men (mostly black or mulatto)[3] married to (or separated from) ethnically white Danish or Swedish women. Both partners were of similar ages, mostly mid-twenties to mid-thirties, though there were a few middle-aged couples. All couples had met in Cuba while the Scandinavian partner was on vacation or studying (Spanish, salsa, drumming, etc.). The interviews were recorded, and the participants' names and identities changed to protect their anonymity.

This chapter starts with an overview on moral discourse and subjectivity. I then examine the Cuban context that frames these relationships, and finally turn to the narratives of the Cuban husbands. I focus on three aspects of their migration stories that are key in establishing the gendered morality of their actions: (1) 'naturalized' conceptions of masculinity and a racialized, national sexuality; (2) narratives of self-making through travel and personal creative pursuits; and (3) family obligations in Cuba.

Male Cross-Border Marriage Migration and Dialogic Morality

Until very recently, a focus on 'gender' and sexualized subjectivities in the transnational sex, migration and marriage migration literature has usually meant 'women'. Only in the last several years have migration studies begun to examine the gendered experiences of migrant men (Batnitzky, McDowell and Dyer 2009; Datta et al. 2009). In the field of marriage migration, migrant brides (particularly from Asia) numerically outnumber migrant grooms, and as a result, women are assumed to be the typical marriage migrant (Williams 2012). There have been very few studies examining men as migrant husbands (Charsley 2005; Gallo 2006; Fleischer 2008), and most of these tend to focus on intra-ethnic couples (such as Pakistanis or Turks in Northern Europe with spouses from their ancestral homelands).

Likewise, most of the literature on sex travel centres on male tourists. It is in this context that scholars developed ideas of 'gendered geographies of power' (Pessar and Mahler 2001) and 'cartographies of desire' (Pflugfelder 1999, in Constable 2005). Though less frequently studied, women are also consumers of sex in the Global South (Ebron 2002; Brennan 2004; Kempadoo 2004), though few scholars (Pruitt and LaFont 1996; Frohlick 2007; Phillips 2008; Karkabi 2011) make these women the primary focus of their research. When female tourists' relationships with local men are mentioned, the analysis is often as Kempadoo (2004) states, that 'women simply become equal to their male counterparts in the consumption of [Caribbean] sexuality'. Studies analysing female tourist relations with local men have been couched alternatively as sex tourism or romance tourism (Pruitt and LaFont 1996), yet as Karkabi (2011) notes, regardless of the label, these studies come to similar conclusions – 'there is a need that foreign women seek to fulfil through their encounters with local men who were inevitably led into these relations due to economic hardship' (Karkabi 2011: 81). Local men are depicted as either being in a subjugated position (foregoing their agency to be with the foreign woman) or they are portrayed as tricksters who dupe the tourists by 'playing at love' (Brennan 2004) in order to gain a visa out of the country. In short, 'female tourist'–'local men' relations are mostly talked about in structurally overdetermined ways as exploitation, prostitution, consumerism or victimization (Karkabi 2011). In commonsense thinking, these characterizations are shrouded in a cloud of moral disdain.

It is not surprising then that, in the context of touristic desire and a growing consumer culture in contemporary Cuba, the dominant view is that marriage to a foreigner is morally suspect. The rise of mass tourism, coupled with the social and economic upheaval since the collapse of the socialist bloc, has plunged Cuba into what many on and off the island see as a state of moral decline. Many Cubans believe that the moral crisis is epitomized in materialist interests fuelling romantic relationships. Anthropologist Elise Andaya, for example, noted that her informants expressed concern about a resurgence of 'anti-values' (i.e. materialist values) in couples (Andaya 2013). This common sentiment is also reflected in the lyrics of popular Cuban songs, which encourage women to seek men who can support their desires for consumption or provide a passport for foreign travel and a life abroad.[4] Havana d' Primera's 2011 song *Carita de Pasaporte* (Face of a Passport), written by Alexander Abreu, opens with the lines:

> And she says that life is really hard
> With problems and censorship
> That's why she needs a passport
> It's essential to walk in other lands
> At any cost
> Without struggle, without war

In counterpoint to expressions of desperation to leave by any means, one can find musical examples proclaiming that bodies are *not* for sale on the island. In the 2004 song *Callejero* (Hustler), the group Moneda Dura (Hard Currency) sings of a middle-aged female tourist who arrives in Havana looking for a young lover to show her a good time. In the song's refrain, the young Cuban man she propositions emphatically replies:

> I don't want your money,
> I don't want you to take me to abroad,
> I don't want to go to Varadero in your car.
> Listen, make no mistake, I'm not a hustler.

This musical debate embodies the tremendous social unease caused by affective engagements with foreign tourists (that sometimes fall under the broad umbrella of *jineterismo* or hustling)[5] and the occasional resulting cross-border marriage. I argue that we can best understand the Cuban men's migration narratives as a response, a kind of dialogic morality, to this commonsense perspective on cross-border marriages in the post-Soviet period. I turn to Ellen Oxfeld's (2010) work on morality in China to help to frame my interpretation of the Cubans' stories.

Oxfeld's focus on everyday morality in China comes at a time of tremendous social change when some intellectuals worry that China is on the verge of moral collapse – paralleling arguments commonly heard about Cuba. She develops the idea of 'dialogic morality' in her study of the daily moral discourse in a rural Chinese village. Based on Bakhtin's idea that utterances are always implicitly or explicitly in response to other utterances, Oxfeld describes dialogic morality as 'a morality that forms in response or in dialogue with the current situation' (Oxfeld 2010: 221). In the Chinese case, she argues that even these preoccupations with a lack of morality are themselves a moral discourse and evidence of moral values. Village residents, as well as published social critics, evince the existence of their own moral beliefs through critique, and gossip about 'doing the right thing', both interpersonally and with regard to the wider society.

Similarly, Cuba finds itself in the midst of social change, a weakening socialist system, and a rising concern over the citizens' morality – particularly in regard to practices of sexuality and kin-making. In this context, the

Cuban men recount their courtship, marriage and migration to Scandinavia in dialogue with the pejorative assumptions attached to cross-border marriages that emerge in the context of tourist encounters. Their narratives are a kind of moral discourse. Through these narratives the men make meaning of their choices and explain their actions, given both the practical and moral considerations of the present moment. Here we see the connection to subjectivity as both an empirical reality and analytic category (Biehl Good and Kleinman 2007). Through the men's narratives, modes of subjectivity intertwine with particular configurations of political and economic conditions. For young Cubans living in the post-Soviet period we can ask, '[how] do people value life and relationships and enact the possibilities they envision for themselves and for others?' (ibid.: 8). As the start of an answer, I offer an examination of three recurrent themes in men's migration narratives that speak to both dialogic morality and masculine self-making.

The 'Naturalness' of Masculinity and a Racialized National Sexuality

While social scientists have long argued the constructed nature of gender, sexuality and race, commonsense understandings of these concepts still prevail. Interestingly, the social upheaval in post-1990 Cuba demonstrates the malleability of these commonsense perspectives, and how they play out at home and abroad.

The history of racial dynamics on the island is complex. As a former colonial plantation society, the island today still bears the legacy of its past in a general denigration of blackness. Despite the Revolution's many achievements, a disproportionate number of darker-skinned Cubans remain in the lower echelons of society (de la Fuente 2001). Although there is a long history of racial mixing, *mestizaje* has always been a contested process, and certain configurations of interracial couples still cause social unease (Fernandez 2010). For black Cuban men, partnering with white Cuban women is neither easy nor common, and when these couples do form, the black men are often highly educated professionals or have steady access to hard currency (ibid.). While sexual encounters between black Cuban men and white Cuban women may occur, particularly among young Cubans, marriage or long-term unions between partners on opposite ends of the colour and economic continuum are less frequent. Racial and class endogamy continues to be the norm, even after more than fifty years of socialism.

In light of this history, the changes in couple formation precipitated by the Special Period and the burgeoning of mass tourism have been remarkable.

Since the 1990s, blackness has transformed from a 'hindrance into an asset' (Hernández-Reguant 2006). Allen notes that 'Cuba is not only cool, but black Cubans are again considered "hot" in the global market place of images and experiences of pleasure' (Allen 2011). In Cuba, like other tourist settings, men can receive social recognition and empowerment as masculine subjects through their relations with tourist women (Karkabi 2011), and they often play on sexualized racial stereotypes (Sanchez Taylor 2006; Simoni 2015).

Echoing social reality, we find exactly this dynamic emerging as a recurrent theme in the hard-driving *timba* music of the post-1990 period. Analysing these *timba* lyrics, Hernández-Reguant (2006) observes that in defending the sexual liaisons between black men and foreign women, the songs simultaneously promote the idea of the exotic and erotic other. *Timba* song lyrics recount how tourism has given black Cuban men new possibilities for accessing white women, namely foreign tourists (ibid.). In the context of reconstructing a positive racially sexualized, masculine self, black Cuban men are rejecting black women and seeking white women instead. The white Western gaze was no longer objectifying black Cuban men; it has turned from the gaze of authority to that of spectator (ibid.).

Like the black Costa Rican men with white foreign girlfriends, the Cubans and Scandinavians could be described as engaging in 'ethnosexual dynamics of mutual desire' (Frohlick 2007). Both partners envision a racialized fantasy of the other. Within this context and the increasingly consumer-oriented economy, these cross-border interracial relations give Cuban men of colour new social capital and status in the racial arena. Against this backdrop of racialized sexuality, I was interested in how Cuban marriage migrants characterized their sexual encounters with tourists (which included meeting their Scandinavian spouses) and presented these histories to me with a mixture of pride and inevitability.

Leonel, a working-class black Cuban who was employed in tourism as a dance instructor in Havana, now lives in Copenhagen with his Danish wife. However, prior to their marriage he had numerous relations with foreign women. He recounted some of these previous experiences as follows:

> So, a student invites me to a *mojito*. Well, after that *mojito*, comes another *mojito*, then the dance, then the conversation, and after a few drinks comes the kiss. And after the kiss come other things. That's the way it is. That's what happens when you work in tourism... Yes, I had quite a few [women] – Spaniards, French, Italians... Imagine! I was enjoying life. I was divorced. I was single. Imagine!... There were blondes; there were some rich women that were really striking... beautiful!... Imagine! They invite you out for a drink, and you can't tell them no.

Another Cuban interlocutor I spoke with, Dariel, a white man with a technical education who worked in tourism in the Cuban city of Santiago, had similar experiences. Interestingly, he too stressed how he did not initiate these encounters. He recalled: 'The first was a pretty young French tourist... well, she fell in love with me [was attracted to me] and well, (laughing) I was weak...' ['weak' as in unable to resist the temptations of her interest]. Dariel went on to describe how tourists he met at work would invite him out dancing after work, and, 'well, we'd go out dancing and then the parties began... you know, the craziness of youth'.

In both narratives the men highlighted the women's initiative in inviting them out, and the inevitability of the sexual encounters in the context of these social excursions. Both positioned their sexual behaviour as part of the social world they shared with the tourists. For the Cuban men I spoke with, sexual engagements with foreign women were simply extensions of their performances of masculinity.

Heterosexual encounters between Cuban men and tourists, like *piropos* (catcalls), are a vehicle for asserting ideal masculinity in a homosocial setting (Lundgren 2011). Dariel commented that his friends envied his access to these foreign women and the ease of his sexual sociability. Dariel and Leonel gained status among peers though their sexual relations with foreign women by demonstrating their heterosexual desirability and male virility. This display of masculinity by marriage migrants echoes Simoni's description of men in Cuba talking with pride about seducing foreign women and boasting of their latest adventures in moments of male sociality, building masculinity-grounded hierarchies among themselves (Simoni 2015).

In addition, both men stressed the inevitability of these sexual liaisons. This is best understood in terms of the interconnection between gender and sexuality, and the negotiation of masculinity in the context of heterosexuality. Analysing Cuban couple-hood among white Cubans, Lundgren argues that heterosexuality is rooted in the complementarity of female needs and uncontrollable male drives. Male expressions of eroticism are easily interpreted as legitimate performances of uncontrollable male virility (Lundgren 2011). Both Cuban men and women reiterate these common gender stereotypes deeply rooted in assumptions about gender differences presumably grounded in nature (Hamilton 2012; Andaya 2014). We see this in how the Cuban migrants I interviewed ascribed a quality of unavoidability to their sexual liaisons with tourists, and furthermore these exploits were valued as markers of virility. Situating these Cuban–tourist dynamics within broader Cuban understandings of gender and sexuality disrupts the '*jinetero*' (hustler) frame, which views these men as hustling the tourists and initiating the encounters by 'catching' the tourist. Gender complementarity naturalizes and normalizes these encounters in commonsense understandings of heterosexual gender dynamics.

Moreover, Hernández-Reguant (2006) argues, sex between a black Cuban man and a foreign white woman must also be understood in the context of constructing a *racialized* masculine self. However, in pairings with white Scandinavian women, all Cubans become racialized as their eroticism is attached to a national-cultural category, and not exclusively to skin colour (Forrest 1999). The Cubans' sexual behaviour must be situated not only within heterosexual dynamics on the island, but also within the context of globalized racial hierarchies, wherein an eroticized 'black sexuality' seems to apply to nearly all Cubans in tourism-related encounters (Roland 2010; Simoni 2015). This positively racialized/national sexuality continues to function in Scandinavia, reinforcing the 'naturalness' of this connection and the 'inevitability' of these relationships with Scandinavian women.

Even off the island, erotic racialized images of Cuba circulate widely in salsa clubs and marketing for Cuban products abroad (such as rum and cigars). Black masculinity, in general, is sexualized through naturalizing global discourse about the erotic other as virile, masterful and attractive (Frohlick 2007). The salsa club scene in Denmark and Sweden provides an excellent illustration of this dynamic. In these predominantly white countries with relatively low levels of non-Western immigration, there is an unspoken hierarchy of immigrants – some are valued more highly and accepted more easily than others in a wide variety of arenas. In the sexual marketplace, Cuban masculinity has a high value. Several interlocutors recounted incidents in salsa clubs where they witnessed black African and olive-skinned Middle Eastern immigrant men trying to pass as Cubans in order to successfully hook up with Scandinavian women. Comically, Dariel retells one such meeting in a salsa bar where he starts chatting in English with a black man. He asks the man where he is from, and upon hearing the man profess that he is Cuban, Dariel rapidly switches to speaking Spanish. Clearly flustered, the man, really an African masquerading as Cuban, responds to Dariel, '*hablo solamente un poco de español*' (I only speak a little Spanish). For the Cuban men married to Scandinavians, their sexual desirability (both in Cuba and in Scandinavia) bolstered their understandings of the 'naturalness' and inevitability of their relationships.

I recognize that there certainly was an aspect of performance and bravado in their sexual recountings to me (a female anthropologist). Hamilton, who conducted research on gender and sexuality in Cuba through life history interviews, astutely reflects on the performance aspect of masculinity as it manifests itself in the interview process: 'The performance of masculinity is found as well in the interview settings, in which a male narrator may boast about multiple sexual exploits … clearly enjoying the opportunity to perform for and even provoke the interviewers [two middle-aged white women] (Hamilton 2012: 111). Similar dynamics were surely at play in my interactions with Cuban men in Scandinavia, but our conversations were never tainted with shame or a sense of moral transgression about what might be considered by some as 'womanizing'. Quite the opposite, the encounters the men described were inexorable and morally unquestionable because of their understandings of their masculine sexual selves. Repeatedly they emphasized the women's initiative, and the 'natural' and 'normal' way the sexual relations developed, deflecting any spectre of instrumentality or ulterior motives that might have clouded these encounters. Their discourse distanced themselves from *jineterimso* (tourist hustling), and bolstered a morally grounded view of their courtship and subsequent marriages.

Self-Making through Travel and Personal Pursuits

Another recurrent theme in the interviews was a tendency to minimize any interest in migration, but at the same time discuss desires to travel or to realize personal goals and ambitions that might be facilitated by travel. There is a long-standing Western view of travel as a vehicle for self-cultivation and transformation, which Amit argues is now heightened by a discourse in many countries that promotes the importance of 'international experience', given the globalizing world economy (Amit 2007). Many scholars suggest that mobility and travel lie at the heart of social life and modernity (Urry 2000). Salazar and Smart add that there is a common assumption that mobility generates change, progress and improvement: 'People link horizontal or geographical mobility almost automatically with vertical economic, social and cultural climbing ... mobility is more than mere movement; it is infused with meaning' (Salazar and Smart 2011). For some Cubans, Suárez argues that, 'in the twenty-first century, travel defines us: travelling beyond the confines of the island; staying, returning, caught in between...' (Suárez 2008). For other Cubans, it is the impossibility of travel, a sense of immobility, that both *defines* and *confines* them. It is not surprising then that the Cuban men engage this mobility discourse in their migration narratives, especially since their spouses have entered their lives through a travel encounter. For some, this desire to travel is combined with personal aspirations for creative endeavours, and marriages are seen by some as a gateway to a new life and opportunities.

Javier, a black Cuban with a technical education who is married to a Dane, commented: 'I never had desires to leave Cuba. I was focused on my art. I wanted to travel. But travel as an artist, travel and return and continue to create with my art'. Ernesto, a conservatory-trained musician, expressed similar sentiments; speaking of his Danish wife he said: 'She returned to Cuba because really from the very start when she met me she wanted to bring me here to Denmark. I told her no, not now, not right now. At the time I was doing things in Cuba that were important to me... there was a really creative wave [in Cuba at that time]'. Later he did go to Denmark, but continued to maintain strong ties and partnerships with Cuban musicians on the island. Dayron, in recounting his courtship and marriage to his Danish wife Pernilla, also downplayed any interest in migration;[6] though like other men I spoke with, he expressed a desire to travel and see the world.

The following narrative highlights the intertwined elements of self-making, travel and career that were echoed in other men's stories. García-Moreno and Pujadas Muñoz note how Cuban women migrating to Spain also cite personal aspirations and professional development as motivation for their migration (García-Moreno and Pujadas Muñoz 2011). Victor, a black Cuban from a middle-class background and now divorced from his Danish wife, has been in Denmark for several years playing music at night and working in a supermarket during the day:

> I always thought about leaving because I was always curious about other things, to see what was outside [of Cuba], that is, to meet other people, see other things. I always liked the idea of experiencing other things that I had learned about only in books. So, yes [I thought of leaving], but always with the idea of leaving and returning. Many of the people I knew, we had the idea to experience (*conocer*) and then return (*regresar*) to Cuba. This is something beautiful and good because you can implement (*realizar*) what you learned in your country ... I hadn't planned to meet someone so I could leave the country. My idea was to travel with my music. We had done auditions for foreign businesses that were looking for musicians to take to other countries ... My relations with foreigners began with friends. I didn't start with [foreign] women. I started with friends singing [and playing music] with friends. Some of them I'm still in touch with, and they have come to visit me here [in Denmark]. Basically, that was my contact with foreigners – friendships. Until I realized, well, this may be a possibility for love also, because Cuban women are very difficult.[7]

It was a Danish musician studying in Cuba who had introduced Victor to the Danish woman whom he later married. She had been in Cuba for several weeks and was interested in taking percussion lessons, and her friend put her in touch with Victor. The lessons began, and were soon accompanied by a romance. When it was time to return to Denmark the couple faced the inevitable dilemma of if and how to continue this binational relationship.[8]

> After some months [she invited me to Denmark]; it was the only way because she couldn't continue travelling [to Cuba]. So she took a gamble and I took a gamble too, to try (*probar*). [After arriving in Denmark] we decided... we talked, now I was already here [in Denmark], we continued trying. Really it was a big test. In those first months I felt really strange. I felt like I had won a scholarship (*una beca*). ... and while I was still married I thought I'd go back to Cuba if there were any problems. I still had this idea of the scholarship. I felt like I was on a scholarship (study abroad). Where was this scholarship going to take me?

Victor's narrative centres on processes of self-making; crafting a modern self in the 'autological' sense described by Povinelli (2006). His relations with foreigners begin from his profession – from his music. The connections he establishes are professional exchanges around music, not hustling or materially motivated. These contacts develop into long-standing friendships as people he met in Cuba continue to be part of his life, even after he moves to Denmark. The longevity of these friendships, despite geographic distance, attests to the authenticity of these connections. With friendship as the foundation, Victor establishes solid moral footing for his connection to foreigners, and ultimately to the woman who becomes his wife. Writing on friendships in touristic Cuba, Simoni reveals Cubans aspirations of becoming free, autonomous, and moral subjects in full-fledged 'pure' friendships with foreigners such as Victor describes (Simoni 2014). Furthermore, Victor's friendships are about a shared art – playing, performing and creating music. His ambitions, inextricably linked to his craft and career, scaffold these friendships he develops with like-minded foreigners. Finally, meeting and marrying the Danish woman emerges at the end of this chain of relationships, whose logic and moral grounding are self-apparent. He presents the marriage itself, not in an idyllic bubble where romantic love transcends material reality, but rather situates it firmly in the practical reality and obstacles of conducting a binational relationship. Recognizing the uncertainty that lies ahead, the couple decide 'to try' anyway, and the marriage becomes for Victor both an affective relationship and an opportunity, a scholarship.

At different historical moments, marriage has served as an avenue for advancement, particularly for Cuban women of colour (Safa 2005); and even in contemporary Cuba, marriage can be a transformation strategy for women, as an escape, a way to make a new life, and a break with the past (Hamilton 2012). With his professional ambitions in mind, we see Victor express a similar view as he speculates where this marriage might lead. While motivations of migration and a residency visa would be viewed as instrumental – a desire to travel, advance a career, pursue and maintain friendships – these things convey inalienable rights of a modern subject.[9]

His grounded view of the risks and potentialities of his marriage framed in the idiom of friendship and career help to create a narrative of an autological individual with morally defensible aspirations.

Family Obligations and Remittances

In Cuba, the migration of a family member may be traumatic, but it also brings with it new possibilities not only for the one migrating, but for the family left behind. The relationship of nurturance and obligation between children and parents is the anchor of the Cuban family (Andaya 2014). Conjugal ties may be fragile, but bonds between children and parents are enduring (Andaya 2013). One way these bonds are expressed and maintained is through remittances. Even relatively small amounts of money sent regularly translate into significantly improved living conditions for family members still in Cuba. Annual remittances arriving in Cuba are reaching record levels, climbing from just under a million US dollars in 2000 to over 3.4 *billion* dollars in 2016 (Morales 2017). While much of this money comes from the well-established Cuban-American community in the United States, more recent immigrants across the globe also significantly contribute to this flow.

For the men in Scandinavia, remittances become part of building both a moral and a masculine self. While models of masculinity in Cuba may be multiple and situational, the archetype of the solid provider still frames gender relations on the island (Andaya 2014; Simoni 2015). This aspect of masculinity is mirrored in the men's migration narratives, where remittances contribute to the breadwinner facet of Cuban masculinity (Simoni 2015). While some of the migrant men may have felt unable to live up to expected male roles as providers in Cuba, for many that changed once they settled in Scandinavia. Nearly all the Cubans I interviewed sent remittances back to their natal families. If able, they did so on a regular basis, sending amounts ranging from $50US to $250US every month. While helping their families in Cuba, this money sent home also legitimized their cross-border marriage. They were being good sons living up to familial obligations. Ariel, a white Cuban working in construction, commented:

> I don't regret leaving [Cuba], because thanks to me being here [in Sweden], my family in Cuba lives. Every month, I send my mother two hundred dollars. This never fails. She shares it with my siblings. They buy food. If I were in Cuba with them, I'd be there in sandals made from [plastic] coca cola bottles. I have a photo [of that]! I'm going to send it to you!

Even those men with strained relationships with their families on the island still feel the necessity to send remittances home to them. Lorenzo is a white Cuban, now a university student in Sweden. Although he rarely communicates with his mother, he has been sending a monthly stipend to her since he left Cuba more than six years ago with his Swedish wife. Reflecting on his regular remittances, he commented:

> In reality I don't know why I do it. Sometimes I'm at the point of stopping. I don't know why I do it, maybe simply to feel good about myself. And I also know it's something very cultural ... you can't abandon your mother, no matter what. So the least I can do is to send her 150 dollars a month.

Even their Scandinavian wives supported these endeavours (within limits), because it positioned their husbands as moral individuals. All of their wives had spent some time in Cuba, and each knew the situation of their husband's family and the general standard of living on the island. As Vibeke and her Cuban husband Misael are both university students in Denmark, the issue of remittances was somewhat sensitive. She commented:

> We don't have a lot of money and this had been a conflict between us, but we agreed to put a limit on it [amount remitted]. And for me it was fine to send 50 dollars a month because she [his mother] is living on nothing there, and her husband [also living abroad] is not sending any money. So [sending money regularly] is fine ... Now we are in agreement. Before we set the limit it was more difficult, because of course, you want to give your mother what she needs.

Even if struggling financially in Scandinavia, sending remittances whenever possible was unquestionably 'the right thing to do'. As Victor noted, 'I send something to my family, I can't send a lot. But it's incredible – my father is a doctor [in Cuba], I'm cleaning floors [in Denmark] and struggling, and I have to send money to a doctor in Cuba'.

For all of the men, sending remittances allowed them to fulfil family obligations in Cuba and also meet expectations of the masculine provider, both in their own eyes and in the eyes of their Scandinavian wives.

Conclusion

Post-Soviet Cuba is often portrayed as being in a state of moral crisis, and cross-border sexual liaisons are often seen as evidence of that moral decline. However, the narratives of these marriage migrants tell a different story. Black masculine sexual prowess was indeed 'a key for upward mobility in a new transnational terrain' in touristic Cuba, as Hernández-Reguant (2006) argues. However, this 'strategic' sexuality was justifiable and 'good' when situated, as it was in the men's narratives, within a naturalized discourse on masculinity, a global understanding of mobility as a modern right, and a continued commitment to family on the island. In the Cubans' narratives, these recurring themes of masculine sexuality, self-fulfilment through travel, and assuming the masculine role as provider through remittances serve to establish them as moral individuals in a marriage believed by many to be motivated by instrumentality. In this way, the men's narratives provide an example of dialogic morality as the men craft their autological selves and give meaning to their choices in the context of Cuba's social upheaval and the reality of global tourism.

Acknowledgements

I thank Valerio Simoni and Christian Groes for their insightful suggestions and comments.

Nadine T. Fernandez, a cultural anthropologist, is an associate professor and chair of the Social Science Department at the State University of New York/Empire State College. Her publications include *Revolutionizing Romance: Interracial Couples in Contemporary Cuba* (Rutgers University Press 2010), and several book chapters. Her articles appear in the *Journal of Ethnic and Migration Studies*, *Identities*, *Latin American Perspectives*, and *Temas*. She was a guest researcher at the Copenhagen University Anthropology Institute (2010), and the Danish National Centre for Social Research (2011). In 2015, she received the SUNY Chancellor's Award for Excellence in Scholarship and Creative Activities.

NOTES

1. Following Williams (2010), I use the term 'cross-border' marriage as a broad and neutral concept that avoids value judgment or reference to social or ethnic traits. Cross-border marriages can refer to marriages within or between communities, and it avoids an essentialist view of culture that is implied in the terms 'mixed' or 'intercultural' marriage.
2. Cubans marrying Danes in another European country would not show up in these numbers.
3. Mulatto is the common racial terminology used in Cuba for mixed-race individuals, and it is the term by which some of my informants self-identify.
4. Charanga Habanera's song *El Temba* is an example.

5. For a discussion of *jineterismo*, see Fernandez 1999, Berg 2004, Kummels 2005 and Cabezas 2009.
6. Garica-Moreno and Pujadas Munoz also noted that in Spain, despite the stereotype of the Cuban *jinetera* (hustler) marrying to leave the Cuba, the Cuban women they interviewed who married Spaniards also expressed that they had no intentions of emigrating nor were they frequenting tourist sites looking for Spanish husbands (García-Moreno and Pujadas Muñoz 2011).
7. During the interview, he elaborated how it was difficult for many Cuban men to have relationships with Cuban women as the women were only interested in men who could provide for them materially. So Cuban men without steady access to hard currency or desired goods or food found it difficult to court and maintain relations with Cubanas (Andaya 2014; Simoni 2014).
8. See Fernandez 2013 for an examination of Danish and Cuban immigration policies that frame and complicate the decisions transnational couples must make.
9. This dynamic is similar to what Simoni (2014) describes with Cuban friendships with tourists, where the Cubans insist on their 'commitment to a disinterested, affection-based friendship'. Faier posits a parallel argument regarding Filipina wives' professions of love for their Japanese husbands, through which they 'craft moral senses of self' (Faier 2007: 149).

REFERENCES

Allen, J.S. 2011. *Venceremos? The Erotics of Black Self-Making in Cuba*. Durham, NC: Duke University Press.

Amit, V. 2007. *Going First Class: New Approaches to Privileged Travel and Movement*. New York: Berghahn Books.

Andaya, E. 2013. 'Relationships and Money, Money and Relationships: Family, Gender and Changing Economics in Post-Soviet Cuba'. *Feminist Studies* 39: 731–58.

_____. 2014. *Conceiving Cuba: Reproduction, Women and the State in the Post-Soviet Era*. New Brunswick, NJ: Rutgers University Press.

Batnitzky, A., L. McDowell and S. Dyer. 2009. 'Flexible and Strategic Masculinities: The Working Lives and Gendered Identities of Male Migrants in London'. *Journal of Ethnic and Migration Studies* 35(8): 1275–93.

Berg, M.L. 2004. 'Tourism and the Revolutionary New Man: The Specter of *Jineterismo* in Late "Special Period" Cuba'. *Focaal* 43: 46–56.

_____. 2011. *Generating Diaspora: Memory, Politics and Nation among Cubans in Spain*. New York: Berghahn Books.

Biehl, J., B. Good and A. Kleinman. 2007. 'Introduction: Rethinking Subjectivity', in J. Biehl, B. Good and A. Kleinman (eds), *Subjectivity: Ethnographic Investigations*. Berkeley, CA: University of California Press, pp. 1–23.

Brennan, D. 2004. *What's Love Got to Do With It? Transnational Desires and Sex Tourism in the Dominican Republic*. Durham, NC: Duke University Press.

Burnett, V. 2013. 'Harsh Self-Assessment as Cuba Looks Within'. New York Times A9, 24 July.
Cabezas, A. 2009. *Economies of Desire: Sex and Tourism in Cuba and the Dominican Republic*. Philadelphia, PA: Temple University Press.
Charsley, K. 2005. 'Unhappy Husbands: Masculinity and Migration in Transnational Pakistani Marriages'. *Journal of the Royal Anthropological Institute* 11(1): 85-105.
_____. 2012. *Transnational Marriage: New Perspectives from Europe and Beyond*. New York: Routledge.
Constable, N. 2005. *Cross-Border Marriages: Gender and Mobility in Transnational Asia*. Philadelphia, PA: University of Pennsylvania Press.
Datta, K., et al. 2009. 'Men on the Move: Narratives of Migration and Work among Low-Paid Migrant Men in London'. *Social & Cultural Geography* 10(8): 853-73.
De la Fuente, A. 2001. *A Nation for All*. Chapel Hill, NC: University of North Carolina Press.
Ebron, P.A. 2002. *Performing Africa*. Princeton, NJ: Princeton University Press.
Fernandez, N.T. 1999. 'Back to the Future?: Women, Race and Tourism in Cuba', in K. Kempadoo (ed.), *Sex, Sun and Gold: Tourism and Sex Work in the Caribbean*. Boulder, CO: Rowman & Littlefield, pp. 81-92.
_____. 2010. *Revolutionizing Romance: Interracial Couples in Contemporary Cuba*. New Brunswick, NJ: Rutgers University Press.
_____. 2013. 'Moral Boundaries and National Borders: Cuban Marriage Migration to Denmark'. *Identities: Global Studies in Power and Culture* 20(3): 270-87.
Fleischer, A. 2008. 'Marriage over Time and Space among Male Migrants from Cameroon to Germany'. Rostock: Max Planck Institute for Demographic Research, Working Paper 2008-006.
Forrest, D.P. 1999. *Bichos, Maricones and Pingueros: An Ethnographic Study of Maleness and Scarcity in Contemporary Socialist Cuba*. London: University of London.
Frohlick, S. 2007. 'Fluid Exchanges: The Negotiation of Intimacy between Tourist Women and Local Men in a Transnational Town in Caribbean Costa Rica'. *City & Society* 19(1): 139-68.
Gallo, E. 2006. 'Italy is Not a Good Place for Men: Narratives of Places, Marriage and Masculinity among Malayali Migrants'. *Global Networks* 6(4): 357-72.
García-Moreno, C., and J.J. Pujadas Muñoz. 2011. '"No es fácil... y aquí tampoco": Trayectorias migratorias de mujeres cubanas en España'. *Revista de Dialectología y Tradiciones Populares* LXVI: 455-86 (doi:10.3989/rdtp.2011.17).
Hamilton, C. 2012. *Sexual Revolutions in Cuba: Passion, Politics, and Memory*. Chapel Hill, NC: University of North Carolina Press.
Hernández-Reguant, A. 2006. 'Havana's Timba: A Macho Sound for Black Sex', in K.M. Clarke and D.A. Thomas (eds), *Globalization and Race: Transformations in the Cultural Production of Blackness*. Durham, NC: Duke University Press, pp. 249-78.
Karkabi, N. 2011. 'Couples in the Global Margins: Sexuality and Marriage between Egyptian Men and Western Women in South Sinai'. *Anthropology of the Middle East* 6(1): 79-97.

Kempadoo, K. 2004. *Sexing the Caribbean: Gender, Race and Sexual Labor*. New York: Routledge.

Kummels, I. 2005. 'Love in the Time of Diaspora: Global Markets and Local Meanings in Prostitution, Marriage and Womanhood in Cuba'. *Iberoamericana* 5(20): 7–26.

Lundgren, S. 2011. *Heterosexual Havana: Ideals and Hierarchies of Gender and Sexuality in Contemporary Cuba*. Uppsala: Uppsala University Sweden.

Mai, N., and R. King. 2009. 'Introduction. Love, Sexuality and Migration: Mapping and Issue(s)'. *Mobilities* 4(3): 295–307.

Morales, E. 2017. 'Analysis: Cuba Remittances and the Shifting Pattern of Cuban Emigration'. *Cuba Trade* magazine, April.

Oxfeld, E. 2010. *Drink Water, but Remember the Source: Moral Discourse in a Chinese Village*. Berkeley, CA: University of California Press.

Pessar, P., and S. Mahler. 2001. 'Gender and Transnational Migration'. Transnational Communities Program Working Paper Series.

Phillips, J. 2008. 'Female Sex Tourism in Barbados: A Post-colonial Perspective'. *The Brown Journal of World Affairs* XIV, 201–12.

Povinelli, E.A. 2006. *The Empire of Love: Toward a Theory of Intimacy, Genealogy, and Carnality*. Durham, NC: Duke University Press.

Pruitt, D., and S. LaFont. 1996. 'For Love and Money: Romance Tourism in Jamaica'. *Annals of Tourism Research* 22(2): 422–40.

Roland, L.K. 2010. *Cuban Color in Tourism and La Lucha*. Oxford: Oxford University Press.

Safa, H. 2005. 'The Matrifocal Family and Patriarchal Ideology in Cuba and the Caribbean'. *Journal of Latin American Anthropology* 10(2): 314–37.

Salazar, N.B., and A. Smart. 2011. 'Anthropological Takes on (Im)mobility'. *Identities: Global Studies in Culture and Power* 18(6): i–ix.

Sanchez Taylor, J. 2006. 'Female Sex Tourism: A Contradiction in Terms?' *Feminist Review* 83: 42–59.

Simoni, V. 2014. 'The Morality of Friendship in Touristic Cuba'. *Suomen Antropologi: Journal of the Finnish Anthropological Society* 39(1): 19–36.

———. 2015. 'Breadwinners, Sex Machines, and Romantic Lovers: Entangling Masculinities, Moralities and Pragmatic Concerns in Touristic Cuba'. *Etnográfica. Revista do Centro em Rede de Investigação em Antropologia* 19(2): 389–411.

Statistics Denmark. 2018. http://www.dst.dk/en/Statistik. Retrieved 7 January 2018.

Statistics Sweden. 2018. http://www.scb.se/en/. Retrieved 7 January 2018.

Suárez, L.M. 2008. 'Our Memories, Ourselves', in R. Behar and L.M. Suárez (eds), *The Portable Island: Cubans at Home in the World*. New York: Palgrave Macmillian, pp. 9–16.

Urry, J. 2000. 'Mobile Sociology'. *British Journal of Sociology* 51(1): 185–203.

Williams, L. 2010. *Global Marriage: Cross-Border Marriage Migration in Global Context*. New York: Palgrave Macmillan.

———. 2012. 'Transnational Marriage Migration and Marriage Migration: An Overview', in K. Charsley (ed.), *Transnational Marriage: New Perspectives from Europe and Beyond*. New York: Routledge, pp. 23–40.

Index

adoptees, 2
affection. *See* friendship and affection
African intimacies, 194
age differences, 80, 88, 125, 132, 172
agency, economic, 193–94
agency of female migrants, 104, 117–18, 140
Agustín, Laura, 14, 101
Ahmed, Sara, 152
ajuda (help)
   concept of, 168, 171, 172–74
   prostitution *vs.*, 174–75, 176
   respect, 182–84
   in Southern Europe, 181–82
   in tourist circuits, 178
Amit, Vered, 222
Andaya, Elise, 216
Andreassen, Rikke, 152
Appadurai, Arjun, 58, 154, 174
arranged marriages
   Chinese, 34, 35, 44–45, 47
   civil registrars' attitudes toward, 89–91, 93
   South Asian, 94n13, 95n14
Asian women, fantasies about, 152, 153
asylum seekers, 53, 56, 71n1
Augé, Marc, 5
au pairs, 2, 8
authenticity, game of, 83–84
autological subject/society, 93, 202, 203, 208n15, 224, 225, 227

Ballard, Roger, 39
Bangladeshi Muslims, 39, 46
Bao, Jiemin, 34
Basch, Linda, Nina Glick Schiller, and Cristina Szanton Blanc, 58
beautification practices, 129
beauty as factor in marriage evaluations, 77
bébés-papiers, 91

Beck-Gernsheim, Elisabeth, 38–39
Belgian civil code, 76–77, 91–92
belonging and exclusion
   Cuban context, 190, 195, 197, 200–201, 202, 204–5
   politics of, 75, 92, 95n14
   state and international actions, 10
   transnational, 33
Berg, Anne-Jorunn, 145
Besson, Eric, 5
Biehl, João, Byron Good, and Arthur Kleinman, 214
binational marriages. *See* cross-border marriages
Bishop, Ryan, and Lillian S. Robinson, 152
black masculinity, 226–27
border gatekeepers, 75, 81–84
Bourdieu, Pierre, 124, 131
Brazilian women. *See also* sex workers
   migratory trajectories of, 20, 139, 167–68, 176, 180–83
   patronage and, 176
   populations studied, 168, 170–71, 185n1, 185n3
Brennan, Denise, 135, 136, 149, 154, 195
brothels and clubs. *See also* global nightscapes
   in Copenhagen (Denmark), 147–48, 150
   in Galicia, Spain, 106–7, 108, 110, 115, 117
   venues for love, 147–48
Browne, Katherine E., 196
Brussels (Belgium). *See also* civil registrars' offices (Brussels)
   civil code regarding marriage, 76–78, 91
   fieldwork study in, 75–76, 93n1, 94n5

interviews with binational couples, 79–81, 82–83
bureaucratic feminism, 74–75, 87, 92
Butler, Judith, 144–45, 153–54, 159, 160n2

Callejero (Hustler) (Moneda Dura), 217
capitalism, 4, 8, 18, 68, 102, 103, 194–95, 207n8
care chains, 14, 124
Caribbean culture, 194, 195
Carita de Pasporte (Face of a Passport) (Havana d'Primera), 216–17
Castro, Raul, 213
Chao, Emily, 45
Charsley, Katharine, 33, 56, 57, 58, 64, 69
Cheng, Sealing, 91, 149, 150, 154
China, morality in, 217
Chinese diaspora, 37, 41, 46
Chinese marriage practices, 11–12, 31–32, 34–35, 40–41, 43, 44–47, 48n3
Chu, C. Y. Cyrus, and Ruoh-Rong Yu, 35
citizenship, fractured, 94n4
civil registrars' offices (Brussels)
    assessment of marriages, 76–78, 84–91, 92–93
    as border gatekeepers, 75, 81–84
    bureaucratic feminism, 87–91
    characteristics of, 78–79
    documentation of interviews, 75, 80, 81, 86–87
    fieldwork study in, 75–76, 93n1, 94n5
    interviews with binational couples, 79–81, 82–83
Clifford, James, 5
Cole, Jennifer, 194
colonialism, 4, 152, 194, 197
Columbian migrants, 109, 110–11, 114
communication technologies, 36, 37–38, 40, 66
community allegiance, 193, 195–97, 198–99, 200, 204. *See also* belonging and exclusion
companionate marriage, 75, 89, 94n11, 208n14
Constable, Nicole, 42, 43, 45
creole economies, 196
cross-border marriages
    assessment of, 74
    in the context of friendship, 224
    Cuban-Spanish, 206n6, 228n6
    distinction with transnational marriages, 56–58
    ethnographic study of Cuban relationships, 214–15
    legitimization of, 225
    and morality, 217–18
    motivations for, 213–14
    Pakistani-Indonesian marriages, 59–65
    Pakistanis, 57
    and sex work, 144, 148–50
    use of term, 227n1
cross-dressers, 150
Cuba
    authorities and *jineterismo*, 207n8, 209n22
    family and community in, 193, 196, 200, 204–5
    fieldwork in, 206n2, 206n4
    moral decline in, 199, 213, 216
    racial dynamics of, 218
    resistance narratives, 194–95
Cuban-tourist relationships. *See* cunning love; true love
Cuban women, 199, 206n5, 228n7
cultural capital, 124, 128, 131
cunning love, 190–97, 203, 204, 209n21. *See also* instrumental relationships; love relationships; true love
curtidoras
    aspirations of, 93n2
    controlling emotions, 195, 209n20
    description of, 122–23, 126
    development of erotic power in, 129–30
    downward mobility, 133–35
    experience of social mobility, 133
    importance of sexual capital, 16, 19, 139
    job aspirations, 138
    kinship ties, 129
    views of white and Mozambican men, 131–32

Daigle, Megan D., 209n22
Danish-Thai liaisons, 16–17, 139, 143, 148, 150, 151–59
Davidson, Julia O'Connell, and Jacqueline Sanchez Taylor, 153, 159
Davin, Delia, 34
Davis, Coralynn, 91
Day, Sophie, 101
de Beauvoir, Simone, 16

deception and trickery. See cunning love
De Munck, Victor, 91
Denmark
　global nightscapes in, 144, 147-48, 150, 151-52, 155
　Thai population of, 146, 160nn3-5
dependency, 134, 135, 139
dialogic morality, 214, 217-18, 227
discrimination. See civil registrars' offices; sham marriages
divorce, 137
Doezema, Jo, 102
domestic violence, 137
domestic workers, 8, 53, 54, 56, 59-62, 63, 64, 130
domination, resistance to, 193-94
Dominican sex workers, 149, 195
dual marriages, 64-65

economic capital, 124, 128, 130, 131
economic hardship, 199, 204, 209n22, 213, 216. See also *la lucha;* remittances to Cuba
Eggebø, Helga, 78, 84, 90
emotion and judgement, 84-86
erotic other, 152, 153, 154-55, 159, 219, 221
erotic power, 123-24, 128, 129-30, 139, 175
'error of the spy,' 19, 188-90, 195, 204
ethnography of moral reason, 214
Europeans, 3, 127, 131, 132
exotic other, 18, 175, 219
exotic women, 111, 158-59
expatriates, 18, 127, 132, 133, 139-40

Faier, Lieba, 149-50, 155, 228n9
familial obligations. See also resource redistribution
　labour migrants, 53
　Latin Americans, 173, 199, 201, 225-26, 227
　reciprocity of, 129
　sex workers, 113, 118
family reunification, 39, 89, 105, 107-8, 146, 160n6
Fan, C. Cindy and Ling Li, 34, 38
Farrer, James, 43, 144, 154, 155, 159
female migration, 101. See also sex workers
　motivation for, 103, 105, 118n4
femininity, 151-54

Fernandez, Nadine, 89, 197
Filipina-Japanese marriages, 150, 156, 228n9
Filipina migrants, 55, 57-58, 149, 150. See also Hong Kong
foreign domestic workers. See domestic workers
Fortaleza (Brazil)
　fieldwork in, 170, 185n3
　reconfigurations of sexual modalities, 176-80, 183-84
　friendship and affection, 169, 173, 180-82, 184, 224, 228n9

Galicia (Spain), field study in, 104-5
García-Moreno, Cristina, and Joan Josep Pujadas Muñoz, 223, 228n6
Gavron, Kate, 90
Gell, Alfred, 94n13, 95n14
gendered geographies of power, 216
gendered intimacy, 67-68, 69, 150-51, 207n10
gendered morality, 214, 215
gender equality, 87-89, 134, 135, 136-37, 179
gender performance, 7, 152, 153, 157-59, 160n2, 220, 221
gender roles, 9, 15, 144
gender stereotypes, 15, 220
genealogy, 208n15
global citizenship, 201-2, 204. See also belonging and exclusion
global nightscapes, 16, 144, 151-55, 159-60. See also brothels and clubs
Global North and South. See also civil registrars' offices (Brussels); Cuba; *curtidoras;* Qingtian (Zhejiang province); sex workers; Thai-Danish liaisons
　migration to the North, 2, 3-4, 9, 13, 14, 92, 123-24, 214
　sex tourism in the South, 9, 123, 216
Goffman, Erving, 206-7n7
'grey marriage.' See marriages of convenience
Groes (Groes-Green), Christian, 13, 76, 93n2, 175, 176, 195, 209n20

Hamilton, Carrie, 221
Hannem, Kevin, Mimi Scheller, and John Urry, 6

Hansen, Mette Halskov, and Cuiming Pang, 46
Harris-Todaro model, 4
Hernández-Reguant, Adriana, 219, 221, 226-27
Hertz, Ellen, 85
heteronormativity, 66, 67
heterosexuality, 8, 15, 17, 53, 144, 150, 157, 220-21. See also gender performance; gender roles; transgenders
Hirsch, Jennifer, and Holly Wardlow, 94n11, 95n14
Hong Kong
   asylum seekers, 71n1
   legal marriage in, 56
   regulatory view of domestic workers, 54
   study of migrants in, 53, 55, 58-65
hopes and aspirations, 200, 202, 208n16. See also social mobility
Hunter, Mark, 174
husbands, ideal, 131-32, 150
hypergamy, 34, 41

Illouz, Eva, 87
immigration policies. See migration policies
Indonesian migrants, 55, 59-65
informal circuit, 103, 114-17, 119n7
instrumentality, 213, 224-25, 227
instrumental relationships, 13, 19, 199, 216-17. See also cunning love
inter-ethnic intimacy, 68
inter-ethnic marriages, 57-58, 69-70, 71n3, 146-47
intergenerational differences, 44, 45, 47, 80, 88, 125, 132, 172
interracial couples, 218
intimacy. See also cunning love; friendship and affection; instrumentality; love relationships; marriages of convenience; true love
   commodification of, 8-9
   fluid boundaries, 151, 159
   and identity formation, 149
   relationship with mobility, 7
   state intrusion into, 78, 79-81, 92
   through racialized gender performance, 145
intimacy, shared, 74, 86-87
intimacy, temporary, 58-65

'intimate conviction,' 84, 94n9
intimate mobilities
   continuum of, 10
   defined, 1-2
Japanese men, 150
jineterismo (tourist hustling), 191-97, 198, 200, 203, 204, 207n8, 209n22, 216-17, 222

Karkabi, Nadeem, 216
Kempadoo, Kamala, 101-2, 216
Kibria, Nazli, 39, 46
kinship networks, 2, 40, 46, 124, 128-29, 132, 139-40, 182

labour migrants, 12, 53, 54, 67
labour migration, 2, 4, 9, 10, 53
Lavanchy, Anne, 77-78
'leftovers' (unmarried men and women), 31-32, 41
Lewis, W. Arthur, 4
Lindholm, Charles, 95n14
Lin Lean Lim, 102
love relationships, 41, 63, 64, 167, 172, 174, 179. See also cunning love; friendship and affection; true love
la lucha (the struggle), 194, 196, 199, 204, 207n8
Lundgren, Silje, 220

MacCannell, Dean, 206-7n7
Mai, Nicola, and Russell King, 90
male migrants, viii
Maputo (Mozambique)
   female-headed households, 129
   fieldwork in, 125-26
   transformation of, 127
marriage, blurred boundaries of, vii
marriage compatibility, 77-78
marriage-like relationships, 12-13, 52-53, 55-56, 68-69
marriage migration. See also marriages of convenience
   from Africa, 124
   and policies of exception, 2-3
   serving cultural expectations, 11-12
   sexuality, love, and desire, 71n2
marriagescapes, 58
marriages of convenience, 13, 76-79, 82, 89-90, 91-92. See also sham marriages

Martin, John Levi, and Matt George, 128
masculine self-making, 20, 214, 218-19, 227
masculinity. See also gender performance
　black masculinity, 221-22
　ideal men, 131-32, 139, 179
　provider, 225-26, 227
matchmaking
　Chinese practices, 31-32, 33-34, 37-44, 45, 46-47, 48n4
　in the Global South, 123
　in Maputo (Mozambique), 124-25
methodological conjugalism, 13, 14, 76, 92, 93n2
methodological nationalism, 13-14
migrant communities, formation of, 38-39
migrants, categories of, 52, 53, 54
migration
migratory pressure in Europe, 81-82, 92
　motivating factors, 4-5, 118n4
　push and pull factors, 4, 14
migration policies, 7, 10-11, 15, 39. See also family reunification
　Belgian, 90-92
　control, viii-ix, 2, 3, 10-15, 57
　marriage loophole, 74
　role of intimacy and emotion in, viii
　role of intimacy in, 2-3
　Spanish, 111, 115, 116
　Swedish, 137
migration streams, 38
migration studies
　centrality of relationships and emotion, vii-ix
　compartmentalization of sex work, 143
　gaps in, 52, 54
　migrant men, 215
　theories, 4
　trends in, 33-34
　trends in transnational migration, 33-35
migratory life, expectations of, 67, 69-70
Milan (Italy), 170, 185n3
Mincer, Jacob, 5
mixed-race children, 68-69
mobility, concept of, 5-6, 5-7
mobility of power and capital, 130
mobility studies, 5-6
modernity, 75, 87, 208n14, 222, 224-25, 227
Moore, Henrietta L., 202

moral decline in Cuba, 199, 213, 216
moral frameworks, 194-95, 204, 222, 225-26
moralities of migration, 20
morality, dialogic, 214, 217-18, 227
moral standards, 202
moral subjectivity, 209n18
Morokvasic, Mirjana, 4-5
motility, 6
Mozambican women. See *curtidoras*
mulatto, 227n3
multi-circuited maze
　concept of, 18, 103, 104
　informal circuit, 114-16, 117-18
　sex worker circuit, 111-13, 117-18, 118n2
　transnational household circuit, 113-14, 117-18
　transnational migratory circuit, 108-11, 117-18
mulungus (whites), 131-32
Myong, Lene, 145
Myrdhal, Eileen Muller, 90

Nencel, Lorraine, 145
Neveu Kringelbach, Hélène, 76
nikah (Muslim marriage blessing ceremony), 56, 59, 63
normalcy, 199, 200, 201-2, 207n8, 208n13, 209n19
Norway, marriage in, 84, 90

'otherness,' 18, 90, 144, 145, 152, 195, 206-7n7, 208n16
Oxfeld, Ellen, 34, 39, 42, 214, 217

Pakistani-Indonesian marriages, 59-65. See also Hong Kong
participant observation, 48n1, 125, 145, 146, 215
'passage to hope,' 12, 47
Patico, Jennifer, 208n13
patronage, 175-76. See also *ajuda*
People's Republic of China (PRC). See under Chinese
Piot, Charles, 208n16
Piscitelli, Adriana, 139
pisos de contactos (in-call flats), 107, 108, 110, 115, 117
Plambech, Sine, 139
plazas (rotation system), 112, 113, 114, 116, 117

police raids, 112, 115
Portugal, migrant experiences in, 133–36
Povinelli, Elizabeth, 87, 197, 202, 203, 207n8, 208n15, 224
power and privilege, 6–7, 9, 19. *See also* erotic power; subjectivity
programas (tricks)
   concept of, 171–72, 173
   reconfigured, 176–80, 180–82, 183–84
   shifts with *ajuda*, 174
promiscuity, 68
prostitution
   and *ajuda*, 174–75, 176
   in Brazil, 168, 170, 171–72
   mixed paradigms of, 177
   in Spain, 112, 115, 116
   victim narrative, 144, 154
   voluntary *vs.* forced, 102

Qingtian (Zhejiang province). *See also* Chinese marriage practices
   economic benefit of migration, 36
   matchmaking in, 31–32, 33, 36–44
   out-migration from, 34, 36, 45–46, 47
   wedding trends in, 40, 48n4
queer migration, 8

racial factors in mobility, 15–16
racialization, 145
racialized femininity, 144, 152, 158–59, 160n2
racialized gender hierarchies, 155, 159
racialized privilege, 18
racialized sexuality, 218–20, 221
racial stereotypes, 132, 219
Rasta men, 189, 206n2
reciprocity, 175, 176, 203
refugee crisis, 3
remittances to Cuba, 225–26
reputation, 195
resistance, 193–94, 208n16
resource redistribution, 178, 182, 194, 196
respect and respectability
   assessment of self-worth, 123
   empowerment and control, 133–35, 137
   relationship to class, 124, 130, 131, 138, 139–40
   romantic love relationships, 155–56
   through *ajuda*, 173, 182
Riley, Nancy E., 35

romantic love. *See* true love
Ruiz, Martha Cecilia, 104

Salazar, Noel, and Alan Smart, 7, 222
Salcedo Robledo, Manuela, 84
Sandell, Steven H., 5
Sassen, Saskia, 9, 102
Scandinavia, immigrant hierarchies in, 221
Schein, Louisa, 34
seduction and flirtation, 151–54, 156–57, 220
self-making, 214, 218–19, 222–24
Sequeiros, Jose Luis, 111
sex industry
   economic role of, 102
   love in, 149–50
   sex work entangled with intimacy, 148–51
   in Spain, 104–5, 180–82
   trafficking perspective, 101–2, 110, 118n1
'sexpatriates,' 18
sexscapes, 10, 154
sex tourism. *See also* Brazilian women; Cuba; cunning love; *jineterismo* (tourist hustling)
   commodification of sex, 9
   in Cuba, 170, 176–80, 185nn1–2, 191, 204
   expatriates, 18, 124
   gendered geographies of power, 216
   Thailand, 154
sex trafficking, 3, 15, 17, 101–2, 110, 118n1, 169, 170
sexual and economic exchanges. *See also ajuda; programas;* sexual economies
   asymmetrical, 174–76
   in Brazil, 168–71, 172
   confused expectations in, 177
   desire and intimacy's role in, 149, 150
   modalities of, 172–74
   reconfigurations of, 20–21, 176–83, 184
   social mobility, 127
sexual capital, 123–24, 128, 133, 135–36, 138
sexual contact zones, 144, 147, 154, 159, 197, 205
sexual economies, 7–8, 124, 125, 128, 149, 150, 169–70
sexual exploitation, 17, 101, 169, 216

sexual freedom, 67, 68
sexuality, love, and desire, 71n2, 132, 149, 174. See also Thai-Danish liaisons
sex work, labour perspectives, 14
sex worker circuit, 103, 111–13, 116
sex workers
  as breadwinners, 113–14
  compartmentalization of identity, 143–44, 149, 159
  Dominican, 135
  exploitation of, 115–16
  family security, 4
  field study of, 104–5
  mobility of, 8, 111–13
  in Mozambique, 126
  social mobility strategies, 105–8, 117, 118, 118–19n5
  social spaces for, 147–48, 151–54
  social status of, 146
  Thai migrant workers, 147
  in tourist trade, 176–80
  working conditions, 110
sham marriages, 75, 76–78, 94n10, 116, 205
Simoni, Valerio, 184, 220, 224, 228n9
Slovenia, 33, 48n1
small-trade networks, 17, 105, 108–9, 118n5
social capital, 124, 128, 219
social mobility. See also respect and respectability
  barriers to, 118
  black masculinity, 226–27
  Brazilian women, 176, 179
  downward mobility, 133–35, 136–37
  from geographic mobility, 2, 7, 11–12, 222–24
  Latin American sex workers, 102–4, 117, 118
  marriage as vehicle for, 32, 34, 40–41, 42, 224–25
  Mozambican women, 127–28
  through *ajuda*, 172
social mobility strategies, 17–18
social workers, 145–46
socio-economic inequality, 13, 117, 127, 140, 169, 173, 185, 193
Sousa e Santos, Dina de, 132, 208n13
Spain
  female migrants in, 102–3
  fieldwork in, 170, 185n3
  sex workers in, 167, 180–82
spousal choice, 32–33, 34. See also matchmaking
stereotypes, 15, 132, 140, 156, 194, 206n6, 220
stigmatization, 173, 178, 183
Stoler, Ann L., 197
Strasser, Sabine, 39
Suárez, Lucía, 222
subjection process, 144–45
subjectivity, 149–50, 190, 214
suspicion, administrative, 75–76, 80, 84–85, 86, 93
Suzuki, Nobue, 156
Sykes, Karen, 214
symbolic capital, 124, 128, 131

Thai, Hung Cam, 39
Thai-Danish liaisons, 16–17, 139, 143, 148, 150, 151–59
Thai migrants
  field study of, 144–46
  multiple femininities, 144
  population in Denmark, 146–47
  subjectivities of, 149, 150
timba music, 219
torture claims, 59–60, 62–63
tourism, growth of, 218–19
tourism discourses, 193
tourists' countermeasures, 191–93, 196, 203. See also *jineterismo*
tourists goals, 206–7n7
transactional sex, 123, 128, 175
transgenders, 9, 150, 157–59
transnational household circuit, 103, 113–14, 117
transnationalism, 58, 65–68
transnational marriages. See cross-border marriages
transnational migratory circuit, 103, 108–11, 116, 117
travel, 222–24
true love (romantic love). See also cunning love
  in Brazilian tourist circuits, 173, 184 (See also *ajuda* (help))
  constructed through money and intimacy, 161n7
  Cuban-tourist relationships, 20, 189–90, 197–203, 204, 209n19
  despite economic hardship, 207n10

failed relationships, 182, 183, 191, 202–3, 209n20
gender equality, 88
marriage assessments, 74, 90–91, 92–93, 95n14
modernity, 208n14, 208n16
as moral category, 75
moral guidance of, 209n18
privileging Western conceptions, 13
respectability and, 155–56
role in mobility, viii
as social construct, 150
Thai migrants in Denmark, 147, 148

undocumented migrants, 103, 112, 115, 116, 118, 119n7
Unger, Roberto, 90

victimization, 15, 104, 144, 154, 185n1, 216

Vietnamese diaspora, 39
virtual dating, 40

Weitzer, Ronald, 102
Wenzhou (Zhejiang province), 36, 48n2
'Wenzhou economic model,' 36
white men, 131, 139
Willereslev, Rane, 209n18
Williams, Lucy, 56–58, 69, 214, 227n1
Wilson, Peter J., 194
Wimmer, Andreas, and Nina Glick Schiller, 13
work life *vs.* intimacy, 54–55
Wray, Helena, 75, 91

Xu, Xiaohe, and Martin King Whyte, 34

Zigon, Jarrett, 209n18

www.ingramcontent.com/pod-product-compliance
Lightning Source LLC
Chambersburg PA
CBHW070920030426
42336CB00014BA/2473